Clusters

Creative Mid-sized
Missional Communities

Clusters

Creative Mid-sized
Missional Communities

Bob Hopkins & Mike Breen

publishing
www.3dministries.com

CLUSTERS
© 2007 Bob Hopkins & Mike Breen

This edition published by ACPI in partnership with 3DM.

Unless otherwise noted, all Scripture quotations are taken from the New International Version 1960, 1962, 1963, 1968, 1971, 1972, 1973, 1975, 1977, 1995 by the Lockman Foundation. Used by permission.

Front cover photograph and cover design by Sally Breen

ISBN 978-0-9559363-0-2

First edition published by 3DM Publications 2007
1st edition ISBN 978-1-932503-67-8

This second edition printed in 2008 in the United Kingdom.

Dedicated to all the ordinary Christians who have sacrificed so much to pioneer these exciting fresh expressions of church. And to the church leaders who have had the vision and courage to release and support them. From all of whom we have learnt so much.

Cluster Summary

- Clusters are mid-sized groups (larger than cells/small groups and smaller than celebrations) which grow together in their relationship to God as they explore relevant whole-life spirituality (UP).

- Clusters build Christian community as places of belonging and participation... on days, times and places that suit (they are quite distinctly different from inherited "Sunday Service") (IN).

- Clusters gain identity and purpose from a united mission vision, being called to a clear geographic or network focus and engaging with the social patterns of that culture and context (OUT).

- Clusters are linked together by a network of support and accountability to a diversity of other mid-sized groups (OF).

- Clusters are led by ordinary unpaid Christians in their non-work time (unless it is a work based cluster), both receiving and passing on Jesus' pattern of discipleship (UP:IN:OUT:OF).

New Wine in the Cluster?

Thus saith the Lord... "As the New Wine is in the Cluster and men say 'Do not destroy it, for a blessing is in it,' so will I do for my servants' sake..."
Isaiah 65:8

This comes from a prophetic interpretation given by Mark Stibbe at St Andrew's, Chorleywood, UK in 2006 as they began to see the potential missionary fruit of their mid-size communities/MSCs.

Contents

Clusters: Building Blocks for a Missionary Movement?

Mike and Sally Breen, Mary and I have had a long relationship since the late 1980's. It started when Mike and Sally were in inner-urban UPA[1] Brixton and we were in UPA Merseyside. We recognised then that we shared a passion for exploring and planting fresh expressions of church that might be more effective in engaging with our rapidly changing culture. We kept in touch when the Breen family moved to Little Rock in the US from 1991 to 1994. Then in 1997 we accepted Mike's invitation to join them on the leadership team of St Thomas', Crookes in Sheffield.

The sense in which this book is co-authored by Mike and myself is that Mike is the pioneer who has initiated most of the concepts and models described here and I am the commentator, analyst and scribe. Mike has sometimes joked that he instinctively does the stuff and I then explain what and why he's done it. Whilst this exaggerates my role, so far as this book is concerned, I have written up what Mike has initiated and which we and his leadership team have brainstormed together and sought to implement over ten years. To this I have added so much that Mary and I have gained as we have wrestled with similar principles of missional church with a host of other churches and contexts.

---

[1] UPA is the accepted abbreviation for Urban Priority Area, a socially deprived context (see Glossary).

Over the past thirty years, Mary and I have had the privilege of working with countless churches across the UK and some other European countries. We have ourselves been members and on the leadership of a local church in the South East commuter suburbs of Chorleywood for ten years, and then in urban priority Merseyside for 14 years and now in a citywide networked church in Sheffield for ten years.

Our relationships in consultation and training with hundreds of other churches have come through our leadership of Anglican Church Planting Initiatives, as link missioners with Springboard and team members of DAWN Europa. More recently we have joined Archbishop Rowan Williams' Fresh Expressions team and are partnering with Church Mission Society (CMS). Our lifelong call has been as missionaries and therefore the motivating focus with all these churches and roles has been to seek to discover effective missionary principles for our Western European context.

This journey has led us to some key themes and conclusions. Clearly, the process of God's mission is summed up in his nature as Trinity – community in mission. We see this most fully and finally expressed in the work of Jesus, sent by the Father and empowered by the Spirit. And Jesus provides the model for all our mission. Firstly, this involves incarnation and the identification with each culture and context, articulating the gospel in their language and addressing it to their world-view, and then allowing the gospel community that arises to be embedded in their social forms but transformed by Kingdom values. Secondly, inherent in this mission of God and the establishment of his Kingdom on earth is the principle of multiplication[2]. The third overarching conviction is that the

---

[2] Expressed in so many of Jesus' parables and in the movement of mission that Jesus initiated through the Gospels and Acts.

mission of God spreads through a context based on a two dimensional rhythm. This is a gathering followed by a sending, or an increase in strength of a powerful centre, followed by a spreading out or dispersion through to the limits of that context. This pattern was exemplified in Jesus' own ministry and also in the account of the New Testament churches' mission through the book of Acts[3]. The fourth linked principle is that once an indigenous church is established in a culture or context, providing its processes and structures are geared to the other principles of multiplication and working with the rhythm of establishing resource centres or "minsters", then the most effective outcome becomes a movement of mission[4].

As we all pray and work towards the re-evangelisation of Western Europe, then it seems to us that one of our tasks is to seek to discern where God is initiating these principles, so that we can work with Him towards various movements of mission that will be required.

In England it appears that there are a number of situations where this may already be beginning to happen. Most notable may be the signs of revival spreading through the traveller (gipsy) communities and through prisons. There may also be signs of emerging movements within youth culture and a couple of rural contexts. It is also our hope that what we are part of here in Sheffield, involving a multiplying pattern of clusters across the city, may also be the early signs of an emerging missionary movement. It is this latter development of clusters as multiplying missional communities that we want to

---

[3] Exemplified in Acts 6:7, 12:24, 19:20 as well as the arrangement of the narrative. This analysis is written up in Enabling Church Planting, Bob Hopkins & Richard White, CPAS 1995 p.5

[4] I expand on this in my contribution to Setting the Church of England Free, Mark Mills Powell (ed), John Hunt, 2003 p139

describe and explore here. We believe that the cluster model initiated and developed in Sheffield and now being adopted and adapted by many other churches, illustrates a number of fundamental principles for effective mission in our post-Christendom culture of the West. Our visits to Australia and New Zealand and Mike and his team's work in the USA and Canada, are all confirming that the principles we are discovering from Clusters are widely applicable.

So, although this book started with the piloting of clusters in St Thomas' Church, Sheffield, the mid-sized missional communities described here are now proving effective in a whole range of contexts. The underlying principles that we have explained are flexible and lead to significant diversity in how the models emerge, according to each situation. More and more churches, large and small, urban, suburban and rural, are seeking help in developing mid-sized communities. Some call them clusters, others use different names like Mid-size Communities (MSCs) and 'Trash Groups' for Youth in Gloucestershire. Through this book we shall most often speak of clusters, but the principles are more important than the name. We are now in touch with churches all over Britain and other European countries becoming "cluster-shaped." And as we write they are yielding most encouraging results in mission, evangelism and growth. We hope that these point to something much wider and more significant in the future.

Bob Hopkins, November 2006

Introduction

Clusters are mid-sized communities in mission. They are not small cells and they are not large celebrations. They are an intermediate size in-between, typically around 25-65 people. And this is not hard and fast. We shall quote slightly different ranges being experienced in different contexts.

These cluster communities have now been adopted and adapted by many churches in the UK and elsewhere. These adaptations have led to quite wide variations in application and form and have enabled effective engagement in mission in all sorts of contexts from rural to suburban and cities.

This essential mid-sized building block has acquired different names – from clusters to MSCs to Trash Groups; and taken on different forms – from a grouping of small groups/cells to more of a mission team with no small group structure. They are developing in small churches, large churches and as dispersed networks of churches, even across cities or rural counties.

The prototype for these groups was first experimented with by Mike Breen in Brixton around 1988 where they were called 'Pastoral Bases'[1]. Later they formed the core of his vision on taking over St Thomas', Sheffield in 1994. And at that time he described them as multiplying missionary congregations and called them CLUSTERS.

We therefore need to explain right at the start that this book may seem to contain a disproportionate reference to this model at St Thomas', Sheffield; whereas it is now just one cluster-based church among many. However, this is inevitable and also right.

---

[1] Bob Hopkins (ed), Planting New Churches, Eagle, 1992, Chapter 10

Firstly, because Mike has been developing these principles for nearly twenty years compared to the more recent appearance of Mid-sized Communities in many other churches. And secondly, because Mike and I as authors have both been part of St Thomas' for ten years during the period when these principles underwent most of their development (see chapter 14).

So as you move through the chapters, recognise that although the more common references are to clusters in St Thomas', this is not because it is the only or even necessarily the best example of the principles... It's just the most developed and the one that we have lived.

Also note that we often introduce references to other churches employing mid-sized cluster principles and sometimes compare and contrast them to the original St Thomas' conception. If a few terms seem new to you, have a quick look at the glossary at the back. And if you want to have in mind the essence and heart of clusters before we get started, refer back to the summary on page six.

Now, in the rest of this introduction we tell some stories to self-consciously start with narrative pictures to paint the background to the later development of the principles and the analysis. They are told as signposts to where we are going. We hope that these varied tales create pictures of the range of what can be, and that they kindle your faith and imagination and whet your appetite for cluster-shaped church.

A WACKY TALE!

Soon after Mike Breen had taken over as Rector of St Thomas', Sheffield in 1994 he began to share the vision for "clusters." These were larger than small groups - in fact were made up of a few small groups - but were much smaller than a Sunday service and quite different in nature. They aren't about an event at all, but rather a group of Christians together as community in mission. Mike encouraged anyone to seek God for a vision for such a new expression of church and he would then release them to form a team which would work as a nucleus and then gather a cluster.

On their return to Sheffield in 1996, Mal and Chriscelle Calladine started praying one night a week with another couple, Peter and Caroline Harris, with a sense of expectancy. They did this for four months before asking Mike if they could start a new small group. Up to that point at St Thomas the pre-existent home groups had been structured into clusters, looking to unite groups around common vision. These two couples in their late twenties approached Mike about starting a new group rather than joining a current cluster. Their vision being that the small group would emerge into a new cluster which would reach those in their generation who had not found a belonging place in the current clusters. Many of the young adults and students who were then attending the Sunday evening service weren't in any small group.

Now one of the couples had just helped lead an Alpha course whose discussion group of young adults wanted to continue meeting. So in January 1997 a new group began, led by Mal and Chriscelle, based around the two couples, the post-Alpha group and a couple of other friends. On first meeting they brainstormed what they wanted to do. And whatever it was, it would have to generate a high commitment to meeting together every Tuesday evening when there were so many other enticing other options available – including favourite TV shows! They agreed they needed to have a strong sense of vision of who they were & what they wanted to do if they were going to truly commit to this group. Basically they were asking one another "what could we invite our friends to? If we want to reach not-yet-Christians from our generation and who think like us, what would appeal to them and draw them in?"

The result of these discussions became known as the 'Twelve Pillars of Wacky' (as an ironic humorous reference to the eastern spirituality of the 'seven pillars of Wisdom'). These were the twelve goals they had agreed they wanted to be defined by and are depicted in Appendix II. The process they used to work this through they later found out is called "the Swedish Method". They got everyone on their own to write down the five things they most wanted to do and then to reduce the list down to their three most important. Then they shared that list in pairs and were asked to prioritise together their joint top four. Next those pairs were asked to join another pair and thrash out an agreed top three. Finally, these were then fed back by the group of four to everyone, and stuck onto the wall on post-it notes. The ensuing feedback and filtering resulted in the twelve dynamics that they all wanted to be defined by and this consensus created a massive ownership amongst the group. It meant that they enthusiastically invited their friends and as a result, a new person came every week for the next six months, until they became a core of about 24.

The cluster name also came out of this exercise because the top three things that everyone settled on, summed up what they all most wanted their expression of church to be marked by. And they were:

"Wild" - a heart's desire that church stuff should be good fun and not seen to be religious, but untamed and dangerous in its pursuit of the kingdom.

"Attractive" - to their friends. Not in the pretty sense, but something they were proud of and would feel confident to invite their friends to; and …

"Community" - in a generation looking for a place to belong, where many had experienced little identity from their natural family and all were conditioned through TV shows like Friends, to aspire to what Bridget Jones called her "urban family."

So WAC became the shorthand for the group and this quickly became 'Wacky Races,' a Hanna Barbera cartoon TV show from their childhoods. They also liked the idea that as their expectation of growth led to multiplication into a number of groups, they could name the different small groups after the main characters in the Races. So... the Anthill Mob, the Slagg Brothers, the Converta-car, the Army Surplus Special and the Arkansas Chugabug were in their sights! And of course these were represented in icons. And a strip-cartoon form both fitted with their ethos and also provided easy visual communication and re-referencing. The dog 'Muttley' quickly became their logo and later the name of their worship band.

This original core grew remarkably quickly as other young adults readily identified with the vision. Walking in the Peaks (local hills); playing football; rock climbing; video nights and generally just hanging out together... all with God and prayer naturally fitting in, was just the sort of non-churchy social context these gen-Xers were looking for to "do church" rather than "go to church."

When I say not long after, it really was moving fast and they soon all went away together to a cabin residential centre in the countryside for a great weekend. This was the time to further clarify and extend the vision (purpose) and values (community choices) that the growing cluster would embrace.

With the core group already about 24, everyone knew they had to multiply since meeting in the front room of a Sheffield terraced house (where the only couple then with children lived) had become extremely cramped. At this point Mal and

Chriscelle started to meet for Sunday afternoon tea with the other potential small group leaders who they had observed taking more responsibility. Light-weight and low maintenance had been a watchword Mike had shared and that resonated with them. They felt church was too much about meetings and their passion was to grow community through natural times of meeting for friendship. As friends they already enjoyed spending Sunday afternoon together – it didn't feel like another church meeting.

As it became time to multiply (they were careful to use the words 'multiply' and 'develop' the vision rather than 'split' or 'divide' the group as those words created negativity), the now larger group was involved in a Vision and Strategy process they called "Processed P's." The last thing they did as one group was to brainstorm ideas for a few weeks using this process. Chapter ten records both the process and the conclusion of this creative time, which produced the cohesion of strong ownership right across the four new groups of the cluster. They agreed a meeting rhythm of two weeks in small groups and one as 'big group,' with the plan to all meet down the pub after small groups, so wider relationship time could be maintained. At their first meeting of 'big group' 40 people turned up! They had created space for those on the fringes to join, and those who had been nervous that becoming four groups would leave each one too small suddenly found their group full.

The "Processed P's" exercise came out of this whole cluster engagement, but was steered by the leadership team of small group leaders. It was their way of systematically doing a planning exercise to move from purpose (vision) and philosophy (values), to their priorities, pattern of activities and then their programs and the people who would do them (Processed P's in Appendix 2). Within a year members of the community had come back to Mal saying, "We've achieved nearly all our goals from the Processed P's document, we need to do another one" – now that's ownership!

Wild attractive community it certainly was. And as many others were drawn to this highly relevant but quite radical new way of doing church, they stretched beyond four small groups to six within the next six months. This rapid growth provided one of the most significant insights for the development of the whole cluster concept.

As numbers grew in 18 months or so to 60, then 70, then 80, the leaders began to sense a dis-ease. To begin with they couldn't put their finger on what was making them lose their peace in what otherwise seemed such welcome fruitfulness. Then gradually hunches became a clear conviction as we talked through their perceptions. Precisely because their founding vision was "wild attractive community" it was becoming clear that they could no longer sustain the very quality that was generating the growth. The heart of the attractiveness of the 'big group' community they had created was getting diluted as the growth pushed them to this even larger size. Once the group went above something like 60 or 70 young adults, you couldn't sustain the dynamic of this sort of "everyone involved together community."

This has become a defining principle of clusters and a crucial insight about this sort of group. Clearly Clusters are a size that provides a social context with good access to leaders for everyone; the potential for all to contribute in interactive gatherings; the facility for knowing everyone and missing them when absent; and the ability for all to own the vision and maintain a strong sense of belonging to the group.

The recognition of this principle led to the multiplication of the Wacky Races Cluster not very long after. But such was the momentum of growth that had been generated, that the total belonging had reached around 100 by the time the plan for dividing up had clarified. So it had to multiply into three new clusters rather than two, each of some 30 to 40 people. This became the "Wacky Clan" of clusters under the leadership of the founders, Mal and Chriscelle. The three new clusters still wanted identity as Wacky so they named themselves after three of the actual races – the individual episodes of the TV show. So the 'Super Silly Swamp Sprinters,' the 'Zippy Mississippi Racers' (later just Zippy) and the 'Speedy (Arkansas) Travellers' were born!

Over the next couple of years, couples had kids and many single young adults got married. Leadership get-togethers were still scheduled as normal social gatherings for Sunday afternoons (with babies) or an evening drink at the pub. Still light weight and low maintenance! But nonetheless, this period led to an uneasy phase, as it wasn't clear how a "clan" fitted with the wider family of clusters that was developing across the church. It took four or five years before we discovered that. But that's another story for a later chapter!

AN EMERGING TALE

In a city in the North West of England there live a couple called Richard and Wendy with two small kids. They have been very committed members of their local Anglican parish church for quite a few years. Wendy has run the Parent and Toddlers, Richard is a lay reader and preacher and leads services. However, over the past couple of years God has given them a vision for the estate of 5000 people where they live.

Through chatting at the school gate and making friends with neighbours they have generally developed a network of relationships in the streets around where they live. With all these contacts God has developed a vision of an expression of church on each street.

They have all sorts of get-togethers, formal and informal. At the more planned meetings there is always the bible and they approach any passage with two simple questions: what truth do you find here, and what do you intend to do about it?! A number of get-togethers are emerging, although they are not like fixed membership "home groups." On a Monday evening adults gather at a neighbour's house in varying combinations. Then Wendy and Richard have a Sunday morning family breakfast church in their home at 8am. This includes a simple prayer, liturgy, bible and food for all ages with lots of interaction, often led by the children.

At most of their gatherings there are lots of not-yet Christians and in the past couple of years they have seen sixteen people converted. They had a baptism for three in an inflatable pool in their back garden on a Friday a year ago!

As friendships develop they find a "Journeys Video"[6] of testimonies is so accessible and compulsive it gets passed round the streets. This opens up new conversations and relationships develop. As the house-based missionary cells grew they began to multiply and they developed the next step of the vision, which was to pray and plan towards a gathering together of a cluster of these groups in a larger venue on the estate.

Up to this point Richard and Wendy and children had rushed off after the Sunday morning breakfast church, to the parish morning service for 10.30am. However, in Autumn 2005 they were then commissioned by that church and released to this new community in mission work on their estate. This is emerging into the planting of a fresh expression of church arising from the informal mission cells that have begun to

---

[6] Journeys – lighthousecc@exemail.com.au

cluster into a mid-sized community with similar principles to those we shall explain here. Whilst it will be under the overall authority of the local Anglican parish structure, it is cluster as a parallel stream, set free to find its own pattern to express its very rooted life and mission on the estate. As God gives further growth, they plan to multiply these mid-sized interactive gatherings, rather than build any sort of Sunday service.

AND A TWIST IN THE TALE

Around the same time in the early 90's that Mike Breen moved to lead St Thomas', Sheffield, Phil Potter took over as vicar of St Mark's, Haydock in Merseyside. He inherited a church of three or four hundred that had a long history in renewal and evangelism but had been through some recent struggles.

Around that time he encountered the Cell Church Movement and the early Anglican pioneers in the UK of Howard Astin (Bradford)[7] and Steve Croft (Halifax)[8] and was convinced. Phil developed strong links to the Cell UK Network led by Lawrence Singlehurst[9] and to the Anglican Cell movement in Singapore, making visits with some of his lay leaders and receiving Pastor Derek Hong in Haydock.

St Mark's had a fairly long tradition of Home Groups, which like most in the UK were rather stuck and not very effective in outreach. Phil reviewed the possibilities for introducing cell. The two principal options are either the gradual route starting with one prototype leader cell which then multiplies through the congregation or the so called "big bang" transitioning of the whole church all at once. Having been convinced of the

[7] Howard Astin, Body and Cell, Monarch, 1998
[8] Steven Croft, Transforming Communities, DLT, 2002
[9] Lawrence Singlehurst, Loving the Lost, Kingsway, 2001

advantages of the Big Bang he then applied his exceptional leadership gifts and excellent supporting team, to achieve a remarkably effective transition to cell.[10]

Within a couple of years they had moved from some 20 traditional home groups to 50 cells. Linked with this transition was a steady growth to 500 and later to 700-800 involved with the church. The other wing of this cell/celebration model was four weekly Sunday services (celebrations) in the parish church. There were two in the morning, one early afternoon with more elderly folk and one in the evening.

Bob & Mary Hopkins of ACPI had been leading the growing network of Anglicans pursuing or interested in cell church.[11] Through their long relationship with Phil Potter and recognition of the significance of what was happening at St Mark's, they moved the annual National Anglican Cell Conferences from venues in the South to Haydock. After two such conferences, it was clear that St Mark's was the appropriate hub of the national network and Anglican Cell Church Network (ACCN) moved from the ACPI team to St Mark's under Phil's leadership. As well as consultations and regional training events, Phil and his team led highly effective leaders retreats to foster the vision and support vicars implementing cell principles.

Throughout this period Phil Potter had strengthening links with Mike Breen and the leaders at St Thomas, Sheffield. They were part of a small group of northern leaders having regular retreats as well as visits to one another's churches. This exposed Phil to the cluster model and principles that were enthusiastically shared with him. However, although he was interested and often raised questions about clusters, he

---

[10] Phil Potter, The Challenge of Cell Church, BRF/CPAS, 2001 and Bob Hopkins (ed), Cell Stories as Signs of Mission, Grove Ev51, ch 4
[11] Bob Hopkins, Explaining Cell Church, Administry Mini-Guide 12, 1999

consistently concluded that this mid-sized group was not for St Marks, which he continued to lead in cell and celebration, a two winged understanding[12].

With lots of mutual respect the leaders of St Thomas' and St Mark's continued to have fellowship together and encourage one another, but recognising that they were following two similar but distinct paths of developing fresh expressions of church for the UK in the twenty first century.

Then quite suddenly in the Spring of 2002 things began to change. Three main factors led Phil to re-examine the cluster level of church that his colleagues across the Pennines in South Yorkshire had been promoting.

Firstly, the writings of Joseph Meyers had brought to his attention the insights of sociology, which explained the four sizes or levels of distinct human social groupings.[13] Meyers identified that for fully developed social interaction there were what he described as four sociological spaces. Intimate space, personal space, social space and public space. Phil recognised that things like prayer triplets and accountability partners at St Mark's corresponded to intimate space, the cells represented personal space, and the Sunday service Celebrations, represented public space. However, this left social space missing in the pattern at St Mark's, precisely between cell and celebration... could this be clusters?

Secondly, there had been regular honest reviews of progress with the Haydock cells over many years now. This had led to adjustments and improvements where appropriate. However, although there had been much encouragement in evangelistic fruit for quite a number of the cells, there was still a sense that

---

[12] W. Beckham, The Second Reformation, Touch, 1995

[13] Joseph R. Meyers, The Search to Belong, Zondervan, 2003

the mission potential was not being fully realised. In particular Phil and his leaders were always reading the mission field in their part of Merseyside and he recognised that it was made up of subsets of both networks and neighbourhoods. It was also becoming increasingly clear that cells on their own that focussed only on individual friendship evangelism did not give the potential to fully engage with this multiplicity of sub-cultures... could clusters provide the missing mission clout for more significant engagement?

Then thirdly, the blessing of growth that cells had generated over the years had led to the church building being full at some of the Sunday service celebrations. There was no solution down the route of extending the building as there had already been two major extension/re-ordering projects in the past ten years. Phil became convinced that the only way to continue the momentum of growth was to empty some of the people from Sunday services! Could clusters provide the cohesion to sustain lay led groups that moved out of the church building on a rota once a month and engaged with different mission and community activities in their chosen context?

Once these issues came together, relatively quickly it was decided that come the start of the new church year in Sept 2002, clusters would be launched. Once again, such is the strength of Phil and his team that they cast this further vision and successfully implemented it in less than six months. And this despite the very considerable challenge of the fact that the scores of well developed cells didn't fit neatly into the mission visions that emerged.

Creative and adaptive as ever, Phil came up with a quite different model of clusters from the one he had observed for so long at Sheffield. He introduced the cluster level but was happy to live with the seemingly untidy mismatch between cells and clusters. So members of any one cell can be in several different clusters! In marked contrast to St Thomas', there is no neat correspondence of clusters made up of distinct cells all sharing the same mission vision.

A multi-visual card was produced just six months after the cluster vision was launched with over a dozen clusters, each with a logo or image to communicate their mission vision and identity as well as their name.

FamLeigh First was started in Leigh Vale School where Phil's wife Joy is a senior staff member. This is not a plant of church folk renting the school hall on Sunday, but a faith community owning the school as it's "parish"... pupils, parents and staff through the week. The school curriculum includes "circle-time" for children. So the cluster introduced after school "circle time" as their version and application of cell church!

Then *Stepping Stones* is a cell-based faith community that after prayer felt called to engage with a residential home for the elderly. Rather than a clergy person or lay reader taking a monthly "service" in the old folks home, this is seeking to be the catalyst to facilitate church amongst the residents of the home. Within less than a year there were stories of families choosing their visiting day and time based on the cluster community get-togethers and staff coming in on their day off! Again the vision of this community in mission is the "parish" of residents, families and staff.

We could describe the *Tango* Cluster which took to a new level the work of those already involved with the most needy and deprived. Or the early steps of *Walkout* drawing together St Mark's members and their not-yet-Christian friends and contacts who share a passion for walking. Though the cell members' involvement in different clusters appears as a "mix-up" it was Eddie Gibbs who said that "mission is messy." And in discussion with Phil as these clusters continued to gather momentum in 2005, we reflected that the current post-modern culture isn't just an array of discreet networks. Rather, people find their relationships and significance in a whole number of multi-layered networks... being involved with networks at work, recreation, location, interest group, etc. So this less neat expression of cells and non-matching clusters can be seen as the church mirroring and engaging authentically with society's patterns... church folk being with one set in a cell, a different set in their cluster and yet another in their Sunday service celebration.

My reflection was that clusters introduced a new social animal to St Mark's – not a neat cluster of cells – but a pioneer mission team drawn from lots of cells. The strength of course is the cross-fertilising of mission ideas and experience in cells and the avoiding of re-shuffling of people to create neat fits between cell and cluster. In fact as these pioneer mission teams have grown and matured into missional communities, Phil has introduced the classification of St Mark's as a mixed economy church of "River and Lake" communities. The "River" expressions being these flexible mid-size missional groups flowing in a "Go" mode well beyond the "Lake" expressions of inherited "Come" mode[14]. The text from Genesis that sums up the St Mark's vision is very inspiring...

*"May God bless you and make you fruitful and increase your numbers until you become **a community of peoples.**"* Gen 28:3.

With these introductory stories to get our imaginations going, let's move to the chapters of the book to explore the principles of this expression of cluster-shaped church.

---

[14] Phil Potter is due to have his book published on these River and Lake principles in 2008, by BRF.

PART ONE

ESSENCE & IDENTITY OF CLUSTERS

*A summary of what clusters are
and how cluster-shaped church works.*

Chapter 1　　**Clusters in a Nutshell**
So what are clusters? How can I understand the essence of these mid-sized communities right at the start?

Chapter 2　　**The Glue that Holds Clusters Together**
How does a group of 25-65 find its identity apart from a special building and a religious event? And how may it gain cohesion as well as connection with the wider church?

Chapter 3　　**The Three Dimensions of Clusters**
How do lay leaders with families and day jobs keep these mid-sized communities as healthy church. Unpacking the relationships UP:IN:OUT dynamics and the OF that makes "Toblerone Church!"

Chapter 4　　**Clusters Mean Radical Change**
So what's the essential difference? The challenge of a biblical system and structure of church.

CHAPTER ONE

Clusters in a Nutshell

What are clusters and why are they important? This is a very reasonable question to address right at the start. We want to give you enough of a broad overview in this first chapter to see why this may be important for you and to identify the main themes. We shall explore the practicalities of how you might best introduce and grow such mid-sized missional communities, what their gatherings may be like and how they work with different generations.

In later parts of the book we will re-visit and expand the principles that we introduce here. We shall look at the mission context and also at some frameworks of doing church and see how these explain the place of clusters. We shall explore the practicalities of how you might best introduce and grow such mid-sized missional communities, what their gatherings may be like and how they work with different generations. Then in the last part, we shall seek to shed more light telling the story of how clusters developed at St Thomas' in Sheffield and have now been adopted and adapted by scores of other churches. This concludes with an honest look at their strengths and weaknesses and some questions they raise.

So we come back to our core question, what are clusters? Are they a new fad or fashion in how to do church? I hope not. In fact I passionately believe not, if we understand them rightly. We believe that they are flexible and adaptable, being based on core principles rather than a rigid model. We have been working with church planting and fresh expressions of church for 25 years and throughout this time our driving aim has been to discover effective missional communities. Communities that engage with changing and diverse contexts to contribute to the re-evangelisation of our culture. We believe that clusters are examples of such missional communities... examples of emerging mode church, in contrast to inherited mode that principally connects with a disappearing Christendom.

Under the following headings we summarise the essence of these mid-sized communities:

CLUSTERS OF SMALL GROUPS OR JUST MID-SIZED COMMUNITIES

Yes, at the most basic level, it was that straightforward when clusters were started at St Thomas, Sheffield. Clusters were simply a cluster of small groups! But they are much, much more than that, as we shall see. Typically a Cluster was composed of two to six or seven small groups or cells. And yes, it's important that the constituent small groups can be of different types. They may be a lot like cells of the cell church movement[1]. Although they may be more like households or house churches[2]. They can draw on base community insights[3] or even be the gatherings of mixed Christians and not-yet-Christians from a New Age background who socialise in one another's houses in different combinations from week to week.

However, as other churches have adopted clusters, they haven't always been made up of small groups. Some churches

---

[1] Ralph Neighbour, Where Do We Go From Here, Touch, 1991, and W. Beckham, The Second Reformation, Touch 1995 and Tony & Felicity Dale, Simply Church, Karis, 2002

[2] Wolfgang Simson, Houses that Change the World, Authentic, 1999

[3] Jeanne Hinton, Walking in the Same Direction - New Ways of Being Church, WCC, 1995

have introduced mid-sized clusters without any sub-structure. In some cases this has been an initial phase and the clusters have later developed constituent small groups. Other churches have a mixture of clusters made up of small groups and others without. It could be that this mid-sized group merely has a sub-structure of accountability partnerships or prayer triplets.

So the more important question is how many people are there typically in a cluster? With between two and six small groups, it's likely that total numbers range from 15 to 65 people. Some have grown so fast that they have gone over one hundred adults and children. But one of the very significant things we have seen is that the essence of cluster as missional community begins to get lost above 60 or 70 people. The ideal size which defines cluster dynamics probably ranges from 25 to 55 adults. If there are children this may go up a little.

The important thing to grasp right at the outset is that cluster or mid-sized community defines a grouping with a specific sociological, ecclesiological and missional identity. The key is how cluster works as a community, as an expression of church and as a missionary band. These are the things we want to unpack in these chapters. As we have indicated here, clusters grow. They grow in quality and in quantity, and yes, they do multiply.

WHAT CLUSTERS ARE NOT

At the outset it's most important to clarify some things that clusters are not. No, they are not just a strategy to re-structure large churches. They embody a universal principle of healthy missional church and as such can be implemented in any size church. A small existing church of 30 to 50 could re-form itself to develop one or two clusters. Any sized church could initiate clusters in parallel to their existing body of people. Then again larger churches certainly can transition into a cluster-based approach. Some churches that tried and failed to introduce cell church principles have found cluster size has been embraced really well. Then later, healthy cells have emerged within the clusters.

In talking too specifically about the size of clusters we have to be a bit careful. Since leadership with vision is the seed for clusters, we have learnt to "call it what God's put in their heart." If a few people have caught a vision to birth a cluster, even if they aren't as big as a small group yet – recognise and respect their faith and call it an emerging cluster. To begin with we were so set on the discovery of this extended family size community that we wanted to be rigorous and only call it a cluster if it was large enough to be bigger than a small group and preferably to already be made up of two or more small groups. But over the years we have seen that vision and faith in the founding leaders are key... so call it what they have caught sight of.

Furthermore, clusters are not just a variation on cell or household church, although cluster-based church can work with and incorporate these models and insights extremely well. In Appendix 4 we explain how cluster has much in common with the cell and base community movements and certainly is a development of their insights. Cluster based church is a post-modern approach to church planting and mission. A cluster is not just another size or level of meeting. When done well, it is much more about community in mission than about meetings, though we will look at what and how they meet (Chapter 11 and Appendix 3).

CLUSTERS RE-DISCOVER BIBLICAL CONGREGATION

To understand clusters we shall need to recognise that one of the principal weaknesses of the western church is that we have lost Biblical and sociological 'congregation.' What we now call congregation, we believe is something different. This is particularly serious because we define church as congregation and it's the word congregation that carries all our assumptions about church. Congregation is at the heart of how we have come to understand church. So this is precisely why it is so important that we re-imagine congregation so as to re-discover its true biblical identity and dynamic. Clusters are precisely such a re-discovery of this mid-sized community. And the avoidance of the use of the word congregation is extremely crucial if we are to break out of the conforming mental map that goes with that word.

In today's western church formed by Christendom, congregation is all about a special religious event (service) in a special building on one day of the week. The historic development of congregation as parish church and gathered chapel has taken from the Cathedral most of the characteristics of what should be celebration. It is western distortion of congregation that has enshrined clericalism and prevents the liberation of the whole people of God in community-based mission (Chapter 6).

Clusters seek the recovery of the biblical congregation. These do not depend on a professional caste of leaders and they express a deep reality of community where absentees are missed and everyone has a chance to contribute. Clusters are about an extended family size community that recovers these interactive dynamics of participation and belonging. They are holistic missional communities. Clusters are not about buildings, a religious event or one special day of the week.

As you read chapters 11 to 14 of First Corinthians, Paul repeatedly refers to "when you meet together." And his descriptions only make sense and come to life with gatherings from 15 to 60 that do extended family community (Chapter 5).

Robert Warren's influential little book *Building Missionary Congregations*[4] gives a wonderful challenge and vision of the church becoming mission centred. My only critique to him was that it should have been entitled *Building Missionary Communities* because so much about the word congregation traps us in inherited mode.

CLUSTERS ARE DEFINED BY MISSION

Clusters are communities that are defined by mission. This is their principle difference to "Pastorates[5]" which have been successfully adopted by some churches and may be a similar sized grouping. It's the cluster mission focus above anything else that sets them apart, holds them together, gives them identity and motivates them (Chapter 2). Clusters that lack a clear unified mission purpose stagnate or die. It is the quality that most strikes a visitor to clusters. Ideally, each cluster should be initiated and gathered round their specific mission context or sub-culture. Their driving force is to seek to be community in that context, of that context and for that context. They seek to be indigenous incarnations of the Gospel. Jon Fox, one of our cluster leaders, summed up that "clusters are small enough to share a common vision and large enough to do something about it" (Chapter 7).

So we have seen clusters proliferating for all sorts of groups in our plural society. Some are engaging with areas that still retain neighbourhood relationships. Others are enthusiastic about a non-geographic social network such as café culture or club

---

[4] Robert Warren, Building Missionary Congregations, CHP, 1995
[5] Pastorates, Alpha International, 2003

culture. A particular need can call for a community to be built that leads to a cluster. For example A2B cluster stands for Addiction to Belief and then Good News is a cluster that has arisen out of a drop-in café feeding the homeless. Then again, several clusters have drawn together those concerned for church in the workplace. Some clusters are multi-generational and others focus on youth, whilst still others reach out to young adults exploring creative community (Chapter 12).

EXAMPLES OF CLUSTER MISSION FOCUS

- Link - Young adults in the workplace
- Banner Cross & Beyond - Suburban local community
- Grassroots - Inner urban local community
- Home - Young adults - creative arts
- Sadacca - Addiction to Belief… Drugs and Homeless
- D3 - Clubbing scene
- Generator - Intergenerational Extended Family
- Devoted - Youth
- Walkabout - Social, Justice and Environmental issues
- Go Global - Integrating internationals

CLUSTERS RELEASE A LEADERSHIP EXPLOSION

These mid-sized communities or groups of small groups, have seen a phenomenal growth of leaders. Over 30 clusters at St Thomas' are currently led by lay leader teams… all supported by secular employment. And this is true in all the other churches we know that are becoming cluster-based. Their model of community is lightweight and low maintenance. Hence the most common and critical limitation in churches, the shortage of leaders, is released by *lowering the bar* and *raising the motivation*. These mission driven communities are exciting, dynamic places to belong and to lead. Once people catch the vision and experience the difference, many begin to volunteer to start a new group in and for the context that motivates them. In these respects clusters present a completely different prospect from traditional congregational leadership which requires a highly competent experienced, up-front leader for a presentational event. When potential leaders experience clusters they begin to think, "I could have a go at this … I might even do it better!" (Chapters 6 & 10)

Leadership development in this mid-sized community or bundle of small groups, also has a crucial difference from the cell church model. Leaders of small groups grow to the next level by leading a slightly larger community of faith. Rather than in Cell Church when good cell leaders cease leading a faith community and just move up a ladder of increasing pastoral support and oversight as they become cell supervisors and then area supervisors. By contrast, in clusters leaders grow in key gifts and skills, such as vision casting, mission engagement, speaking and community development, in manageable steps. And exactly the same is proving true amongst teenagers involved in leading youth clusters (Chapter 12).

CLUSTERS GIVE A KEY TO EVANGELISM & MULTIPLICATION

Cell church has brought many blessings and crucial insights for discipleship. However, what is proving the hardest barrier is cell church's highest goal – that of growth and multiplication through effective evangelism from small groups. Aggregating cells together into clusters seems to solve the two underlying barriers.

First, a mid-sized group or cluster of cells can be more effective in evangelism by giving a more substantial pool of relationships when the cells combine to work not just with the 'Oikos' (relational network) of 6 to 12 people but engage a significant neighbourhood or network focus. The evangelistic effectiveness is further increased by the combined energy, gifts and ideas of 25-60 people working together in mission. Hence there is a more significant mission resource to respond to a more sizeable and significant mission opportunity.

Secondly, there is the resistance to growth and multiplication because cell members don't want to loose their friends. With cells grouped in a cluster, multiplication of a cell keeps all the relationships in this wider community.

WHAT'S THEIR PATTERN OF MEETING?

Here we are back to a basic functional question that's always one of the first to be asked. But like most questions addressed to this way of doing church, the answer is "it depends." Because clusters are mission driven communities, leaders will vary their pattern of life to serve the stage of their vision. They are not like a church program that runs to a certain schedule and never changes. They aim to be seven days a week holistic community rather than a one day event.

Some of these clusters may meet on a weekday, every week with no small groups. But typically a cluster of cells might meet three times a month in small groups and once all together. However, to start a cluster, leaders may want to establish the vision and so reverse the order, or even meet only as cluster and later break down into cells.

Lots of circumstances in the life of clusters can lead to other variations on these patterns. Similarly there is flexibility in whether clusters meet on Sunday or weekdays. When they are normally meeting midweek, there may be a 'cluster Sunday' once a term. St Thomas' and one or two other churches have had periods when clusters have regularly met on Sundays, but this is more challenging. It doesn't have to be like that necessarily and usually it is not advisable in the early stages of implementing clusters.

Their venues are as variable as their mission focus, and they are likely to be 'on pilgrimage' since their venue needs to change as they grow. So this flexibility both serves their missional nature and is a mark of a missional community in our mobile and rapidly changing social context (more on meetings and venues in Chapter 11 and Appendix 3).

CLUSTERS CREATE NETWORKED CHURCH

The result of developing church, based on a variety of clusters engaging with diverse contexts, can be a networked church. This is distinct from a network of churches, because the clusters stay together and periodically gather in larger celebrations. Again the frequency of combined celebration gatherings can vary from weekly on Sunday if clusters are midweek, to monthly or at other longer intervals.

Most important for this networked arrangement of clusters, is the fact that the "small church" cluster expression is supported by "large church" central resourcing. This can be thought of as a matrix, with the missional communities on one axis and central teams on the other axis to provide things like finance, training, children's resources, youth work, etc. (see chapter 2, with diagram).

This networked structure may allow the twin benefits of combining maximum diversity of mission points with increasingly effective releasing of pooled resources. However, with more churches adapting the model, this networking can vary from a tight-knit array of closely linked clusters to a much looser confederation of semi-autonomous cluster plants.

Furthermore, as we saw in the emerging story in the introduction, church can arise based on cluster principles with no such network.

BUT IS IT OUT OF CONTROL?

With the explosion of leaders and a loose networked structure, how is the whole show kept on track? If, in such a releasing environment, everyone is encouraged to develop vision and creativity, and such diversity is permitted, what is there to protect orthodoxy? The simple answer here is in a substantial shift from the system in most churches, which relies on high control.

Leadership at every level in a healthy cluster system reverses the norm and is based on high accountability and low control. We shall see later how this can be delivered (Chapter four). So it's important to recognise at the outset that cluster-based church may still have recognisably similar overall church leaders: vicars, senior pastors, etc. But they will be functioning in a different leadership style and within a different structure. Again, we say much more on this in chapters four and nine.

Clusters uncover a profound challenge to how we disciple children. When clusters first started no-one thought much about how they would affect children. There was enough to do working out how adults make this new community in mission really work. However, a progression followed from occasional adding of events to include children, to evolving family clusters and then fully inter-generational communities. And in the process we are discovering the need for an upside-down transformation of thinking about discipling children. This exposes much existing church practice as consumerist provision of children's programmes that robs/enables parents to abdicate their God-given role to disciple their own children. Cluster-

41

based churches are moving profoundly counter-culturally when they begin to resource parents to re-assume the responsibility. This is also true when they equip mid-sized family communities to provide a vital supporting role to parents in this discipling of the next generation (Chapter 13).

CLUSTERS BY ANY OTHER NAME!

So what's in a name? Must it be clusters and can they be adapted? Certainly they don't have to be called clusters. One church is calling them 'Mid-Size Communities'... or MSCs for short! And another calls youth clusters 'Trash Groups.' Yet another network of rural church used the term cluster for three years while it established the practice of these mid-sized, all involved, missional communities, but has now reverted to calling them congregations! (Assuring us that they are still functioning as the real biblical thing). Nor do they have to be structured or supported in exactly the way St Thomas' initially developed them or exactly as we have described them here. As we have said, they may start as an aggregation of cells, or they may start with no cell sub-structure at all.

But they do need to recover the dynamic of missional communities inherent in Biblical congregation. Their flexibility makes them highly adaptable to your context but the underlying principles are what give them their remarkable effectiveness. And it's the underlying principles, just touched on in this summary that we hope to develop for you in the rest of the book.

MIKE BREEN'S SUMMARY OF CLUSTERS IN 1995 AND 2000.

When Mike Breen launched the cluster vision in 1995 he characterised them as "Missionary Congregations" expressing the three relationships UP:IN:OUT in their life together (Chapter three). Then when the first formal Cluster Leader Training course (then called Lifeskills 3) was run in 2000, he summarized clusters as being about...

1) A place of **Identity**, **Belonging** and **Ownership**... containing elements of wholeness and maturity. This was to be their "texture."

2) A point of **Gathering**... in fact a gathering together of small groups in wider community. This was to be their "structure."

3) A context of **Training**... the opportunity for all to raise to their capacity beyond the small group.

4) And lastly, **Embryos**... embryo church plants... though by no means all will be or should be. This is still intrinsic to the vision.

Mike also noted that key qualities of these mid-sized communities were energy and leadership; momentum and direction (Acts 11:23).

READ ON!

This first chapter has merely given a brief overview of some of the central characteristics of clusters. These characteristics, which I have summarised, make it clear that this is a whole new way of doing church, which requires a radical shift from both leaders and those led. If this summary has caught your attention, then read on. But whatever you do, don't think you have already got the essence and all you need for implementing clusters. If you plan to put any of this into action please, please read on because the church is littered with half understood failed concepts.

CHAPTER TWO

The Glue That Holds Clusters Together

This new dispersed way of doing church poses this question – where is the glue?! And the question needs addressing at two levels. First, what is it within a cluster that holds it together? Then second, what is it that holds together a number of different and possibly widely spread clusters? We shall address each question in turn.

THE GLUE WITHIN A CLUSTER – INTERNAL GLUE

If clusters have their existence apart from a building or special service, what holds them together? We are so used to our expression of church taking its identify from a Sunday service, that it is a very real question. How do clusters get their identity, coherence and stability? We have described them as communities in mission and that is their essence. They gain their identity and integrity as a place of belonging (community) and a people with a common purpose (mission).

Vision and Values: When asked, "What church do you belong to?" it's a whole new challenge when you can't refer to a building and a Sunday service. We found that we were forced back to describing the body of people we worshipped and walked with in our cluster. Very biblical of course, and how we were led to describe our cluster was by the sort of community it was (values) and who we felt called to reach (vision). As we experienced more and more clusters developing at St Thomas' these were always the things that they had in common. They always spoke of who they felt called to reach and of what were the characteristics of the sort of social grouping they wanted to become. Linked to this was the identifying of a name for the cluster which was chosen as far as possible to sum up these aims and characteristics. (So we had clusters called Gritstone, Archway, Vine, Chrysanthemum, Nut, Kernel, Wacky, Airborne, etc.)

In this the cluster leadership teams were mirroring at the level of their small faith community, the same principle by which Mike Breen lead the whole church. This was by a clear presentation of vision and values. For the whole of St Thomas' the vision was summed up in **Kingdom** and the values summarised by **Covenant of Grace**. Each year Mike launched the annual plan within this framework of Kingdom Vision and Grace Values. The clusters functioned under this overarching umbrella and found their own vision (mission) and values (community) as a subset of this wider whole church picture and direction.

The way Mike visualises the working together of vision and values to create momentum, keep direction and hold it all together is like the hairsights on a rifle. The diagram overleaf illustrates this with the horizontal crosshair being vision, which generates momentum to move us to our God-given purpose or mission. Then the vertical crosshair represents how shared values build us up into community.

As clusters have been adopted by countless other churches we see this same pattern repeating itself over and over. Emerging leaders get a vision for a mission opportunity and an appropriate style of community and give a name to it. As they pray and cast the vision a team forms and off they go!

As St Andrew's, Chorleywood moved from the first four pioneer Mid-Size Communities (MSCs - Open Door; Friends International; The Grand; TGIB) to eight, to seventeen... so appeared The Ark, WD3, Golden Doors, The Anchor, Transform, Breakout, etc. One did end up being called MSCXVII since no other inspiration came!

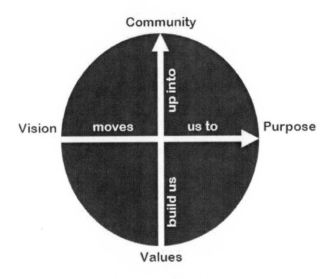

PVa – The Formula for Glue! At the first training session for cluster leaders that Mary and I led at St Thomas in 1988, I was explaining what I had identified that held clusters together. I described it as glue and broke it down into three constituent parts. First, was the key role provided by a sense of **Purpose** summed up in a clear mission focus. Second, I identified the **Values** that created the style and quality of community. And lastly I noted how clusters used a name and some common agreed language to express these characteristics and to articulate their shared story.

At this point a Cluster Leader with a science background (or perhaps a handyman!) called out, "Do you realise that the formula for glue is PVa!" So there you are, it stuck! Purpose, Values and Agreed language are at the heart of giving coherence and identity to Clusters... communities in mission. No sooner had this observation been shared with much laughter, than Mike chipped in and brought us into line with the St Thomas' principle of alliteration, with the catchy alternative of "Vision, Values & Vocab."

GLUE THAT HOLDS CLUSTERS TOGETHER

P	PURPOSE	Mission Focus
V	VALUES	Community Qualities
A	AGREED LANGUAGE	Name and Story

Vision and Values and Vocab

Strong Identity Produces a Healthy Cluster: In describing this glue as the shared mission purpose, community values and associated language, we were not only recognising common characteristics developing in most clusters. The increasingly strong evidence was that the clearer these were and the better they were communicated and owned (helped by the agreed language), the more vigorous and healthy was the cluster.

So we had clusters like Archway with a clear Vision and Values, spelt out in a written document and even with a graphic design to sum up a prophetic description of their call. This enabled one constituent small group to recognise over time that they didn't fit and needed to relocate in another cluster. These characteristics of clusters help every Christian disciple work through their vocation. Cluster leaders need to be reassured that a sifting process around purpose and values is not only ok, it's healthy. There will be losses and gains, but it's important to gather the right people.

Airborne was another example of health and growth that came in the second wave of new clusters. Every get-together involved a shared meal even as numbers rose to 30, 40 and then 50! This community building was matched by leaders with real evangelistic gifts and then a visionary apostolic leader joined the team who added vital momentum and direction. Here again the communication and ownership of the vision was helped by a graphic designed logo, shown opposite, of an eagle in flight linked to the memorable slogan, "Airborne... don't flap... soar!" At some consultations we did with the leaders and then the whole cluster we were able to explore how the cluster rated on the eight quality characteristics of National Church Development.[1]

In both Appendix 1 and 2 we illustrate how strong clusters like Airborne have developed this glue of clear vision and values, communicated through their sort of language. The examples also show how these are then worked through with consistency into the planning of their cluster life and activities.

As we visited different clusters it was not difficult to pick up which were dynamic, motivated, and with a real sense of common commitment and a quality of belonging. Healthy clusters had strong caring relationships and also a "buzz" about them as somewhere that was going places.

---

[1] Christian A. Schwartz , National Church Development, British Church Growth Association, 1997

"DON'T FLAP! SOAR!"

WORSHIP

To worship in spirit and truth, being real to ourselves and giving thanks to God in GRATITUDE

WELCOME

Our aim is to welcome the stranger. Be it that you are a stranger to St. Toms, cluster life or small groups. Or a stranger to God the Father, Jesus as Lord, Teacher, Saviour, Friend or the work and presence of the Holy Spirit. As a cluster we would aim to do this with GENEROSITY.

SERVE

As a cluster we seek to extend the Kingdom and build our community. This involves a lot of food! Our aim is to serve in all things with GRACE

A Cluster like Chrysanthemum had a lovely feel with warm relationships and many gifted leaders. But as we asked what the vision for the cluster was, it emerged that there were not just two but four or five different visions which seemed hard to hold together. We were not surprised that over the next year or so the cluster dissolved with members linking up with other clusters where their passions had a clearer fit.

Vine Cluster was another which didn't meet the PVa test! It had great strengths in community and loving relationships and three clear mission areas that were well supported. However, intercession for unity in Northern Ireland, a passion for Israel and involvement with an orphanage in Romania were all excellent but pulled resources in three directions. Even more important was the lack of any common vision for engagement in a clear mission focus here at home in Sheffield. Such was the quality of community that this cluster survived some seven years in which it did good things.

Cluster Leadership: Needless to say the quality of leadership in the clusters is crucial for the health of clusters. In fact everything we have said about the identity of clusters is created and facilitated by the leadership. The quality of the "glue" is a direct result of the quality of the leaders. It depends on their ability to listen to God and to the people, and from this listening to discern a clear vision and values.

They also need to have the skills to communicate these, first to gather a team and then to gain ownership from cluster members so that they are enabled to contribute and play their part in implementing the vision, creating values-based community and developing the shared language.

Just as lessons from Mike's leadership of the wider church were carried down to the cluster level in the area of clear and communicated Vision and Values – so too were other principles of leadership. For example, the square of Lifeshapes illustrates the need to shift cluster leadership style from visionary/directive in the early cluster forming stage, to coaching in the next testing and turbulent stage.

Leadership should then become collaborative in the growth and exciting phase; leading to a delegating style as the cluster really performs and prepares to multiply. Then again the Lifeshapes pentagon helps cluster leaders recognise and use the different five-fold gifts within their mid-sized community. They are particularly helped to see how apostolic and prophetic gifts motivate and guide the cluster, the evangelists energise everyone to reach out and the pastors and teachers build up and care for the growing community[2].

Is Specific Cluster Language Excluding? Some who hear the principle that cluster identity is based on Purpose, Values and Agreed language, express discomfort. Isn't exclusive language both excluding and cliquish? This charge can sound justified with clusters like Wacky even having small groups like Zippy and Penelope Pitstop, not to mention other Gen X "in phrases." Certainly cluster leaders need to manage this aspect carefully to avoid excessive jargon being a put-off. There must always be lots of explanation to bring new people into the shared expressions and experience.

However, it's really important to recognise that this development of common terms, rituals, nicknames, favourite jokes and shared traditions is what gives identity and a sense of belonging to all healthy groups. Strong families are full of it, every club and society have it and denominations get their identity from it... standardised liturgies are all about this familiarity with which one comes to feel "at home." So we certainly don't want to misunderstand and try to minimise these important bonding and motivating elements, but leaders do need to handle them in an open and welcoming way.

---

[2] These principles are developed much further in chapter 10 on launching and growing clusters and are of course drawn from Mike Breen & Walt Kallestad, A Passionate Life & The Passionate Church, Nexgen, 2005 & 2004.

THE GLUE BETWEEN CLUSTERS – LEADERSHIP HUDDLES, CELEBRATIONS AND A MATRIX

Now we address the question, how do you hold together such a dispersed cluster-based church as it grows and multiplies and becomes a networked church. It is not so much about public events as about the network of missional communities held together by a shared overall vision, some broad common values and by leadership relationships, plus an evolving matrix structure. A normal parish church, even with small groups, is principally about the Sunday service in the parish church building. The mega church even with its many programs, is primarily perceived through its three, six or twelve services each with hundreds or thousands in the big venue. The defining identity of these approaches is centralised. By contrast, as clusters develop it becomes dispersed. Now when clusters first began to form and establish themselves at St Thomas' in Sheffield, there were still four services on Sunday in the parish church. However, as they grew in strength and number, the centre of gravity of the church shifted to these relatively small and much more precarious expressions of life. Increasingly the cluster was where you belonged. Your cluster was what became your Christian family and where you found your role and ministry to serve others. But all within the sense of being held in a web of something wider and more significant, spreading across the city. And these are the things that we have discovered, which hold the dispersed clusters together.

Huddles – Cluster Leader Support Groups: The first thing that links and holds diverse and sometimes distant clusters together is at the leadership level. The lay leaders of these lightweight mid-sized communities can only sustain their role and grow if they are supported and mentored in the task. Ideally a group of leaders from a number of clusters are mentored together. In St Thomas' these took on the name of "Huddles" from Carl George[3]. It took a while after clusters were well established to introduce the huddles and to realise the vital role they play. The principles taken on by these discipleship groups for up to twelve leaders, were drawn partly from the G12 movement[4] and partly from Phil Potter's adaptation of John Wesley's class system questions[5].

These huddle groups in fact provide accountability as described in the previous section of this chapter, as well as support and apprenticeship. The system developed at St Thomas' is based on LifeShapes, but addresses in turn issues of cluster leaders' character, prayer, faith and skills[6]. These mentoring groups not only provide relational unity between leaders of different clusters, but a common development process. And because the cluster leaders in turn huddle the small group leaders in their cluster, this provides a real cohesive glue across a network of clusters.

As other churches have implemented clusters, some form of group support and accountability for their leaders has usually emerged. We would recommend it wherever clusters become the heart of how you do church. But we would see it as indispensable to hold things together in a healthy network once there are a significant number of clusters.

Celebrations – Gathering Networked Church: As the number of clusters grows and some begin to multiply, you are

---

[3] Carl George, Preparing Your Church for the Future, Revell, 1991
[4] Joel Comiskey, Groups of 12, Touch, 1999
[5] Phil Potter, The Challenge of Cell Church, BRF, 2001, Ch.4
[6] Copies of the leaflets used to explore these areas can be obtained from tom@stthomaschurch.org.uk

increasing the outward movement or mission dispersion effect. This needs to be balanced by some level of gathering if the movement is to be held together. This can take all sorts of forms according to the history and context.

In many cases, continuing weekly Sunday services provide a celebration-style gathering, which sustains a looser level of relationship and enables wider vision and issues to be communicated. However, this can develop into lighter patterns of networked church. This can happen by less frequent combined whole church gatherings and/or by the growing number of clusters being grouped into more than one celebration-style gathering to which they then belong.

Both these developments have happened at St Thomas' and to some extent with MSCs at St Andrews, Chorleywood.

Depending on tradition and denomination, Holy Communion may be a focus of combined Celebrations. In some denominations a more formalised Eucharist may be suitable for the gathering together of clusters, which may enjoy a more informal agape meal in their mid-sized communities. Weddings, Funerals and Baptisms may normally be combined events although the cluster and small group may play a prominent role in baptism of new members. Certainly some clusters have held their own baptism, inviting in a leader of the wider church to share it with the cluster leader.

The result of dispersed clusters and gathered celebrations is that this way of doing church can combine really earthed mission clusters having little sense of highly visible public face with celebrations that can be as accessible to the casual visitor as parish church (they may even be held there!).

So these celebrations or specific different Sunday services, become the much larger community made up of four to ten clusters. These celebrations have their own leadership team and periodic gatherings – anything from weekly to monthly. At one stage in Sheffield three such celebrations emerged. The first Sunday celebration was formed of clusters embracing the vision of parish mission at Crookes. The second celebration was formed around those clusters linked to the morning city Sunday service and third were those clusters making up the evening city celebration with a strong youth, student and young adult mission focus. This is illustrated in the family tree below.

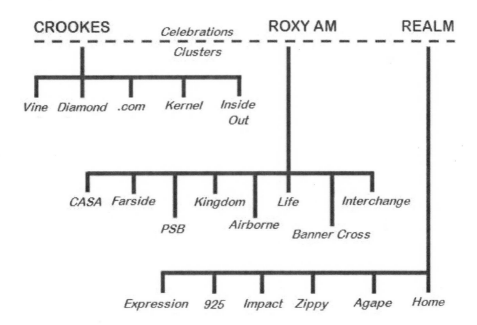

So a well developed cluster-based church begins to take on the form of a mission movement. Multiplication processes begin to be worked out and become natural at small group, cluster and celebration levels. Vision motivates the movement and shapes the resulting network. Hence, as clusters begin to emerge which share a new mission vision in common, a new celebration may be born. So the shared vision at the celebration level is broad whereas the common vision of small groups in a cluster is much more specific and sharply focussed within that overall wide umbrella vision. In general, clusters continue to be led by lay teams, whereas the celebrations or continuing Sunday services can normally justify a paid leader.

A Matrix – Resourcing from the Centre: We have repeatedly emphasised that clusters are light weight and low maintenance. That's why they can be lay led and grow and multiply. But this leads to the question, "how are they resourced?" Those used to the inherited congregation program fear the loss of deeper teaching and of the quality of provision for children and youth. These are real concerns and not easy to address. The last eight years at St Thomas' has seen much effort to address this challenge (see also chapters 12 & 13). The development of Mid-Size Communities (MSCs) at St Andrews has also seen breakthrough in these areas.

What has emerged is just one way to structure and manage a networked church, which both resources dispersed clusters and provides another inter-connection. It takes the form of a resourcing matrix as illustrated opposite. The vertical columns represent the cells, clusters and celebrations, the communities of faith, the places of belonging. The horizontal axis is how the central church provides backup and resources in communication, training, financial management, materials and other needs. And this type of matrix is common to interpretation at St Thomas, Sheffield; Holy Trinity, Cheltenham; and St Andrews, Chorleywood.

The historic *Minster Model* has helped inspire, inform and shape these developments at St Thomas'. This model emerged in the middle ages as Celtic and Roman mission models cross-fertilised to provide a strong settled centre or Minster (led by the Abbot) in the more settled market towns, that resourced and provided retreat for mobile teams and mission bands (led by the Bishop) which evangelised and planted church in the surrounding areas of more scattered population and unstructured society[7].

	Celebration	Celebration	Celebration	Celebration
	Clusters	Clusters	Clusters	Clusters
	Cells	Cells	Cells	Cells
Worship				
Training				
Children				
Youth				
Finance				
Communication				

With this matrix arrangement, experience has shown that you have to work hard to ensure that the emphasis continues to be at the edge not the centre. If a mission movement is the aim, then the resourcing roles must serve the outward momentum but all too easily "large church" programs can trump the plans of small church (clusters).

One example of resourcing from the centre arose at Sheffield and Chorleywood, as clusters began to meet regularly on Sundays. A series of large portable boxes were provided at the centre with everything that the clusters and MSCs could need

---

[7] John Finney, Recovering the Past, DLT, 1996

during the week. A member of each group picked these up with everything from resources for children's activities, to notice sheets to processes for the finances. In addition the senior staff leaders "rode the range" visiting several clusters/MSCs during a session to connect and cross fertilise vision and encouragements.

Having explored the principles that provided cohesion and glue within mid-sized groups and also how they can be held together effectively in a network, let's discover more of what makes them tick.

CHAPTER THREE

The Three Dimensions of Clusters

Just as Cell Church has established that a "Jesus community of disciple-making disciples" is fully church irrespective of its size[1] – so Clusters are fully church. The flipside of this truth, is the recognition and challenge that clusters have to express their corporate life in all three dimensions... UP, IN and OUT, the three primary relationships of church[2].

These correspond to the three essential components of church – the *Upward* relationship to God, the *Inward* relationships to one another within the cluster and the *Outward* relationships with the chosen mission context and the world[3].

UP:IN:OUT

These three dimensions of the relationships are again explored and explained in Lifeshapes. This simple three-dimensional

---

[1] My definition of church in Michael Green (ed), Church Without Walls, Paternoster, 2002, p.143

[2] In fact we originally heard these three essential relationships as the heart of church described by George Patterson in the 1980's. They were later incorporated and expanded in Lifeshapes by Mike Breen in the 1990's and published and further expanded to a fourth dimension in the Mission-shaped Church Report, CHP, 2004, p96-98 and A Passionate Life, Mike Breen & Walt Kallestad, Nexgen, 2004, ch.9-11

[3] Robert Warren described these relationships as the three components of church using overlapping circles – Building Missionary Congregations, CHP, 1995, page 20.

understanding of what clusters are and how they work is another part of the core identity of clusters. It is also what makes these mid-size communities in mission lightweight and low maintenance - faith communities both of a size and of a conception that lots of lay leaders feel well able to have a go at leading.

COMMUNITIES IN MISSION

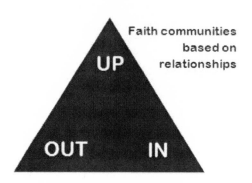

Whilst there is the widest variety in the way that clusters may pray and worship they all develop their distinctive style of relationship to God (UP). Again clusters are encouraged to explore their own pattern and style of community appropriate to their context as they build relationship together (IN). And lastly, as they sharpen their focus on a particular mission calling, so the way that they engage with that sub-culture will vary dramatically from the homeless, to the workplace, to the creative arts, to professional families (OUT).

However, it's precisely because such a wide diversity is encouraged that a simple framework is needed to keep these three relationships vital, growing and in balance. Each dimension should also be in dynamic interaction with the other two as we shall show later. Since clusters are always led by lay teams with day-jobs and families, a simple diagram like the one opposite is needed to plan and develop cluster life.

Now this triangle of relationships is the framework through which the "glue" or essence of clusters described in the previous chapter is worked out. It is precisely through these three dimensions that each cluster expresses its mission vision and its community values. And the language that it develops to communicate these things will also pick up these three characteristics.

To illustrate how central these UP:IN:OUT dimensions are to clusters, we give a few examples in Appendix 1. The first is from Home Cluster which is of young adult creatives connecting with the arts and music world. The next is a cluster called Rise which again is of young adults but which brings together the able and disabled. Then Generator is an example of how an inter-generational family cluster interprets its vision and values through UP:IN:OUT. The logo of Airborne cluster in the previous chapter further illustrates how the cluster idenity is developed from this triangle.

It should be clear that the **upward** cluster relationship can embrace the liturgical or the entirely spontaneous; the alternative worship scene; the contemplative or the very charismatic. It can be wordy or emphasise the symbolic and icons, emphasise the conceptual or the experiential; value quality of presentation or encourage any contribution to empower everyone, including the marginalised. Such upward expressions of cluster relationship to the Trinity can be developed in evening or daytime meetings, in retreats or weekends away, as well as in everyday networking and telephone or email prayer.

Then for the **inward** relationship, clusters may build community either with formality or informality; with light snacks or three course meals; favouring a single cuisine or a variety of ethnic dishes; with outdoor sports and pursuits or high brow culture with intimate sharing of feelings or with story telling of personal history; with lots of caring and prayer for one another or with practical and financial help; with lots of phoning and e-mail connecting or with swapping keys to each others houses! Again this opens up seven days a week community building possibilities and includes weekends away together. When the cluster gathers community can be built by spending some time all together and some breaking down into smaller units.

Similarly the **outward** relationship will vary as widely as the many neighbourhoods and networks within our plural multi-cultural society. And just as the chosen mission focuses are extremely diverse, so will be the patterns of engagement with these contexts. They will be shaped by the gathering points and patterns of the particular social sector. It is evident that appropriate patterns of engagement and evangelism will be quite different from a professional estate, to the art community, to the addicts and homeless, to the workplace and to prostitutes. The gifts and interests of cluster members will also shape the outward dimension in all sorts of creative ways. Prayer and the prophetic can further complement the passion of members for involvement in local issues and all sorts of action on social justice and the environment.

Some outward involvement will flow out of small groups that make up a cluster – others will be done by the whole cluster working together. To give examples of such varied OUT processes to connect with so many contexts and subcultures, could limit rather than illustrate the breadth of what clusters get up to in relating beyond themselves. The main principle is that they listen to their chosen context to identify the needs, aspirations and social patterns. Based on the discernment this gives they get involved in serving and relationship building with as many new people as possible beyond their circle. Often they will do events and programs in partnership with non-church folk rather than have to make everything happen themselves. They may just join in as a small group or cluster with what non-church folk are doing anyway!

So, one cluster that is focused on young adults principally relating through their sporting interests may start a football team or regularly go climbing with their non-Christian friends. Another reaching the same age group may run musical events in a performance venue and plan an exhibition in an art gallery. The work-based cluster can lay on a regular get-together in a function room with invited speakers on work topics, form a discussion forum and organise a golf tournament. One working among the homeless and addicts may do late night city street walks, set up a drop-in cafe and empower the homeless to take on many of the roles themselves. Family all-age clusters focused on a neighbourhood have done all sorts of outward activity from tea parties, to firework nights, to outings, to inviting new folk to Sunday lunch, to starting a father's support group, running parenting courses and providing baby-sitting. And a cluster among the elderly can mobilise all sorts of support, outings, recreation, dominoes, lunch club... and so on. Any cluster can extend beyond its outward engagement with its chosen context by taking action on wider social and environmental issues.

LEADERS PLAN THE LIFE OF CLUSTER THROUGH UP:IN:OUT

Since these three relationships express and develop cluster life, they form the planning framework for leaders. As leaders engage in the early stages of developing the vision and values of an emerging cluster (chapter ten), they can brainstorm and formulate ideas around UP:IN:OUT. Then later, as these leaders begin planning their programme for cluster life and events, these processes will also be greatly helped by being worked out through these three dimensions.

In the previous chapter we used the Airborne cluster logo to illustrate the communication of vision and values. You will have noted that it was built around this triangle and the three core elements of their identity. In Appendix 1 we illustrate the three dimensional vision and values of "Generator", "Home" and "Rise" mid-sized communities. Then in Appendix 2 we present the planning tables used by both Wacky and Airborne to plan processes for UP, IN and OUT involving all the details like "who, how, where and when" for their programmes.

HOW THE DYNAMICS OF UP:IN:OUT GROW CLUSTER

It is also important to see the way that UP:IN:OUT are in dynamic relationship to one another with the life of clusters. In this way they reinforce one another and it can work like a cycle, which can go either way round. Here are some examples.

As the cluster relates to God in worship, prayer or listening they get a new sense of their calling to engage in their mission context. They may even sense some new strategy or activity. This is the UP releasing the OUT. But equally as the cluster engages in mission they become even more aware of their dependence on God and the need for Him to give them the gifts, the openings and ultimately breakthrough. This is the OUT turning us back to UP.

As the cluster seeks more of God they are drawn close together, gifts of the Spirit build one another up and create more inter-dependence. God may point out relationships to restore or challenge to greater love of one another. The UP is enhancing the IN of the cluster. Alternatively as the members of a cluster share their needs with one another they exercise faith in God's provision. As they share their struggles and weaknesses they grow closer through vulnerability but are stimulated to pray for one another. Closer trust and love growing in the cluster overflows in thanks to God. The IN directs us or even erupts into the UP.

Then again, as cluster members talk about the needs in the mission context, share about the "people of peace"[4] that they have been led to... then teams form to respond to the opportunities. As cluster members tell one another about their situation in their neighbourhood, at work or in their network of friends, the sense of mission call sharpens. Folk within the cluster find one another who share a common mission passion, they brainstorm evangelism possibilities... and mission action teams can form. The IN is leading to and resourcing the OUT.

Then as mission teams step out in faith and press through insecurities to reach beyond themselves cluster members learn more about each other than they can in any other way. As they take on even simple tasks together, like planning and running a neighbourhood barbeque or event for workmates, the bonds of support and love grow deeper. Doing mission together can create community like nothing else! The OUT builds and strengthens the IN.

The diagram (overleaf) illustrates how this dynamic cycle grows and enriches the life of clusters. Just as the three pairs in

---

[4] Jesus in commissioning his disciples in the OUTward dimension of mission always taught them to look for and expect to find a "welcome" among people who responded to them (Matt 10:11-14; Mark 6:7-11; Luke 9:1-6). In Luke 10:1-9 he called them "People of Peace." To understand more of this key liberating insight for mission and evangelism see Breen & Kallestad, The Passionate Church, NexGen, 2005, chapters 23 & 24.

the triangle work together in either direction to build cluster life, so the dynamic works round all three relationships. You can start at any of the three points and work in either direction. Encounter with God (UP) can draw a group together (IN) who together get involved in a new project (OUT). Or the strength of relationship between some cluster members (IN) leads them to fast and pray together (UP) during which they are challenged to new acts of love and service to their community (OUT).

A DYNAMIC CYCLE

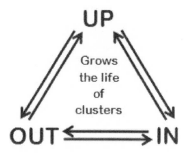

UP:IN:OUT + OF – Toblerone Church

Now clusters also need to relate to each other and to the wider church. This can either be seen as expanding circles of the Inward dimension, as clusters and Christian communities build healthy inter-relationship, or as a fourth dimension – OF. We are always part OF other expressions of church and of the church universal.

The Mission-shaped Church Report, in affirming and exploring fresh expressions of church, unpacks these four dimensions, with George Lings expanding on Mike Breen's UP:IN:OUT.[5] He relates these to the historic credal formulary of church... One (IN), Holy (UP), Catholic(OF) and Apostolic (OUT).

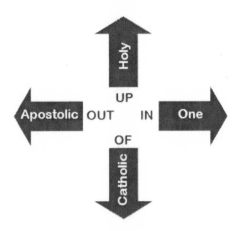

This two dimensional flat representation does helpfully establish these four relationships and their link to the historic convictions about the essential nature of church. However, if we liberate the principles from the flat page, we get the much preferable representation of the four relationships in three dimensions (see diagram overleaf) – toblerone church! This is such a helpful visual representation of individual clusters each defined by and finding their identity and coherence (glue) in their unique UP: IN and OUT relationships, but linked together to other clusters... and beyond to other churches in space and time.

At one level the OF dimension is expressed by clusters forming part of and regularly meeting with others in a larger celebration gathering. Also an organic link is formed by the huddling of leaders from a range of different clusters at which

_____

[5] Mission-shaped Church, Church House Publishing, 2004, Chapter 5, page 99.

all sorts of exchange can occur. This is further extended by whole church gatherings at festivals and whole church involvement in some shared mission events. There are links and common mission activities and meetings with other churches of the city. And clusters often develop practical links with the global church.

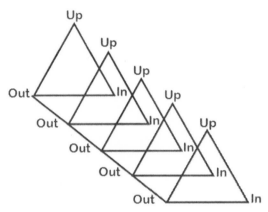

One lovely expression of the Toblerone linkage of different cluster church expressions was the request of children in the intergenerational cluster of families (Generator) to regularly share an activity with the clusters working with the homeless and addicts (Good News Cluster). Each term they go with their parents and share a joint meeting. The children have chatted and prayed with the homeless, baked cakes, taken clothes and sleeping bags that they've collected, performed a nativity and distributed gifts – all the children's ideas!

TRADITIONAL FUNCTIONS OF CHURCH BUILD UP:IN:OUT AND OF FOR CLUSTERS.

Many have asked what happens about those traditional offices of the Church like baptisms, weddings and funerals. The answer, like many questions of cluster-based church, is that "It depends." Sometimes baptisms have been held within the cluster community into which the new convert has been drawn. Often the ceremony will be conducted jointly by the cluster leader and the overall church leader. Here there is the UP relationship expressed in the grace of God in baptism and the thanks and praise of the cluster. There is powerful building of new members into the IN dimension of community. Also the baptism is the fruit of the OUT of the cluster mission and not-yet-Christian friends and family may attend. Then lastly the OF dimension is represented by the leader of the overall church. Alternatively if the cluster take their new convert for baptism into a gathering of the wider church then the OF dimension is even stronger.

Exactly the same involvement of these four essential dynamics of healthy church are expressed in the different ways that weddings and funerals are conducted. These events will normally be marked with clusters joining together and the overall church leader officiating (the OF relationship). But the cluster leader and members will play special parts and be prominent in ministry and thanksgiving, prayer and worship (UP), in welcoming and serving refreshments and meals (IN) and in inviting and supporting their not-yet Christian contacts and friends (OUT). All of these will build into the life of the cluster itself as well as strengthen its relationships beyond itself.

So in this chapter we have explored the simplicity of seeing the essential dynamic of clusters worked out through three relationships of UP, IN and OUT combined with the OF relationship to other clusters and expressions of church. Now we shall move on in the last chapter of this part, to the challenge of just how radical a change is represented by these clusters.

CHAPTER FOUR

Clusters Mean Radical Change

A DIFFERENT WAY OF DOING CHURCH

I have made it clear from the outset that clusters are not just another church program to add on, and nor are they just a re-structuring of larger churches. Underlying the cluster is a re-discovery of biblical congregation, which in turn is a whole different way of doing church. Now this description, "A new way of being church," has been applied with justification to other recent church innovations, such as cell church[1], Base Ecclesial Communities[2] or Household Church[3] (See Appendix 4 for comparisons).

In embracing cluster principles or any of these other approaches, it is vital to understand the radical change in both system and structure involved, which dramatically affects both leaders and led. So in this chapter I explore the specific system underlying cluster church and the associated structures. To illustrate this I happen to use the specific way that St Thomas' in Sheffield has organised and networked this new cluster system.

---

[1] Cell Church – Ralph Neighbour, Where Do We Go From Here, Touch, 1999; Michael Green (ed), Church Without Walls, Paternoster, 2002; Ian Freestone, A New Way of Being Church, Sold Out Publications, 1995
[2] Base Ecclesial Communities – Jeanne Hinton, Walking in the Same Direction: New Ways of Being Church, WCC 1998
[3] Household Church – Wolfgang Simson, Houses that Change the World, Authentic 1999; Tony & Felicity Dale, Simply Church, Karis, 2002

But again it is important to recognise that the underlying system can work with clusters that are being implemented differently in other churches. For example, they may not be networked in a matrix and accountability may work differently.

TWO SYSTEMS OF CHURCH

Here the insights of cell church have been so helpful. It was the training material of Bill Beckham that first introduced me to the concept of a church system. Drawing on the discipline of systems analysis we can arrive at a whole new understanding of church which most have previously taken for granted. Ask yourself! What is a church system? What is the church system that you are part of or that you lead? What was the New Testament system... Jesus' system of church? We so often focus on the externals, that we can take for granted a non-biblical church system[4].

A diagram always communicates principles quickest! On the next page is a slightly adapted version of Bill Beckham's diagram to illustrate two contrasting church systems.

Most of us will be familiar with the one on the left that Beckham calls the program church system. If you are reading this book you have probably been part of the 20% running the programs for the other 80%! It will also probably strike you as immediately convincing that a more satisfactory system and one closer to the New Testament, is the one on the right. 20% resourcing 80% to do the work of ministry sounds much better! But it should probably be even better described as 100% doing the work of mission and ministry, with that work done together

---

[4] W. Beckham, The Second Reformation, Touch Publications, 1975, Chapter 14

through missional communities, in which a certain proportion are equipping and apprenticing others in the process.

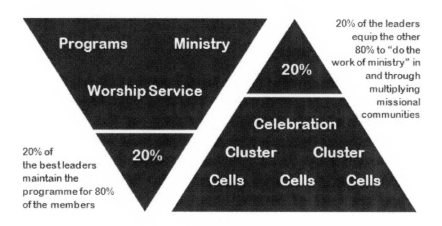

Although these insights have been well developed for the cell church system, we believe that the foundational shift in system can underlie a variety of smaller missional community models. Certainly this is how we see clusters or mid-sized communities working best. In the following table, I have summarised and adapted the cell church literature on the two contrasting church systems of inherited mode and missional community mode. These two descriptive profiles that I contrast below are set above Robert Warren's comparison of inherited and emerging church.[5] At its root, it's a difference between a one day per week event and a seven days discipling community in mission lifestyle.

---

[5] Robert Warren, Building Missionary Congregations, CHP, 1995, page 26

Inherited Church System	Mission Community System
– A gathering of adherents that meets on a special day ... – In a special building for a formal worship event... – And is led by a professional (who may have a team) ... – Who organises programs with them and their resources ... – To meet their needs and to express their mission ...	– Is disciple making by activity and accountability ... – In communities of small groups and clusters of small groups... – Which express their relationship upwards to God ... inwards to one another and outwards to the world... – They grow and multiply through engagement with their mission context ... – And organise apprenticing leaders and resources for their equipping and support
Inherited Church { Priest + Building + Stipend	Emerging Church { Community + Faith + Action

THREE AUTHORITY STRUCTURES - A MOVEMENT OF MISSION

Behind the cluster model is the conviction that the need of the times is to learn from the fact that throughout church history, from Jesus and the Acts of the Apostles onwards, movements of mission have been initiated by God. These movements arose from effective engagement with a culture or context and resulted in indigenous expressions of community that had within them the potential to grow and to multiply, remaining sufficiently flexible and outwardly-focused, that a spreading wave of community-in-mission moved through that part of society.

Most churches in Europe are not well adjusted to enable such a system or process. Their inherited mode of church tends to be static rather than mobile and better serves its own members and fringe rather than being effective in reaching beyond in mission. Furthermore the momentum and multiplication that produce a movement are usually alien. Our western churches originally helped to produce a christianised culture, and have then evolved in a society based on Christendom. This has led to structures that tend to be static and highly institutionalised.

Here again diagrams are helpful to highlight and clarify the issues. We use a modified version of three figures used by Alan Roxborough to best illustrate where we have come from and where we are seeking to explore.[6]

Those denominations whose histories have been inter-twined with the state, such as Catholic, Anglican and Lutheran, tend towards institutional hierarchies that can be represented by a pyramid. Authority flows down regionally from Bishop to Archdeacon, to area Deans to Vicars. Locally this same pattern

---

[6] Alan Roxbourgh, The Missionary Congregation, Leadership & Liminality, Trinity Press. 1997, p65.

has come to be replicated at parish level with Vicars, to wardens, to PCC, to members. This structure is illustrated in the diagrams that follow (overleaf) in which it is contrasted to two other structures.

The typical free-church inverts the pyramid, considering a hierarchy inappropriate. They seek to invest the authority with the membership who work through deacons and elders to direct, hire and fire the minister. This seems to be just a reaction to a system, which is understood to be authoritarian and which has been replaced with one that seeks to be more democratic. However, what lies behind both these historic structures appears to be authority which is worked out through **control**... either through the hierarchy or through the people.

The third diagram seeks to illustrate the mission movement. It keeps two sides of the pyramid and turns it 90° (not 180°) and puts it on its side as the point of an arrow. This represents the penetration of the mission context. And the third side is open to illustrate the expanding wave as missional communities multiply behind the advance.

In this system the authority is given to those recognised and respected as bringing the apostolic and prophetic vision that is energising and shaping the movement. These leaders provide both momentum and direction rather than control, the over-riding principle is rather the **release** of leaders and teams to exercise initiative, creativity and responsibility to support multiplication.

We appreciate that whatever structure or system is in place, the motivation and attitudes of the leaders will significantly modify how it works out in practice.

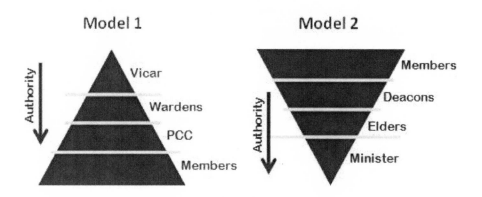

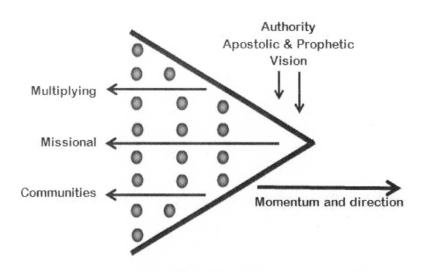

We are aware that there are releasing leaders operating within the two inherited pyramid models. However, these two environments still tend to pre-dispose the system towards control and certainly the degree of releasing rarely achieves significant multiplication. The underlying drives may be to control either practice (who takes initiative and what gets initiated), or orthodoxy (what is communicated or how worship is conducted), but the result still stifles multiplication. A clergy team may aim at an ideal of collaborative working but still operate in control mode. Releasing the whole body of Christ to seek their own calling and creativity and grow into responsibility and maturity, that is a much more dynamic but messy place to be.

Using these diagrams and descriptions, we have tried to answer the question, what is the over-riding nature of a healthy cluster-based system of church? But these analyses make it abundantly clear that it's a radically different sort of church we are talking about. It's a whole different way of life!

FRAMEWORK, FOUNDATION AND FRIENDSHIP

But if we move away from control as a shaping principle of the system and structure, the immediate question arises... how can we guarantee the health and orthodoxy of the multiplying communities of faith? In such a dispersed model of church, how can you protect from deviation? There is a right concern that things don't "get out of control!"

The first and most important answer is that we can't! When a desire to protect orthodoxy and achieve risk minimisation are the dominant concerns, then mission and movement are discouraged or even stifled. The disciples desired to control others who ministered in Jesus' name... but Jesus' response was that "those who are not against us are for us, do not seek to prevent them" (Mark 9:40). Paul's model of mission seems to have been similar. He planted the seeds of the Gospel, called forth new disciples and encouraged them to remain true as he went on his way trusting others who did the watering (1 Cor 3:6) and God who gave the increase. He then later returned to appoint leaders and to encourage them further. Still later he had to write letters, in part to address the problems that his risk-taking mission had allowed. On one level, we could say that we only have much of the New Testament because the missionary movement initiated by Jesus and continued after Pentecost, was so releasing and permissive of initiative with dispersed responsibility, that letters of adjustment, correction and explanation had to be written.

However, having affirmed the inevitable risk involved in a releasing approach to developing leaders, this system is not irresponsible. There is every bit as high a concern to avoid anything destructive and to protect healthy growth. But the difference is that the mechanism is through an emphasis on accountability rather than control. It is crucial to understand that an effective mission movement based on healthy clusters (biblical congregations), depends on overall leaders developing an environment that is high on accountability and low on control. This I believe is the only way to deliver appropriate levels of protection without restricting the release of creative mission energy.

It is our observation and experience, that although accountability is a widely espoused value in the church today, it is very little understood and even less practiced. Institutional church may establish formalised processes that are called accountability but I don't believe they deliver because they do not possess the key elements that we describe here. Instead, because of the strong desire for accountability, we fall back on mechanisms of control. These do not deliver accountability, they just limit freedom, creativity and dynamic mission endeavour.

So a key question is how do you deliver high accountability within a highly releasing environment. My observation from living within a cluster based system for 10 years has led me to conclude that there are three key elements. First we have to create a changed framework of understanding with regard to accountability from one perceived as threat and criticism to one of welcomed support and biblical encouragement. Second, we have to build up a simple but sufficient body of foundational values that are commonly held. Then thirdly, there has to be a relational bond growing from both friendship and frequency of meeting to provide the appropriate trust for accountability to be fruitful.

Delivering High Accountability & Low Control

C	-	Changed Environment
A	-	Agreed Core Values
R	-	Relational Trust

Framework – A Changed Environment: To achieve high accountability we need a new framework to work in, nothing less than a changed atmosphere or attitude. Unless we change how accountability is perceived and practiced at every level of the church we operate in, we cannot grow into a high accountability mode. Even if we impose accountability processes, we are all too adept at hiding for these to deliver. Or they revert to being inappropriate and are rightly critiqued as "heavy shepherding"... and we are back to control. We need to change both the perception and the process if we are to create healthy accountability that will be welcomed not endured. The negative has to be turned to a positive view.

At the outset we need to recognise that this is a change of culture within our society as much as within the western church. Asking questions that call us to account are automatically seen variously as an imposition, implied criticism, intrusion or even rejection. We instinctively tend to regard them as threatening and respond with evasion and self justification. How can this be changed to the point that it's seen as loving support and concern to help my discipleship? What we have seen at St Thomas' is that this has to be tackled on several fronts if it is to be overcome.

First, a grassroots, bottom up movement of accountability has to be initiated. Preaching and teaching have to explain and affirm accountability. This will be supported by every member being regularly encouraged, both in public messages and one to one, to voluntarily find their own accountability partner or partners. Their immediate leaders will offer help to find the right accountability relationship and check from time to time whether it's being found helpful. This will gradually help to spread throughout the church an individual expression of peer accountability that begins to give it a positive image as being helpful and even a channel of blessing. It becomes a significant building block to strengthening the fabric of community.

At the 'every member' level of being accountable to 'one another', it is both voluntary and non-prescriptive in the content. This avoids heavy shepherding. In fact I have observed 'accountability evangelists'! When a new young adult joins the church I have heard conversations with developing friends and cell members that has included the spontaneous encouragement... "Oh, you should find an accountability partner, they're great, it's helped me so much to grow in Christ!"

Another safety factor and contrast to heavy shepherding is that such accountability always relates to "What do you want to see change in your life, what do you sense God is challenging you on?" Accountability partners and groups aren't there to tell you how to run your life but to help and support you in the direction you sense God is leading you and which you want to take. This is the key difference and must often be reemphasised.

Secondly, a more formalised accountability framework has to become the norm of folk at every level of leadership. At St Thomas' this grew through the introduction of a 'huddle' system. Church leaders huddle with the cluster leaders and cluster leaders in turn huddle with their small group leaders. These were started to deliver much needed support and encouragement and were warmly welcomed.

Further accountability grew with the introduction of accountability questions. We got the idea and many of the questions from Phil Potter, who based them on John Wesley's class meeting system. These were helped to be received positively by alternating the focus from skills to build up the competence and confidence of the leader, with questions exploring personal formation and character. Again these sessions were set in the context of mutual sharing with "one another" in vulnerability. This balance of skill and formation with agreed questions provides the framework to give both a positive perception and process for accountability – it's for us and it's good. Furthermore, this dimension of accountability is modelled from leaders, down.

Foundation – Agreed Values: Just as important as this changed environment and positive framework for accountability is a foundation of agreed core values to work from. Without this there is no basis for accountability and everything has to be constantly re-negotiated. Again, we have seen this dimension work out so clearly as the cluster-based mission church at St Thomas' has grown and developed. At St Thomas' the common foundation of shared values and principles is brought together in what is called LifeShapes[7].

LifeShapes is made up of core biblical truths, which have been distilled into eight areas each of which is conveyed through a simple shape. In this way, in our visual culture, they are easily memorable and hence quickly become common currency. True to biblical principles, these foundational theological concepts of Lifeshapes are both simple and profound. They can be introduced in a few minutes or developed into a book on each. These eight core concepts are taught in church training sessions as basic individual discipleship (Lifeshapes 1). The same eight concepts also serve as the foundation to train small group leaders (Lifeshapes 2). They also under gird and crop up throughout the cluster leaders training.

The result is that the principles of LifeShapes will frequently be heard in the conversation of church members, in small group meetings and right through the senior staff strategy discussions. Hence in any accountability context, informal or formal, there becomes a corpus of commonly held convictions and values that form the immediate reference points. This both enables and enriches accountability. It gives everyone the tools for analysis and evaluation as well as a context of equality.

The common values and principles that St Thomas' have developed in their LifeShapes concepts and courses don't have to be adopted as a foundation for accountability by others initiating clusters as missional communities. However, it is my conviction that you would do well to develop your own

---

[7] Lifeshapes principles are published in Mike Breen & Walt Kallestad, The Passionate Church (for leaders) and The Passionate Life (for disciples), Nexgen, 2005.

equivalent to LifeShapes if you don't find the St Thomas' version matches your core theological values and principles of discipleship. You will need commonly held principles as easy reference points for accountability, leadership development and strategy. And whatever you choose, they will work best if they share the LifeShapes characteristics of simplicity, memorability and transferability.

Friendship – Relational Trust: This is the third and last component to facilitate effective accountability and it is often weak in institutional mechanisms of accountability. In the Gospels we can see Jesus' model of accountability that he worked out constantly with his disciples as he gave them tasks, reviewed their progress and repeatedly confronted as well as encouraged reflection with searching questions. This was always set in the context of relationship... a relationship that grew from followers to friends (John 15 v15).

I have observed that accountability has flourished exactly as relationships have grown and deepened so that trust has opened the door to vulnerability. Relational rather than institutional accountability is entirely different and if missional communities are to be that, then relationship is indispensable. And such relationships depend on commitment to one another, on taking the risk of transparency, on practical expressions of support for one another and on something as basic as frequency of meeting. It can't come from an annual review! Hence the adoption of huddles referred to earlier, not only enable relationship because they are frequent (usually at least fortnightly... though they can be short.... even 1 hour) but also when they are clearly experienced as loving support to see one another's lives and ministries blossom. Relationships grow and friendships develop through planned as well as spontaneous encounter.

So the delivery system to support high accountability and low control could be spelt CAR. *Changing* the environment, *Agreed* core values and *Relational* trust.

RADICAL CHANGE IN CHURCH REQUIRES LIFESTYLE CHANGE

We have explored how mid-sized cluster based church represents a substantial change to inherited mode church. We first saw how it was a change in church system and then also a change in structure of how authority works to release rather than control. Taken together these amount to a church so different that it can't be seen as just an extra programme to be added.

This is a lifestyle change both individually and corporately. We have described it as "Jesus communities of disciple-making disciples." This makes it clear that the essential lifestyle foundation is discipleship. It is therefore no coincidence that St Thomas' church, where clusters were first pioneered, at the same time developed the LifeShapes process of discipleship to which we have already referred in this chapter. Several of the LifeShapes principles will crop up in later chapters. Not because we want to push this approach to lifestyle discipleship or the particular application of clusters at St Thomas', but simply because it evolved to its present form alongside the original development of clusters. Hence several of the principles most readily illustrate and support important aspects of introducing and leading a dispersed church based on mid-sized missional communities.

PART TWO

BIBLICAL, HISTORICAL & MISSION RATIONALE

The recovery of biblical congregation and why this mid-sized fresh expression of church has real mission potential today.

Chapter 5   **Biblical Cell, Congregation and Celebration**
How did the biblical people of God build community? And how have these social dynamics adapted and changed through Christendom to today?

Chapter 6   **What's Wrong with Inherited Congregation?**
If the social patterns of congregation as practiced today has more to do with celebration in Temple and Cathedral, what are the drawbacks?

Chapter 7   **Mission Context Shaping Clusters**
How do these mid-sized communities connect with post-Christendom? How do clusters facilitate mission in our changing plural society?

Chapter 8   Clusters as Transitional Church

How can we bridge between church as we have known it (and so many love it) and the radical models of pure cell, household and liquid church, that many can't attain and others fear as deconstruction?

CHAPTER FIVE

Biblical Cell, Congregation and Celebration

One of my pursuits over the past 20 years, together with Mike Breen[1], has been to seek to gain an understanding of the way the people of God express their life together at different sizes, levels or social dynamics[2]. It has seemed to us that the practice of the church now and in previous centuries, together with some analysis by the Church Growth Movement, all fall short of the biblical norms. Furthermore, we also suspect that the inherited Western patterns are not the most sociologically effective, unlike those in biblical times. To get a clear understanding of clusters, it is essential that we get as sharp a focus as possible on the form and function of each of the different social expressions of church.

CHURCH GROWTH INSIGHTS

The church growth movement pioneered by Dr Donald McGavran and developed by C. Peter Wagner, researched church life in many continents over the past 50 years. One of their key findings was the fact that healthy church could be expressed at three different levels which they described as cell, congregation and celebration[3]. These insights were incorporated into the Leaders Seminars run over several decades in the UK by Bible Society. The section was called

---

[1] Bob Hopkins (ed), Planting New Churches, Eagle, 1992 p132-6
[2] Bob Hopkins, Explaining Cell Church, Administry Mini-guide No 12, 1999; Michael Green (ed), Church Without Walls, Paternoster, 2002. Ch 4.
[3] C.P. Wagner, Your Church Can Grow, Regal, 1976, Ch 7.

'Groups for Growth' and the diagram in the training manual looked like the table below[4].

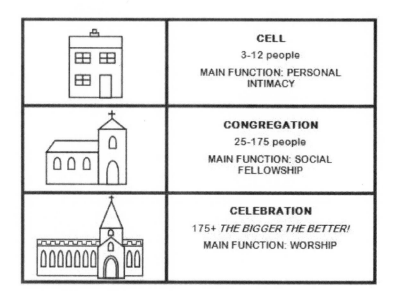

	CELL 3-12 people MAIN FUNCTION: PERSONAL INTIMACY
	CONGREGATION 25-175 people MAIN FUNCTION: SOCIAL FELLOWSHIP
	CELEBRATION 175+ *THE BIGGER THE BETTER!* MAIN FUNCTION: WORSHIP

Whilst the recognition of three effective levels of church life is groundbreaking we believe that more precision is needed to get the most helpful understanding of each. Firstly, we think that the numbers range for each size needs qualification. Cell church certainly sets small group size small at up to 12, but we believe that different social and cultural contexts may point to smaller or larger small groups. Most important, we propose that true congregational dynamics are lost as numbers rise between 60 to 80 people and certainly can't be sustained to 175, as suggested in this diagram.

Secondly, we take issue with the categorisation of the main functions of the three levels. We believe passionately that all

---

[4] Bible Society ran these workshops in the 70's to the 90's. We understand the manuals are out of print.

three should seek to balance worship (UP); fellowship (IN); and mission (OUT) dimensions. It seems significant that mission does not figure in any of the three levels in this table. Beyond this we shall make different suggestions for specific characteristics and contributions of each. Like discipleship for cell; community building, mission and leadership development for congregation; and unity, vision and momentum for celebration.

Thirdly, the buildings used to illustrate the three sizes carry helpful connotations for the cell as nuclear home and celebration as cathedral, but are most unhelpful at equating congregation to local parish church. But we shall see why this is our conclusion as we explore the biblical and historical background.

BIBLICAL ROOTS

I can obviously only present a brief survey here of some of the general strands of biblical tradition and practice. Nonetheless I hope that this will be sufficient to illustrate some fundamental principles relating to different sized groups and sociological functions.

Old Testament: The people of God are defined by being a people in covenant relationship with God. This covenant was first instituted by God in Genesis 12:1-5. Here God calls Abram as a nuclear family, commissions him with his extended family and promises blessing on him, for themselves to become a great people, but also as a means of blessing every nation. From the outset, God's people were defined by Covenant to him (UP), inheriting his blessing to be shared among them (IN), and sent out on a mission with a commission to bless all others (OUT).

The family, extended family and nation later becomes the family, the clan and the tribe. It is in the nuclear home that the next generation are discipled with values founded upon biblical principles... talked about in the home, throughout daily life, written on the doorposts and written and worn on special clothing (Deuteronomy 6:1-9). It was in the nuclear home with children that the Passover was celebrated and the Sabbath cup, bible reading and worship psalm were shared (Exodus 12:3, 21-27 & 46 and Deuteronomy 16:1-8). Then the extended family would have its worship shrine (Judges 18:19). Mission still had a specific application with the exhortation to welcome the alien into your home (Numbers 9:14; Exodus 12:48). Later it became customary to include an alien at the family Passover meal. Local places of worship and sacrifice became the focus for clan and tribe celebrations (e.g. oak at Mamre, Genesis 13:18).

During the Exodus, worship was in every family tent (Exodus 33:10), clans had their community role (Deuteronomy 33; Numbers 2:34) and the tabernacle was the focus for celebration of the whole people of God (Exodus 33:10; Leviticus 23:1). Also, leadership and community was broken down in tens (family), fifties (extended family), and larger celebration sized units of hundreds and thousands (Exodus 18:21). Later, as the people entered and settled the land, the tabernacle continued as a symbol and celebration of their nature as a pilgrim people with a 'God on the move' present among them.

Much later came the building of the temple as the focus for the largest celebration gatherings. This still became associated with pilgrimage as the tribes went up to the temple (Ps 122), and celebration level experience of community and worship focused around glorious and elaborate festivals with colour, pageantry and creativity (Tabernacles – Leviticus 23:23-34; Deuteronomy 16:13-17; Nehemiah 8:13-18. Atonement – Leviticus 23:26-32; Weeks – Deuteronomy 16:9-13).

From the establishment of the tabernacle as the focus for the celebration level, and as the holy places became the focus of a tribes celebration, there was the associated development of the Levitical priesthood to lead the consolidated people's worship and sacrifice. This representative priesthood, necessary for ordering large gatherings, not only fulfilled key leadership roles but also developed gifts in musical performance to enhance the grandeur of worship (1 Chronicles 9:33; 2 Chronicles 5:13). These festival celebrations were definitely performance style dynamics with highly developed skills and differentiated roles (2 Chronicles 5:2-7:6).

During the exile, when it was more difficult to maintain the covenant relationship with Yahweh and disciple the next generation in the shared faith, Synagogues emerged. These were extended family sized, just ten circumcised males being required. They were extended family in their dynamics, with interaction and roles shared (anyone who sat at the reading of the scripture indicated a readiness to bring an exposition or application and this practice continued into New Testament times (Luke 4v20 and Acts 13 v14-15).

New Testament: The record of the life and ministry of Jesus gives us lots of further illustration of how the social pattern of the Old Testament people of God had continued into the first century AD. Jesus grew and was formed in his nuclear home (Luke 2:39-52) although the family were clearly all known at the local synagogue (Luke 4:14-30) and made pilgrimage to the Temple for special occasions (Luke 2:41-52 and John 7 v1-9). The large celebration nature of these festivals is illustrated by the fact that Jesus could get lost in the crowd (John 5:13; Luke 2:43-45). People are not missed at celebration sized gatherings which by nature are impersonal and anonymous. The temple celebrations were also especially appropriate to gather in the gentiles who were being reached through the mission dimension of all three levels of the people of God (Mark 11 v17 and Acts 8 v27).

After Pentecost, the disciples continued expressing their common life in homes (Acts 2:46; Romans 16:3-4 & 10-11), the temple courts (Acts 2:46; 3:2-3; 21:26-39) and synagogue size (Acts 6:9; 18:7-8; 19:8; 20:7-8). In fact, the details of 1 Corinthians, chapters 11-14 give the best description anywhere of New Testament Christian mid-sized dynamics. We shall explore these further in chapter 11.

Biblical Functions: This short review of some biblical themes illustrates the different sizes, dynamics and activities of the people of God. From this we can see that there was a small social unit, represented by nuclear family, the home or the 12 disciples. This functioned in individual formation, discipleship, learning prayer, worship and the scriptures and being apprenticed in life and the ministry, and finding a place of identity and significance. This we would now see working through nuclear family, small group or cell. Secondly, at the intermediate size of the extended family, the synagogue or the 72, there is a building up of a community identity, a place of belonging where everyone is recognised and all can participate. More developed gifts can grow here and the mature bless the whole group, although there are no professional leaders. This we believe works now through extended family, cluster or mid-sized group (biblical congregation).

Lastly, the larger gatherings are where it's the bigger the better to celebrate periodically at the regional holy places or the Temple. The aim is to do things on a grand scale to get the benefit of best quality performance and to feel that you are part of something much more substantial that God is doing. The extra dimension of a special visit to a special venue adds to the quality, giving the pilgrimage dimension. Such gatherings are appropriately led by a professional or "priestly caste," trained and experienced for these wonderful events that bless and motivate the wider whole. And this we suggest functions best in festivals, camps, pilgrimages – celebration gatherings.

If I had to pick one defining characteristic of the three levels or sizes, then it would be disciple-making (the mission and commission of Jesus) for cell; community and ministry development for congregation and unity and momentum for celebration.

CHURCH HISTORY

Now we can try to assess how these characteristics have developed and shifted through the sweep of 2000 years of church history. Again, we are generalising as we take the broad view.

Cell: From the gospels to the Acts and Epistles, small groups and mission teams of up to twelve were involved in disciple-making. These almost certainly continued through the first three centuries as the church in the nuclear home[5]. Where whole households were converted (Acts 10:1-2; Acts 16:33) these would follow family lines, but often the converts might be rejected by family (Matthew 10:21) and gather into their new Christian family group for support in the context of persecution. After Constantine and the legalisation of the Christian Faith, Christendom developed. Here the basic unit of discipleship was the nuclear family. I believe that wherever Christendom

---

[5] W. Beckham, The Second Reformation, Touch, 1995. Ch 10.

was effective, this basic disciple-making cell unit continued the mission of the church to disciple the next generation.

This was still evident until a century ago with family bible, family prayers and family socialisation into biblical story and values. To reinforce this or to replace it in parts of society where it was failing, Christians instituted Christian schools – discipling groups of about 12 to learn the basics of the faith and later, Sunday schools. This function was also carried out by the Wesleyan Class system or method for re-evangelisation. It is only in the last hundred years that all three of these discipling functions (Christian nuclear family, Christian school and Sunday school) have broken down or ceased altogether, that the mission of discipling the next generation in Christendom has lapsed. These three structures were not called by the name of church, because in Christendom they became a universal process. However, they fulfilled this most essential function.

I believe that it is the loss of this disciple making function in the cell size, combined with the loss centuries earlier of a complementing function of the congregation size, that enabled secularisation to sweep in with such rapidity in the UK in the twentieth century. The scientific led Enlightenment had been the prevailing culture for centuries before, but discipling cell sized units were largely proof against this undermining the faith within society. As we are now in a largely post-Christendom context, this is why there is the greatest need to recover effective cell-sized communities for disciple-making. This is a basic difference between our situation and the catholic Christendom of Latin America where base communities emerged with a primary mission focus on social justice. Our situation has more in common with countries in pre-Christian Asia where cells emerged with a full-blooded discipleship emphasis linked to the evangelistic dimension of mission.

Celebration: For our purposes of clarifying the issues, we jump to the largest social unit, the celebration level of the church through history. Here the picture of the Cathedral building in the diagram at the beginning of this chapter is actually most appropriate. Once persecution was over and large gatherings were possible as they had been at the first in the temple courts, the celebration level was recovered. As special buildings for these grand events were developed through the centuries, we get the magnificent cathedrals of the medieval period.

In this cathedral tradition we can trace so much that is in common with the best biblical celebration that was worked out in the tabernacle or temple. Cathedrals were associated with pilgrimage; they were the bigger the better; their architecture was a visual story; they had pageant and procession; their lives revolved around great festivals of the Christian year; they had a professional cast of specialist leaders to act as representatives of the crowd and to provide a quality of performance, especially musically (first the orchestra then the organ).

As with biblical temple worship, the gatherings were such as to be impersonal, anonymous, the pilgrims being not exactly spectators but in minor roles, combined participants all together in one great "mass". It was and is inappropriate as well as impossible to look for interaction, every member using their gifts and ministering one to another in any significant way in this largest size social gathering.

Congregation: As we come to this third, intermediate or mid-size we reach the climax and crunch point of our argument, so far as clusters are concerned. The Bible Society church growth diagram uses the parish church building to illustrate this mid-sized faith community. This is certainly congregation as we have inherited it.

However, I imagine that you have already begun to see from the trends and principles that we have explored here, just how far local parish church has drifted from biblical and sociological congregation characteristics and dynamics. We have seen that these biblical characteristics and dynamics of congregation were based on the extended family and synagogue. Now certain aspects of extended family processes were preserved in our society into the last century with gatherings for anniversaries which would involved Uncle Jo getting us started, Great Aunt Flo giving a recitation, Grandfather reading a poem, mother singing an accompanied song and then off we go with everyone doing "a turn". However the inherited parish church congregation could hardly be further from this.

We shall explore in detail in the next chapter what may be so wrong with inherited western congregation, but lets try to understand what may have led to such a shift from the biblical original. It would be hard to undertake retrospective research into the motives and steps in the process but I believe we can see enough to get the picture (until someone makes it their PhD!).

It is my contention that the majesty and mystery of the great celebration has a magnetic pull. First this is properly expressed in the pilgrims reminiscing on the great times they had celebrating together when they returned home (Psalm 42:4; 68:24-27; 118:27). However, human nature means that, whenever it becomes possible, there is a strong temptation to try to perpetuate and repeat at the local what was so memorable at the "mountain top" (Mark 9 v5). We can certainly see the results of this. Whereas the sparse rural population of the pre-medieval local parish would have had no sophistication and little education, its gatherings must have been of the nature of extended family, in both size and dynamics. But as the means became available, it would seem that we can see the results of innovation following the lines of wanting to mimic the special cathedral experience.

So as the local building gets more grand, it mirrors the cathedral in layout. As local gifts develop, the single sackbut is replaced by the orchestra, and then a smaller version of the cathedral organ. Then the parish church added the cathedral procession with robed choir and associated servers all adding to the colour and pageant. And subtly begins the segregation into a non-congregation. Linked to the introduction of elements of more sophisticated quality performance, presentational style and a growth in size (population), would come the development of a local leader as a representative priestly caste. The parish church became a "dummed down" cathedral experience.

Amazingly, even the impersonal, anonymous characteristic of the cathedral seems to have filtered down to the parish 'congregation'. As a child I was taken religiously to our parish church but no one would speak to each other (let alone minister to one another with gifts and interaction), except perhaps to say 'nice sermon vicar' on departure! So the result over the centuries seems to have been complete. All the good qualities that make the Cathedral celebration such a blessing, have turned up as curses of the local congregation to make it what it's not supposed to be! True biblical sociological congregation was lost. We even called it *celebration* of Eucharist or Mass.

In this over-simplified summary, we can note that plenty of movements recognised the seriousness of the loss of true congregation communities. Some sought to recover the interactive dynamics and schism resulted as with the Quakers (before they went silent!) and the Brethren Assemblies (before they tended to be dominated by one or two!). More recently we can see attempts at partial recovery within the Church of

England with innovations such as the Parish Communion Movement with parish breakfast added on!

Lest we are too judgemental of our forebears, Mike Breen has pointed out that we can probably see the same trends cropping up today and taking over even faster. In the past 50 years or so there have been movements recovering aspects of true celebration which had been lost as pilgrimage patterns declined. So came the proliferation from Keswick, to Spring Harvest, to New Wine, Greenbelt, other Bible Weeks and Walsingham. Very large, but very infrequent jamborees that celebrated everything that's best in the stream or tradition.

The bigger, the better and the higher the quality and sophistication of performance, the better. All consistent with temple/celebration - creating momentum, something memorable and a sense of being part of something much wider. Necessarily dependent on high quality performers and big personality, representative leaders. But can't we trace in even a few years of these big festivals, the returning campers (pilgrims) not just sharing remembrances to encourage and sustain one another, but beginning to whisper "can't we have here locally a worship band, can't we have banners, why can't we have deeper teaching; and wouldn't it be good if a celebrity leader led our congregation, oh! and that smoke on stage was nice, what about …"!

SOME RESULTING GUIDING PRINCIPLES FOR MID-SIZED CLUSTERS

These convictions lie behind the gradual emergence of clusters at St Thomas' in Sheffield and then at Holy Trinity, Cheltenham and now many other churches. Usually the insights of Cell Church have been adapted in some form to the small group life to recover this healthy expression of church. Then the need to re-discover appropriate biblical congregation has followed. But such are the distorted assumptions about congregation that we carry because of our experience of it as a celebration style event, that we have to start all over again. Take a different name, 'clusters', to break the link and grow into the extended family size and social dynamics, once again.

So the pictures we use to illustrate the three levels or expressions of church are given overleaf. These use triangles because, since each level or size is fully church, each must have UP, IN and OUT dimensions. Celebration is at heart more of an *event* whereas congregation *is community*.

The diagrams on page 105 also make the explicit links to the biblical roots we have tried to explore here in both Old and New Testaments. You will note that we actually consider holistic church to be made up of four sorts and sizes of relationship. We start with the accountability partner relationship as the smallest building block. This picks up Jesus' intimate association with Peter, James and John and links to our exploration of accountability processes at the end of the previous chapter. These four community dynamics also correspond to the sociology insights of Joseph Meyer, picked up by Phil Potter and referred to in the introduction. You will remember that he described the four as "Private space, intimate space, social space and public space."

In this chapter we have traced how far we have changed from biblical mid-sized communities over the subsequent centuries of Christendom. In the next we shall assess what we lose when our thinking about mid-sized congregation is so shaped by celebration social dynamics (public space).

Old Testament

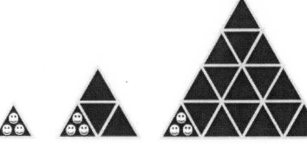

New Testament

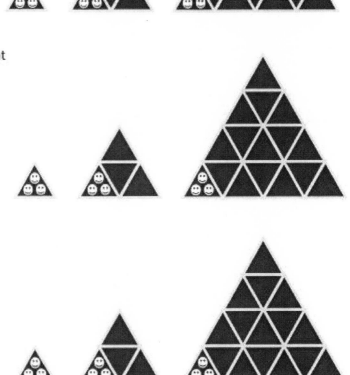

St Thomas'

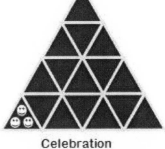

Accountability   Cell   Cluster   Celebration

CHAPTER SIX

What's Wrong With Inherited Congregation?

BREAK OPEN THE BOX

It would be easy to think that I am exaggerating the case against the present form of the parish congregation and the gathered free church or chapel congregation. Some may instinctively feel that it must always have been as it is now. Another view could be that if it came to us in this form after so long, it must be right. The trouble is that not only is the inherited congregation not what it should be, but the new mission context combines the challenges of secular pluralism with that of a disappearing Christendom.

This makes the situation extremely serious. The matter is made even worse when a) most local churches do not have an effective small expression (small group or cell) and b) cathedral has often ceased to be the centre of pilgrimage for local congregations at regular festivals through the year and c) the parish church that is functioning like a mini-cathedral celebration, can't do it nearly as well and lacks the power to draw outsiders.

So at worst, we end up with no small expression of church; a mid-size that has organised itself as though it were the large celebration and therefore failing to be congregation and doing celebration badly, and a loss of connection with what could be quality celebration at cathedrals.

Many have spoken of the need to "think outside the box." Chris Neal has written to this effect and described our present situation as "vacuum packed and hermetically sealed[1]." He is quite clear that not only our thinking but our practice has to break out. The picture I have is of an alabaster box of perfume. Biblically, we the church are together not only the body of Christ, but the aroma of Christ (2 Corinthians 2:15). Our corporate expressions should spread the knowledge of Christ everywhere, way beyond ourselves. But we have ended up being boxed in, limited, contained.

It is really good when local churches recover effective small groups, cells or the like. However in most cases, their cell/celebration model limits their cells to the existing parish congregation... they remain linked to "the box." Let's look at the aspects of inherited congregation that represent the walls of the box that needs to be broken open. And for which cluster provides one way for break out. These walls are as much our internal mental assumptions as the external practical processes and structures that shape the box.

CLERICALISM

There has been a gradual shift into the parish congregation of a professional priestly caste which is good and necessary at the cathedral celebration level. This has effectively extended clericalisation to the whole church and disempowered the people. Local congregation has become our only or primary understanding of church and with that understanding goes a requirement for leadership focused rather than shared. And what is more focused than a highly theologically trained specialist who requires to be full-time paid? With this clericalisation came the concept that the local cleric was not a

---

[1] Chris Neal, Article C.E.N. 25.11.03

leader who developed mission, vision and empowered the people, but rather a chaplain to service the faithful.

Furthermore, the celebration style, presentational event at the heart of inherited congregation is a demanding model to lead and few lay people can sustain it. In contrast, St Thomas' has some 30 clusters, all are led by lay teams, many with families and demanding jobs. And the scores of other churches adopting these principles all have their clusters lay led. This recovery of biblical congregation liberates the ministry of the whole people, which is so effective at this level. Over and over, from adult clusters, to youth clusters and inter-generational clusters, the overwhelming report is about the explosion of leadership.

CONTROLLED NOT RELEASING

Because parish congregation modelled itself as a mini-cathedral, it required a highly controlled environment. The principles of extended family, biblical congregation and synagogue are much more open and releasing. This mid-sized community experience is as good as the sum of its parts. Everyone owns responsibility and grows in involvement. At its worst the controlled environment of the inherited congregation, so inappropriate to this level, leads to fear and a loss of confidence. Combined with clericalism, it can produce subservient people not just passive people.

PROVIDER: CLIENT

When we model congregation on the cathedral, we can end up becoming consumers. And consumers look to providers! Did the vicar deliver the goods this week? We have seen that at celebrations there is a right element of performance, presentation and refined quality. It is then appropriate for pilgrims to be *recipient participants* whereas at authentic congregation we should all be *initiating participants*. In inherited congregation we have almost completely lost the 'one another' dynamic that grows ministry and leadership across the people and builds community. There is little so debilitating of congregation missional community as provider: client assumptions.

Many attending parish congregations sense they are doing the vicar a favour by turning up! In true congregation, such as clusters seek to create, if we the members don't turn up, it doesn't happen. And what does happen is as good as we all make it! As we have already seen from reference to 1 Corinthians chapters 11-14, the congregation-sized meeting is designed to be highly interactive, not front led and the product of all our contributions.

BUILDING CENTRED

Here again the legitimate emphasis in celebration/cathedral on special and imposing buildings is no longer appropriate for congregation. However hard it is taught that church is not about buildings but people, this will not be believed, practiced and experienced while there is no congregation level apart from the gothic or mock-gothic, parish church building.

Sacred space certainly has its place in the life and development of the people of God. But the congregations should principally be about building community. This is an organism and emphasis needs to be on relationships not relics, internal issues not external. The introduction of pews merely reinforced the impersonal nature of celebration dynamics. Taking the pews out (after much conflict) doesn't change the underlying expectations. And it's not just the pews that set in stone the wrong structures and assumptions.

The borrowing of cathedral architecture in separate sections of nave, chancel, altar and of screens and choir stalls, all provide the sort of endo-skeleton appropriate to support a large and highly complex affair, but quite unlike the exo-skeleton sufficient to contain a highly fluid and flexible smaller organism.

SUNDAY CENTRED/EVENT CENTRED – LOST GATHERING POWER

The inherited congregation not only meets in a special building, but only gathers for a religious event on a special day. Again we hear echoes more of the essence of celebration. It is of the nature of celebration that it is event centred. Congregation is community centred and this is built differently. This inherited aspect of local parish means we speak of "going to church" rather than being church or doing church. This extends further so that mission for inherited congregation tends to be limited to "come to church" or special "mission events." That works at the cathedral level but not the local inherited congregation.

When the local church is a small, pale imitation of cathedral and it becomes the only commonly understood expression of church, it may be doomed to become a ghetto in Post-Christendom. It can't do a celebration anything like as well as a cathedral with less resources, less imposing place and much less people. In today's media culture the local congregation trying to do celebration, rarely achieves a "come to us" factor or pull.

On the other hand when cathedrals make the most of their potential, they still do have scale with sufficient of the spectacular and the dramatic to match the media and also sufficient of what's different (not available on the box or at Sainsbury's) to attract an increasing spiritually aware and hungry populace. The cathedral with the power of pageant and place can provide the impact to deliver the drawing power that is the appropriate mission dimension of true celebration. No wonder many cathedrals that recover their founding dream, are growing significantly!

In contrast, when the local congregation ceases to be true congregation, loses community and becomes event, it is impotent to fulfil its mission role. It has lost its right power to gather, which is its ability to do real community. It has become separated from family, from neighbourhood and from the workplace in today's society and has neither the qualities to attract nor the mechanisms to connect. If church just happens on a Sunday, then the rest of the week becomes something else and we have created secular space. And tragically we have lost a golden opportunity, since true mid-size, extended family community is what society has lost and many are desperate to discover.

WHICH WAY "SUCCESS"?

There is another ironic problem with local congregations as we have allowed them to become. That is that we have an unspoken understanding that a successful congregation in the parish church or gathered chapel, is over one hundred people... and that's already way too big for true congregation and quality mid-sized community dynamics. Of course most of our buildings silently proclaim the opposite message, with seating for 150 or 250 or... oh dear! 450!

But again the real seat of the problem is not in the number of pews, but in our heads. Everyone is shocked and surprised that recent statistics show that churches in the range 150-250 are the fastest declining and churches at 35-50 are amongst the most likely to be growing[2]! If we don't get the message and let go of our credo that one structure congregation fits all, then we shall merely reshuffle which churches grow and which decline. As the 35-50 grow as they begin to become community and a little more like the congregation... oops! They will reach 75 and 100 and then join the fast declining group! Unless of course, we change our assumptions and practice and multiply mid-sized cluster groups to keep them mid-sized!

THE CURRENT DECLINE OF LARGER CHURCHES CONFIRMS THESE FAILINGS

The national statistics show that larger churches (over 200) are declining, whilst smaller ones (especially 50-100) are growing[3]. This does not surprise us and we believe exactly bears out our analysis of what is wrong with inherited congregation. First, as an inherited congregation defining its identity by a Sunday service goes over 150, it is forced to get more and more presentational, with the little remaining potential of interaction and participation of biblical congregation, squeezed out altogether.

Then secondly, efforts at sustaining some sort of real community and sense of belonging (the other main feature of biblical congregation) that may have borne some fruit up to 100 people, become impossible over 200. Whilst small groups can

---

[2] Bob Jackson, Hope for the Church, CHP, 2002; chapter 11, entitled Acting Small – whatever your size, develops this at length and refers to the 1989 Church Census, the 1998 Church Survey and wider research: Christian A. Schwartz, Natural Church Development Handbook, BCGA, 1996

[3] Bob Jackson, Hope for the Church, CHP, 2002; chapter 11, entitled Acting Small – whatever your size, develops this at length and refers to the 1989 Church Census, the 1998 Church Survey and wider research: Christian A. Schwartz, Natural Church Development Handbook, BCGA, 1996

compensate for these losses of participation and community, they can't deliver the full measure of biblical congregation/synagogue dynamics. Only cluster (mid-sized community) can fully recover these essential qualities.

WE ARE NOT FORMING LEADERS FOR BIBLICAL CONGREGATION

In this context, we have reflected that in most of our theological colleges and seminaries, we train church leaders to **lead services** not to create and **build community**. As we watched the development of our lay cluster leaders we have noted that they grow in skills of forming community. As they get familiar with these skills some can go a long way to create the dynamics of community in a single gathering of a pick-up group.

In the mission context of today's western society, with community breaking or broken down at every level, these are core skills of the missional leader. But they are not academically taught but rather caught through apprenticeship and immersion in effective community. If we are right in our analysis here, then it casts a whole new light on the pastoral epistles stating as the prime requirement for local church leaders – those who can "manage" their own extended family - the gift of creating real community (1 Timothy 3:4-5).

WHAT'S SO RIGHT ABOUT CLUSTERS?

We are not suggesting that clusters are the ultimate solution to the problem of inherited congregation. However, they are one approach which clearly tackles head on the problems we have identified and so seek to "break open the box."

There may be other models that will deliver similar qualities of missional communities for our new culture and context. But we sense that they will share many of these same principles of clusters and their mid-size that we summarised in the first chapter and which we are developing further in these following chapters.

Clusters aim to be small enough to enable "one-another" community, so often referred to in the New Testament. They break free from buildings and are not tied to a special Sunday event. They are essentially not about meetings (young adults hate these) but about shared lives and shared lifestyles. They can express their life anywhere, on any day and at whatever intervals serve the building-up of their community and the effectiveness of their mission.

They are lay led with no professional theologians and no stipend bills, although they may be as large or larger than many parish 'congregations'. The passive consumer culture of inherited congregation is broken as everyone is encouraged and enabled to contribute and to grow in their calling. If a significant character of our society and culture is the loss of extended family and community, then the planting and multiplication of clusters as true congregations, may even help to make the Kingdom contribution of rebuilding the fabric of society.

AND WHAT HAPPENS TO OUR SUNDAY SERVICES?

A key question for most Western churches considering clusters in order to recover biblical congregation, is what happens to our Sunday services? There is so much invested in our traditional buildings and so much expectation in the minds of traditional church goers of a weekly special event, that its hard to make rapid radical changes in this area. Weekly services as we have seen here, are expressing biblical temple/celebration, although biblical celebration developed only around the festivals as seasonal highpoints.

This movement of clusters recovering biblical congregation is very new. And so far this is probably why most clusters develop their life during weekdays – modifying small group/cell patterns and leaving Sundays largely unaffected. The Sunday service can of course develop a strong link to clusters as cluster members share testimony, become a prayer focus and provide hospitality roles. However, time will tell whether there is an increase in what is at present a minority of churches that face the challenge of adapting Sunday service patterns so that those biblical style celebrations are less frequent and the mid-sized cluster life can strengthen further.

AND AGAIN, WHAT ABOUT BASE ECCLESIAL COMMUNITIES (BEC'S) AND HOUSEHOLD CHURCH?

With the perspective we have gained of biblical congregation in these two chapters, we can see Base Communities and Household Church in a new light. We say more in Appendix 4 to compare and contrast clusters to these other smaller community expressions of church. But they are also clearly breaking free of inherited congregation and working out many of the principles we are exploring here. BEC's born in a highly institutionalised Christendom in Catholic Latin America have, in effect, re-created a hybrid cell/congregation sort of community. They have re-gained much of lost biblical congregation dynamics in their lay led, highly interactive, extended family missional group focused around the word and social transformation. Whilst at the same time they have left what is called the Catholic parish "congregation" to fulfil its actual function as a priest-led mass celebration!

Household church on the other hand was born out of persecuted contexts such as China. It has lost the celebration dimension as was also largely true in the periods of intense

110

persecution in the first three centuries. Furthermore, as Household church also aims to recover extended family sized congregation dynamics, and is explored in the West where there is no persecution, there has still been little emphasis on celebration size gathering together. However, we must remember that biblical and medieval celebration with pilgrimage was confined to a few times a year. So maybe as the household church loose networks gather to encourage one another in regional and national conferences, they may be much nearer the biblical norm than so much of the Western church which pursues the very rich diet of weekly celebration (New Wine or Spring Harvest or Walsingham every week!).

CHAPTER SEVEN

Mission Context Shaping Clusters

Much has been written about the rapidly changing social and cultural context today in the Western World. This is the challenge facing the church in the UK, which has been losing members and attendees as well as losing connection with these multiple mission opportunities. Many excellent books have been written analysing the changes and the resulting emerging culture and proposing the sorts of church that can meet the challenge. Books like *Church Next, Changing World: Changing Church, Liquid Church, Invading Secular Space, The Shape of things to Come, Emergingchurch.intro, Post-Christendom* and *Emerging Churches: Creating Christian Community in Post-modern Cultures*[1].

This is not the place and there is certainly not the space here to unpack and build on all the insights of these authors. Clearly it is important for leaders to draw on all the detailed analysis that these works provide of the complexity and subtleties of our situation. However for our purposes we are looking for a big picture summary that can give a clear understanding of where

---

[1] Eddie Gibbs, Church Next, IVF, 2000; Michael Moynagh, Changing World: Changing Church, Monarch, 2001; Pete Ward, Liquid Church, Paternoster, 2002; Martin Robinson & Dave Smith, Invading Secular Space, Monarch 2003; Michael Frost & Alan Hirsch, The Shape of Things to Come, Peabody Hendrickson, 2003; Michael Moynagh, Emergingchurch.intro, Monarch, 2004; Stuart Murray-Williams, Post Christendom, Paternoster, 2004; Eddie Gibbs & Ryan Bolger, Emerging Churches: Creating Christian Community in Post-modern Cultures, SPCK, 2006.

clusters fit[2]. What we want to give is a simple overview of the three main shaping influences that we see on the way ahead. These are first, where we have come from... Christendom; second, where things are going... Pluralism; and thirdly, the structure of culture itself. To help us quickly gain a framework of understanding in these first two areas, we find the diagrams used by Robert Warren in Being Human: Being Church[3], most helpful.

FROM CHRISTENDOM...

To have any chance of plotting a course into the future we have to know where we have come from. In the UK and most of the rest of Europe, Christendom describes the relatively stable and uniform culture that has predominated for centuries. Robert's diagram illustrates the main features. It shows that the church was at the centre in more senses than one. Firstly the church was at the centre of every community and neighbourhood (almost all relationships were geographically based). From villages, to market towns, to the parish subdivisions of cities, the church provided the focus and fabric of community life. Secondly the church was the location and provider for all the rites of passage, festivals, events and high points of local life.

Thirdly and most importantly, the church provided and sustained the biblical worldview and Judeo-Christian values and ethic that underpinned all of societies institutions and structures from monarchy, to legal system, to education, to agriculture and business. The white background of the whole society circle in the Warren diagram represents this universal foundation of worldview and values.

---

[2] I have given some summary analysis with diagrams in Bob Hopkins (ed), Cell Stories as Signs of Mission, Grove Ev51, 2000, p.5-8
[3] Robert Warren, Being Human: Being Church, Marshall Pickering, 1995

Christendom

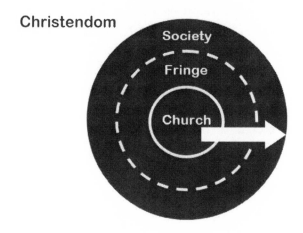

Robert Warren then also helpfully addresses the mission task of the church in this Christendom Culture. This he represents by the arrow, from the centre circle of church, to the margins. He then identifies this mission challenge as the church calling the structures and institutions of society to behave faithfully to the biblical, Christian worldview and values.

As I have argued elsewhere[4], this is only one of the two primary mission tasks in Christendom. Since the diagram is not static, time must be seen as the third dimension, there is always the work of discipling the next generation in the core Christian worldview and value system.

My observation is that most significantly, this mission task has never principally been fulfilled by the institutional, Christendom Church. Rather, in the periods when it has been done effectively and Christendom remained strong, this disciple-making of the emerging generation was done by extended Christian family (family bible, prayers and

---

[4] Michael Green (ed), Church Without Walls, Paternoster, 2002, Chapter 4, page 41-44,

socialisation in Christian values and worldview), Christian schools (small discipling groups for children invented by Christians not the state) and Sunday schools.

It is my contention that the loss of these small to medium-sized places of discipleship is the main reason why secularisation has come in like a flood in the last hundred years. But even more important, for the future, it is essential for the mission of the church to recover effective discipleship in small social groupings. **This is the first foundation for the mission rationale behind clusters.**

TO PLURALISM...

The last hundred years or so has seen the erosion of Christendom and a massive cultural shift that has often been described as secular pluralism. Secular it may only have been for a generation or so, since there has now been a rise in multi-faith, in spirituality and a churchless-faith.

However, while there has certainly been a move from something more mono-cultural and strongly bound around church and faith. The church has not only lost its hold as the social and community's centre, but the worldview has also shifted to commercialism and individualism, which in turn has led to a proliferation of a host of competing value systems.

Robert Warren's second diagram (overleaf) attempts to illustrate this new situation. The church is small with a tiny, tight-knit fringe. It is pushed to the side, no longer seen as relevant or providing answers to today's questions. Then the many different shapes represent all the subcultures in the changing and proliferating pluralism of our society.

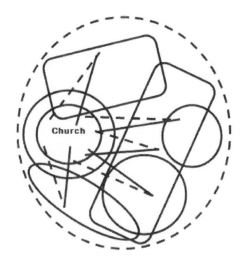

Obviously, the situation we now live with is even more complex than can be represented by this two dimensional diagram. There is a far greater diversity of neighbourhoods and networks than illustrated by these few different shapes. People's relationships are now formed around work, family, leisure, lifestyle, interests, the web, etc.

One of the best summaries of this plural culture and the forces shaping it, is given in the first chapter of the report Mission-shaped Church.[5]

Robert's diagram above also shows a solid line and dotted line between church and each new sub-culture. These summarise some of the lessons learnt from (often the mistakes of) mission engagement in past centuries and other continents. The solid line represents the first task which is to "*sit and listen*" rather than to "*stand and tell.*" We have to learn the "languages" and the values of these sub-cultures before we know how to address

---

[5] Mission-shaped Church, CHP, 2004, Ch1.

the Gospel to them. Then we see the dotted line as indicating that in most cases it is not appropriate and often not possible, to church those who respond back in inherited mode church.

This is where the lessons of Bruce Olsen[6] from mission among the Amazonian Indians, and Vincent Donovan[7] from mission amongst the Massai in Africa, have given us a whole new understanding. Again, the theology and practice of this incarnational mission is well summarised in Mission-shaped Church, chapter 5. There the principle is summed up as "dying to live." We the church have to die to our forms and traditions and allow the seed of the Gospel carried by a small team to take root and emerge in each setting in a contextualised, inculturated form.

The way we have re-drawn Warren's diagram shows that some subcultures have a few people represented in the church fringe. Others actually have folk within the committed membership of the church, even though they may find the church culture rather "foreign."

These folk represent "bridging people" and can form the core of such cross-cultural mission teams to create (plant) fresh expressions of church in their sub-culture. In any event, the clear challenge is that the church has to become plural to reflect our plural culture. Only then can these gospel communities in mission begin to play their part in the transformative effect of the kingdom worldview and values on each sub-culture. **This is the second foundational mission rationale for clusters**. These mid-sized communities in mission enable the church to take on a plural structure of flexible, contextual, fresh expressions of church to match the many and changing shapes

---

[6] Bruce Olsen, Bruchko, Creation House, 1973
[7] Vincent Donovan, Christianity Re-discovered (2nd edition), SCM, 2001 (1st 1978).

of our society. Clusters can seek to be communities in mission doing discipleship in ways appropriate to a whole range of contexts and sub-cultures.

The Threshold churches in Lincolnshire (described more in chapter 9) are a prime example. Their network of clusters hold together and release mission cells in both deep rural villages, expanded satellite villages and a UPA city estate.

St Andrews, Chorleywood are another case embracing mid-sized missional communities across a whole variety of urban, suburban and rural conurbations in the North West London home counties. Then again "The Path" in Holy Trinity, Cheltenham has adapted clusters for youth ministry and their "Trash Groups" have networked to teens in other churches in other towns and villages across Gloucestershire and Worcestershire. And these examples have all developed since Mike's original vision for clusters at St Thomas' to serve the mission strategy of engaging with any and every neighbourhood and social network across the city of Sheffield.

FIVE CATEGORIES OF OUR POPULATION IN RELATION TO CHURCH

Research undertaken in the second half of the 90's and written up by Richter & Francis[8] established that the UK population could be roughly divided into five groups according to their relationship to inherited church. Their findings can be represented by the following pie-chart, also reproduced in Mission-shaped Church, page 37.

---

[8] Richter & Francis, Lost but not Forgotten, DLT, 1998.

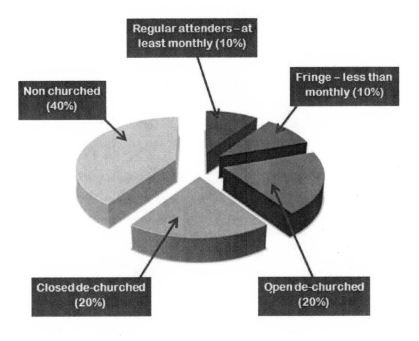

From this we see that, with regional variation, some 10% are actively involved with church. Then another 10% are in loose connection as fringe. There are then 40% of folk that can be described as de-churched. They were once involved and active in church, but have become disconnected. The really helpful insight from this research is that roughly half this group... 20% are 'open de-churched'. This means that it is neutral factors like growing out of a children's or youth group, getting a job, marriage, a move, etc. that has resulted in disconnection. But given the right circumstances they would be quite open to come back.

In contrast, the other 20% of the de-churched are described as "closed" precisely because they have clear reasons for their leaving, such as falling out with the Vicar, disillusionment with formal institutional religion, loss of faith, etc. These folk have strongly negative attitudes to inherited church and may be the hardest to re-incorporate into any form of church.

Lastly, the fifth group are the non-churched. They have never had any significant involvement or even connection with church. They are the largest group... 40% having little or no knowledge, let alone understanding of the gospel.

What is even more significant is that this research was only of adults in the population (over 18 years). And other statistics make it very clear that children and youth are the furthest from church. An estimate of the age adjusted figure of non-churched for the whole population may be as high as 60%!! Unlike the closed de-churched these people don't have any barriers to church from personal negative attitudes caused by pain and disillusionment, only generalised negative impressions from media portrayal. But they are likely to share with the closed de-church, a suspicion of institutions and a dislike of hierarchical authority.

Now this is the third foundational mission rationale for clusters, since it should already be becoming clear that Clusters have real potential to connect with some of these sections of the population in a way that is much harder for inherited church. Inherited church done well, can connect with the fringe and some of the open de-churched.

However, we can begin to recognise that clusters as we have described them, could be effective in reaching and incorporating both folk in the fringe, the open de-churched and the non-churched. These mid-sized groups can even have some effectiveness with the closed de-churched, since they offer a completely contrasting experience of non-institutional faith community.

Many fringe folk need something different to "kick-start" them from passive connection to active involvement. A Cluster may achieve this by being closer to their culture and style, or by having a different more releasing leadership or by building much more belonging and involvement. This can happen whilst still relating to the more familiar gathered expression of church.

The open de-churched are more likely to be reached by clusters which motivate and release Christians to be much more engaged beyond themselves. They can also offer a very welcoming mid-size where everyone can be noticed. Again the combinations of the familiar gathered with the dispersed cluster with real community can offer several of the factors that can encourage back those that have slipped away. These same factors will enable clusters to be effective in mission to the non-churched. Clusters will need much more energy to "go" in mission engagement for this group who have never experienced church or the gospel, but plenty are demonstrating this.

Lastly, it is true that the closed de-churched may be wary when there is a connection between clusters and a large resourcing matrix with celebrations. This may resonate with aspects of very institutional church that they have consciously chosen to leave. However, there is evidence that clusters that develop radically different faith community with non-professional leader teams can overcome barriers to those closed to traditional church... and then have a loose enough connection to the "large church" matrix not to scare them off. These principles are summarised in the table overleaf, which illustrates that cluster-shaped church can engage right across the range, whereas both inherited and radical emerging church are more limited to one end or the other.

Likely Mission Effectiveness of Type of Church	Fringe	Open de-churched	Closed de-churched	Non-churched
Inherited Mode	✓✓	✓	X	X
Clusters and Mid-sized Communities	✓✓	✓✓	✓	✓✓
Radical Emerging Models	X	✓	✓✓	✓✓

REMOVING CHURCHES' "DEFECTIVE GENES"

From the 1980's through the 1990's and into the twenty first century, church plants and new ways of being church have attempted to break through in effective mission. Many observers,[9] including ourselves, have noted the apparent failure of these brave initiatives to break free of certain conforming aspects of inherited church. This had led some to classify these attempts to multiply church as "cloning."

I have repeatedly critiqued this analogy[10] since a clone has every gene the same as its parent. In complete contrast, as I have listed elsewhere, many new missional genes were introduced by these church plants. Furthermore, the analogy seems to me to miss the key point. This is the fact that leaving just a very few but critical things the same disables a church plant or fresh expression in mission. These are much more like defective genes than a clone. And my assessment is that they

[9] George Lings & Stuart Murray, Church Planting through the 90's, Grove Ev61, 2003; Stuart Murray & A. Wilkinson, Lessons from the Margins, Grove Ev49, 2000

[10] Bob Hopkins CEN Articles, 1st July & 8th July, 2005

are our instinctive understanding of church being building centred and Sunday event centred.

Once we recover church as seven days per week, any place any time, community in mission with any configuration of members... then we have church with mission feet on. It's shifted from attraction to infiltration as it combines gathering and dispersing. Flexible and organic not static and institutionalised.

So here is our fourth foundational mission rationale – clusters, as we saw in Chapter 1 and further developed in chapter six, precisely replace the defective genes of inherited congregation as mini-cathedral – building bound and locked into a professionally led, presentational event.

SMALLER CHURCHES GROWING FASTER

As discussed earlier, research in the UK over the past couple of decades has surprised many by showing that larger churches over 150 are generally declining, whilst smaller churches are generally growing. In fact churches from 50 to 100 show the potential for fastest growth.[11] These findings would support all the arguments that we are making here for the cluster, especially our last point about the recovery of biblical congregation as extended family community. Whilst the research can't confirm the cause of smaller churches growing fastest in today's mission context, clusters do share the likely key characteristics. These would include such things as a) the ability to create real community with a ready sense of

---

[11] Bob Jackson, Hope for the Church, CHP, 2002; chapter 11, entitled Acting Small – Whatever Your Size, develops this at length and refers to the 1989 Church Census, the 1998 Church Survey and wider research: Christian A. Schwartz, Natural Church Development Handbook, BCGA, 1996

belonging; b) making people feel needed as participators rather than being spectators; c) easier to spot the newcomer and provide welcome; and d) releasing time and energy for mission engagement rather than sucking them into programs to support a large central machine.

This is, therefore, our **fifth and last foundational mission rationale** - clusters of 30 to 75 folk in fact share much in common with the average smaller UK local church, where most growth is happening. Clusters also share their sense of fragility and vulnerability and certainly don't threaten like the mega churches. And since leadership is always so important, there are many more people with the leadership scope needed to fit them to oversee this smaller sized community.

If we need to "Build Missionary Communities" rather than "Build Missionary Congregations," we also need to multiply and release thousands of missional leaders nationally. And that certainly doesn't mean thousands more vicars! But thousands of self-supporting young adults, middle-aged and elderly folk exercising missional oversight in clusters, as a normal part of their whole life.

CHAPTER EIGHT

Clusters as Transitional Church

In the last chapter we gave the rationale for clusters based on the mission context of where we have come from and where we seem to be heading.

Firstly, our analysis of the degrading of Christendom, identified the crucial need to recover the loss of small socialising communities that delivered discipleship (in the way that Jesus did). Secondly, we saw how the proliferation of a plural society made up of multiple, multi-layered networks and neighbourhoods, required the church to respond with a flexible model of multiple incarnational communities in mission, such as clusters. Then, thirdly we used the analysis of different groups in their relation to church... fringe, de-churched (open or closed), and non-churched.

This gave us yet another perspective on how mid-sized clusters with quite different community dynamics to inherited congregation, could play a significant part in connecting to most of these mission challenges.

However, another way of understanding mid-sized cluster-shaped church is by unpacking Mike Breen's description of it as "Transitional Church." The experience at St Andrew's, Chorleywood also led Mark Stibbe to describe church based on mid-sized communities as providing the opportunity to shift from attraction to "infiltration," whilst combining both dispersed and gathered modes. Now to gain this further understanding of where clusters can fit in the array of developing models and mission responses we shall draw on some more analysis and diagrams to illustrate this transitional quality. We will see that they are transitional, both in the sense of bridging between a range of options but also because they can represent steps on the way to more radical approaches. So let's use these tools to further explore the question of, "Why clusters in our context?"

ATTRACTIONAL, ENGAGED OR EMERGING CHURCH?

The authors of books on emerging church, cited at the beginning of the previous chapter, have introduced some of these concepts, although sometimes they don't all use them in exactly the same way! Frost and Hirsch[1] repeatedly distinguish between attractional church and emerging church, and often with a rather disparaging tone towards the attractional.

We have added the "engaged" category as a third approach, between the other two. And in fact, our view would be that in our context of decaying Christendom, which has certainly not yet disappeared completely, there are significant roles for all three categories. The pie chart from the previous chapter will help us see how this works and relate it to the place of clusters.

As the term implies, **attractional** church works by taking church as we have known it and seeking to make it more attractive and accessible to non-attenders. This will be a lot about giving a real and effective welcome and follow-up to the occasional visitor (often the weakest area of our churches). Then it is also likely to be about making what we do in inherited mode church a lot easier to understand, a lot more relevant to everyday life and a lot more contemporary in style. Not only

---

[1] Michael Frost & Alan Hirsch, The Shape of Things to Come, Peabody Hendrickson, 2003, ch.2, p.18

will this be more likely to hold the casual visitor... its likely to create rumours of change and of pleasant surprise, into the wider community. Attractional Church done well is proving to be effective missional church for connecting to the fringe and to some of the open de-churched. It is unlikely to make significant inroads beyond that.

We could sum up the heart of attractional church as seeking to be the best "COME" mode.

We introduce the category of Engaged Church between attractional and emerging church, since we think this is a fuller explanation of the range of what is happening in response to the new social realities. Engaged Church moves beyond the attractional, researches contexts beyond the fringe, and intentionally mobilises for mission activity there. It will engage with the aspirations and needs and may work in partnership. However, as folk in that sub-culture are drawn to respond to the gospel, they are expected to make the cultural journey to inherited mode church (which hopefully will have made attractional adjustments).

This sort of engaged church is not only effective as missional church in reconnecting with the fringe and open de-churched, but has some significant potential among the non-churched. It is however, unlikely to gain a favourable response from the closed de-churched since, however effectively it engages with them, it expects them to return to the sort of church they chose to leave.

We could sum up the heart of engaged church as moving outwards in "GO" mode, but then inviting folk to "COME."

Then the term **Emerging Church** seems to us best reserved for the mission dynamics described by Frost and Hirsch. It's not just about a slightly different form of church, but much more about a radical process of creating quite new sorts of churches.

Here, as with the engaged church, missionaries identify and research a social setting beyond the fringe. Again, as with engaged church, they then become a part of and get involved with these cultures. However, as they develop relationship and respond to aspirations and needs, rather than inviting to come to inherited church, instead church in a new and thoroughly indigenous form literally **emerges** in the heart of the culture. Such a church that emerges may not be recognisably church by our old expectations of special buildings and religious events. For example, emerging church amongst surfers may just be increasing numbers of Christian surfers who pray together, play together and present Jesus to other surfers together! This is the fullest expression of the Mission-shaped Church principles of "dying to live" expounded in that report. Implicit in this approach is the planting of a fresh expression of church.

We could sum up the heart of emerging church in this sense, as moving outwards in "GO" mode and "STAYING" to see what ARISES.

Three different approaches to Missional Church

- **Attractional Church**   = COME!

- **Engaged Church**   = GO! and invite to COME!

- **Emerging Church**   = GO! and STAY ...
                            see what ARISES

With these understandings we can now see one of the ways in which clusters fit as transitional church. Just as we have seen that mid-sized clusters can engage right across from the fringe to the non-churched, so also this cluster-shaped church is again transitional in the sense that it can adjust right across the three categories described here.

Clusters can function in **attractional** mode, providing welcoming and relevant community that acts as a stepping stone to Sunday service (COME mode). Then again clusters can have GO dynamics when they effectively **engage** in servant mission to their chosen mission field, and then invite the responsive to COME to their community and to Sunday service. Lastly, clusters can GO to their mission context and STAY, allowing a completely new indigenous cluster to ARISE. This **emerging** missional community nonetheless has loose links to a COME type of Sunday or other celebration gathering. All three are possible.

On the other hand, radical expressions of Emerging Church usually mean starting from scratch and with no expectation of any link to inherited type structures and gatherings to which new converts would not be expected to "COME." In this sense emerging church assumes the planting of a distinct fresh expression.

At the other extreme, inherited church can't become an emerging church... it can become attractional or even engaged... but could only plant a completely separate emerging church. The two tables that follow sum up this greater flexibility of networked mid-sized communities to journey outwards from inherited mode church.

This explanation of Transitional Church clarifies Mark Stibbe's observation quoted at the start, that clusters or mid-sized communities in mission (MSCs), provide the opportunity to truly shift from attraction to "infiltration" whilst combining both dispersed and gathered modes.

Clusters can also be seen as transitional in that they are planting fresh expressions within a wider "womb" but are not resulting in conventional "church plants." Mike Breen has always seen this as a strength of the cluster approach since some church plants on their own have proved weak and lacked any growth dynamic.

Mission Engagement

- Emerging Church usually means starting from scratch and staying a distinct church plant

- Inherited Church can't do emerging church

- Clusters are "Transitional Church" as they can emerge and stay in the context but are linked back to inherited church

Effective Mission Engagement	Attractional Church	Engaged Church	Emerging Church
Inherited Church	✓✓	✓	✗
Clusters/Transitional Church	✓✓	✓✓	✓
Radical emerging church plant models	✗	✗	✓✓

WHAT'S HAPPENING TO OUR CULTURE REQUIRES TRANSITIONAL CHURCH

In the previous chapter we used Robert Warren's diagrams to illustrate the shift in our culture and context from Christendom to a plural post-Christendom. It is most important to recognise that although this change is happening relatively quickly (cultural change usually being gradual over many generations/centuries), it is not a shift that involves one ending and the other beginning.

A gradual decay in Christendom is associated with an increasing spread of post-modern pluralism. Hence both are present together in our society but to different degrees. Thus there is generally more residue of Christendom in the North of England than in the South, more in rural areas than in the cities or suburbs.

We can illustrate this with the fact that, in the 1980s converts drawn to a church plant into a Bolton bowling club community that met in the club bar and restaurant, were sure that this wasn't "proper church." It didn't have stained glass and gothic arches! So many who were drawn in chose to continue discipleship by transfer to the parish church. Again, into the twenty first century, most villagers who never attend the church on the green, still proudly consider it their church and express concern and actively oppose changes inside that might suit the few that still come, let alone the youth and children of the village!

These differences in the erosion of Christendom vary even more from country to country, as I developed at length in my chapter to Church Without Walls[1]. There is a stronger residue in Scotland, and in Northern Ireland Christendom is still alive and

---

[1] Michael Green (ed), Church Without Walls, Paternoster, 2002. Ch.4

well. These variations can also be traced across Continental Europe, from Catholic Italy and Poland to Lutheran Scandinavia and more secular France and Belgium. However, since the media, music and films influence the decay so much – the emerging generation across the whole of Western Europe is much more strongly effected by post-Christendom.

To better understand these patterns we need to understand the structure of culture itself so that we see how these shifts and changes are progressing. Culture is not a random association of characteristics and artifacts. Rather it is ordered with a degree of inter-connectedness. This diagram illustrates the main components of our culture and how they are arranged.

The core of any culture is the World View. Around this and shaped by it, is the value system. Then connecting the values to behaviors are what are called Forms and Meanings. These are conventional understandings. For example, a greeting that means a polite welcome may take the form of a handshake in our culture, or a kiss on both cheeks in another, or rubbing noses in yet another. Getting these mixed up will give very different signals! Then again sitting with the sole of my foot pointing at someone means a serious insult in the Middle-East, but communicates relaxed informality in the West! Same form... different meaning.

Now when we take this to a church context we have already begun to see some examples from a church plant in a bowling club in Bolton and from the place of the rural parish church in the social life of the village. Forms and Meanings in Christendom involve lots of understandings and assumptions about the place of Sunday, rites and symbols, the pattern of services and the traditional forms of religious buildings.

Crucial to mission engagement in Europe in the twenty first century is the recognition of exactly how Christendom culture is decaying to form plural post-Christendom. The key insight is that the erosion is happening from the inside out! The worldview and values have already undergone radical transformation... while it is the forms and meanings and the behaviours that they shape that are still hanging around to varying degrees in what some describe as folk-religion, or nominal Christianity.

Most western worldview is now hardly shaped by Judeo-Christian understandings... it rather centres around individualism, commercialism and the free market. In turn values based on biblical ethics are being largely replaced by pick and mix morality... based on a Political Correctness tolerance that allows whatever is OK for you and affirms that if it feels good, do it.

However, there is much memory of Christendom forms and meanings. Otherwise no-one would read "The Da Vinci Code," and scores of adverts that use Christian art or quotes or misquotes of the bible wouldn't sell their products!

The big picture conclusion of all this for mission and church planting in the West, is first that discipleship is key to restore biblical worldview and values. But second, expressions of church must also take account of where expectations are still based on residual forms and meanings from Christendom. At a more detailed level, these understandings can now give us another perspective on why clusters as transitional church, are appropriate communities in mission for many parts of the twenty first century Western Europe.

Firstly, a matrix of several clusters combines smaller faith communities on the one hand, which are NOT the familiar forms of Christendom, with more traditional forms of leadership, structure and celebration gathering on the other hand, which DO connect with Christendom expectations. This linked, twin expression of the mid-sized clusters combined with their gathered celebration can relate to the two aspects of our society – both to where Christendom is going as well as where it has gone!

Then secondly, at the same time, clusters provide stronger discipleship and community, which are appropriate for post-Christendom. Hence it is transitional church in the sense of combining elements of the familiar forms with the unfamiliar.

To illustrate this further we can draw on examples of fresh expressions of church that are cropping up and proving effective in different European contexts. Different approaches have been fruitful, depending on the strength of the echoes of Christendom that are present. These are explained here but also represented on a matrix below. This matrix contrasts whether Christendom forms and meanings such as church building and Sunday, or use of Christian rite and symbol still carry a high meaning or very little meaning.

WHICH APPROACH WOULD YOU USE WHEN?

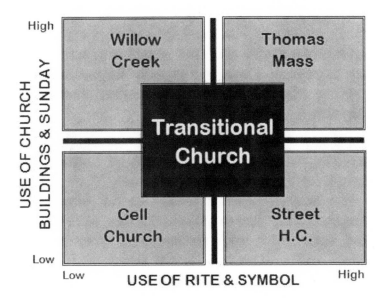

The first example (top-right) is from Finland, where residual Christendom is very strong. Over 90% are confirmed as children and are lifelong, church tax-paying, members of the State Lutheran Church. But less than 2% attend church! Here the prevailing worldview and values are overwhelmingly post-Christendom, but there are very strong elements of Christendom forms and meanings influencing behaviour and expectations.

This explains why the "Thomas Mass" has been so effective. It takes place in the (Helsinki) Cathedral, in the city centre. Using the Greek classic building on a Sunday evening, it picks up on Christendom *forms* that still draw on the *meaning* that there is a proper place and day for church, if you were to go. It is led by priests in sacramental robes, uses candles and liturgy, again since all these rites and symbols (*forms*) still carry strong Christian *meaning*.

However, these are combined with modern band music and post-modern interaction, including tables for everyone to write prayers and bring them to buckets round the altar. When we visited it was packed with some 1000 worshippers of all ages, when neighbouring parish churches would only have a handful on Sunday mornings. However, equally important are mid-week discipling cells that address post-modern worldview and values with biblical truth.

The second quadrant (bottom-right) contrasts this with a project in Oslo, Norway. Here a couple of Lutheran priests created church for the marginalised of society. They gather on a weekday in a busy city-centre square. In full view of all the passing shoppers, they don sacramental robes, set a trestle table as an altar, covering it with embroidered cloth and lighted candles. Then with guitars and formal Eucharistic liturgy they draw the homeless, addicts, prostitutes and punks and offer blessed bread and wine. These are the disenfranchised who would never enter a church building on Sunday – which to them is the *form* that carries the *meaning* of all the oppressive power systems that push them to the bottom. But Christendom is also still strong enough for the *meanings* of bread and wine to speak of a Saviour who accepts them and gave his life for them.

Here is another creative mission initiative rightly interpreting the remaining Christendom opportunity to engage beyond the fringe to the closed de-churched. Those that respond regularly are drawn into a small discipling community in a nearby rented shop-front, where their worldview and values can be rebuilt around the biblical revelation.

Third on our matrix is top-left, which might represent the Seeker Service. In middle American Willow Creek as in middle-class England, folk may still expect church in a building on Sunday. But take out all the recognisable Christian rite or symbol and just address their life situation and needs in message, drama and song... and many come.

Last of the four quadrants at the bottom-left, is low on the *meaning* of church building and Sunday and also low on the *forms* and *meanings* of rite and symbol. This is where pure cell church fits, which minimises the large gathering and emphasises the small intentional discipling group. This model comes from pre-Christian Asia, where there are no echoes of Christendom *forms* or *meanings* either to draw on or to hinder. So pure cell works wonders. Significantly in the UK pure cell seems to work best among youth, where Christendom is weakest (the most non-churched sector of our society).

With these four quadrants explained and illustrated, we can see the place of transitional church in the centre. This central position means it can combine both a high and low expression of *meanings* like Sunday and religious building. Clusters can be midweek and in any secular venue... but can also gather with other clusters to celebrate on Sunday in a special or even traditional building. Transitional Church can also combine high and low use of *forms* and *meanings* from Christian rite and symbol. Again, this can be by minimal use at cluster gatherings but more expression at larger celebrations. However, this networked church can also hold together clusters that are rich in use of rite and symbol... recovering and reinterpreting stations, candles, icons, etc... with other clusters that may use little or none.

CLUSTERS OFFER TRANSITIONAL CHURCH STRUCTURES

This is the last aspect of Transitional Church we shall explore. Carl George introduced the concept of Transitional Church in his book "Preparing Your Church for the Future."[2] He came at it

---

[2] Carl George, Preparing Your Church for the Future, Revell, 1991

from the point of different church structures. He, like other analysts, recognised the common western trend of restructuring the church if it is to successfully grow through various 'size banners.'

The Alban Institute paper[3] also picks up the transition from Family to Pastoral to Program and then to Corporate sized churches – with the need to restructure to break through each barrier. Carl George then identified that the pure cell model has the potential for infinite growth through cell multiplication without a change in structure[4].

However, he recognised that in the West (especially his native North America) the change to pure cell church was probably too great a challenge for inherited mode congregations or leaders! Hence, whilst he described the movement of cells as "the bulls eye," he proposed what he called "Meta-Church" (changing church), or "Church-in-transition" as more generally attainable. An intermediate structure which aims to release most of the benefits of cell or house churches, without the excessive challenge to leaders and people socialised in inherited modes of church.

In this sense, we believe that clusters of cells or mid-sized groups, resourced through a central matrix, can be one of the best expressions of this transitional structure. Cells, Clusters and Celebrations can multiply and the matrix system with huddle support for leaders can expand without crisis points of having to be reinvented.

---

[3] R. Oswald, Alban Institute Report, March/April 1991

[4] This same principle of multiplication without restructuring would also apply to models such as house churches (Wolfgang Simson, Houses that Change the World, Authentic, 1999) or household or simple church (Tony & Felicity Dale, Simply Church, publisher unknown, 2000).

ONLY HALF DECONSTRUCTED!

Before leaving Transitional Church we should refer to the fact that many church leaders fear the challenge of emerging church, which often describes itself as "deconstruction." This fear sees the more radical new forms of church that leave behind all traditionally accepted structures as risking losing the very essence of church and of corrupting the Gospel.

Advocates of radical emerging church may counter by saying that this is the reaction of controlling leaders who rightly recognise that these models involve them losing inappropriate authority over the flock. Only more time to prove these new experimental models will establish which view is more justified. However, in the meantime, a movement of clusters is a transitional position that releases some structures whilst retaining others. A half deconstructed church! It is deconstructed in the area of seeking to shift from control to release but retains accountability through huddles and connectedness, and through the networking or matrix of clusters.

We could sum up the rationale for transitional church like this: The changing context requires a church that's on a journey of change rather than making a quantum leap! Most church leaders can't shift that far that quick anyway; and also those people in post-Christendom, rather than pre-Christian culture, can't cope!

We could conclude this chapter by summing up the potential flexibility of clusters in three areas. They can bridge cultural diversity; they are a socially intermediate mid-size; and they can connect with any residue of Christendom or none.

Truly cluster-shaped church can express the "Mixed Economy" vision... it offers within its diversity a "Both/And" expression of church!

CLUSTERS

PART THREE

IMPLEMENTATION

Practical processes for the whole church as well as for growing an individual Cluster, and the challenge of the generations.

CHAPTER NINE

Introducing Clusters to a Church

The process of introducing clusters to a church can take a whole variety of forms but many of the underlying principles are common to managing most significant change[1]. And we have made it clear that introducing clusters does involve really significant change.

It is a shift from Sunday Christianity to seven-day church in mission. Hence it is important to be clear right at the start that it takes time if it is to be done well. Realistic expectations are crucial and with a church of any size, to lay the foundation and transition to clusters as missional communities, we should be thinking of a three year process.

Before outlining the different principles and practises of implementation it is perhaps important to review some of the factors that will influence the choice of the most appropriate way.

FACTORS INFLUENCING THE METHOD OF INTRODUCTION

The first factor is the leader and her/his style of leadership and her/his relationship to the church. This will be a principal issue determining the extent and rate of change. Those leaders who naturally function in a visionary/directive style will manage the change in a different and probably quicker way than those

---

[1] For excellent change management principles see John Finney, Understanding Leadership, DLT, 1989

whose preference is collaborative. Also these leaders who have established with their church an experience of regular change and a trust based on positive outcomes, will be able to move more purposefully.

Secondly, the size of church will make a significant difference as will its past experience with small groups in particular and change in general. The spirituality and tradition of the church may also affect how clusters may be embraced. Lastly, mission demographics and the social and cultural context may play an important role, as will the history of the church's relationship to its context.

THREE OUTCOMES OR STRATEGIES

There are three possible outcomes or strategies with regards introducing clusters or mid-sized communities. Most of this book assumes that a whole church is **transitioned** over time to be based on some form of adaptation of cluster described here. However, it may be judged that a significant part of the existing church is unlikely to embrace this change. So rather than incur destructive conflict and loss, it may be preferred to introduce clusters alongside the existing pattern.

This will create a separate stream or **parallel** expression, held together through leadership with the existing congregation. Lastly, it may not be felt best to hold together two different models within the same church and so **planting** of a new cluster church is entirely possible. At the most radical extreme, a series of only loosely affiliated clusters could be planted.

TWO PROCESSES AND A RANGE BETWEEN

Assuming that the more common outcome is envisaged, of a transitioning of the whole church to clusters over time, then there are two principal processes. These are similar to the two routes to introduce cell church principles. They can be described as either **evolution** with a pilot or prototype approach, or more of a **transformation** ("big bang") aimed at shifting everyone to a cluster model at the same time. These are obviously two extremes on a scale and it is important to revisit the factors influencing such choices that we explained above.

An example of one of the most gradual introductions would be St George's, Deal in Kent in 2004. They have a pastoral style senior leader with an apostolic associate and with some 400 in attendance. They had transitioned all their Home Groups to cell just a year before. So the Cluster vision was introduced gently and initially just one cluster was established and developed well in the first year. There were leaders keen to develop a second cluster nine months later, but some local factors delayed that.

By contrast, the story of St Mark's Haydock, told in the introduction, was one of the faster processes. A church of over 700 with an apostolic overall leader, St Mark's had very successfully transitioned to cell by "big bang" in 1998. These cells were well bedded down and performing effectively so in 2004, a cluster vision was shared, which was distinct from the cells. People from different cells gathered round a particular mission vision or social interest.

Hence the clusters that emerged represented a new structure and were more like mission teams and not groups of cells. The first clusters launched only a few months later and within six months, although many folk in cells hadn't yet joined a cluster, nonetheless ten clusters had successfully emerged.

Somewhere in the middle was St Andrew's, Chorleywood, which had some 700-800 in attendance, a prophetic teacher as overall leader with a gifted implementer as associate. Home groups had been rather set and inward looking, many having been together for up to 15 years. The vision for Mid-Size

Communities (clusters by another name) was launched on 5th November 2003.

By Easter 2004, five MSCs had formed and then a building project meant that everyone was going to have to leave the building in the autumn for at least six months. This led to the decision for MSCs to be launched for everyone right across the church – 975 signing up for 19 MSCs after the September launch weekend! Nine months later as they prepared to move back into their building, about 90% of the MSCs decided to continue and they have made allowance for a second stream of the minority opting not to be in MSCs. Crucial here in shaping things is their context, which is made up of a mosaic of commuter suburbs, villages and towns over a 25 mile radius.

This is quite different from a dense spreading city like Sheffield, but the cluster/mid-sized community is proving effective and adaptable in both. Mid-Size Communities (MSCs) at St Andrews have transformed many commuting spectators at their previous teaching celebrations into enthusiastic participants in mission where they live. The diagram opposite illustrates the range of MSCs in the autumn of 2004.

Threshold is a rural network of churches that has been going in Lincolnshire villages for a dozen years or so. It had also successfully transitioned to cell, at the second attempt around 2000. By 2003 those cells were spread across five villages and one UPA estate in Lincoln City itself. As those cells continued to grow and multiply, it became clear that a clustering of them according to their geographic mission focus would be most effective. So from 2004 clustering has evolved and enabled continued fruitful conversion growth. There are currently three clusters in Nettleham village, one covering the twin villages of Whetton and Dunholme, one that links Wragby and a cell further out in Hemmingby and one in the Lincoln UPA.

This is not only an example of the gradual evolutionary process of implementation, but also of ongoing evolutionary adaptation as mission arises in new contexts and cells then clusters emerge and the best way to connect them is worked out. The larger gatherings for celebration style, have also had to change more than once to adjust to the pattern of mission on the ground.

Mid-sized Communities at St Andrews, Chorleywood. Sept 2004

The North London Vineyard Church presented a much more straightforward situation. It is small with some 75 members and a strong apostolic leader. So here the vision was shared and the whole church transitioned in one go to just two clusters. A couple of years later they have now released a third cluster.

On the other hand a church with several services on a Sunday has decided to introduce clusters in just one of these services.

There are pros and cons of either the gradual **evolution** or the more direct **transformation** option. The faster, more revolutionary "all at once" method has the advantage of working with a single model right across the church. This avoids some people feeling left out and frustrated. Also supporting structures can be introduced across the board.

However, it is less organic and tends to suffer from "social engineering." This usually results in a significant number of weak and stagnant clusters as they aren't based on either strong relationships, or clear common vision and values having emerged. Hence with this all at once transformation approach, there may then need to be substantial reshuffling over a period, to get the quality and mix right.

By contrast, the slower evolutionary approach with pilot or prototype clusters, gradually multiplying through the church, does mean living with two systems.

These organic clusters are likely to be stronger. But care is needed to ensure they keep mission focused and don't just grow by drawing in more from the pool of those not yet committed to cluster. Certainly a few strong vibrant clusters can help "sell" the idea to the slower adopters. They also have good models to learn from.

PRINCIPLES FOR HEALTHY CLUSTER INTRODUCTION

As we mentioned earlier, many of these principles are common to good management through change and can be more fully read up elsewhere. However, some of the key principles are:

a) The visions have to be birthed in prayer and the introduction/transition process surrounded with prayer, involving both intercessors and the whole church.

b) The leader or leaders have to change first and this is principally at a heart level. Leaders have also to embrace significant shifts in role as we shall see next. So they need to have faced the cost themselves first and to have sifted their motives.

c) Change must be based on values rather than structures. So the leader needs to bring the proposed change to the church by first preaching and teaching the underlying values until they are owned by a significant proportion. Values lead on to the vision and only then are the new structures outlined. Clearly foundational values will be mission, community, growth and multiplication. The vision will be of church breaking free from institution and formalism related to building and Sunday. It is likely to involve principles related to the recovery of biblical congregation as missional community with vibrant relationships... UP:IN:OUT.

d) Its good to get outside help and input from those who have been this way before. Bring them in to review your situation and your plans, as well as to envision and train. Also take your key people to see clusters working elsewhere.

e) This will all form part of your training for those who will lead and be core members of early clusters. Consider attending a 'Cluster Conference' as a team.

f) Prepare the new support structures and create an apprenticeship culture in the church. You will also need to prune a little and probably dispense with any competing programme.

g) If you have discerned it's right for a slower evolutionary approach then spot those who are responding to the values and vision and getting excited. Test their call and release them.

h) Alternatively if you are led to a broader introduction across all or most of the church, then still spot the early adopters. But then work with them and the early majority to win the later majority in order to gain a critical mass of support.

i) In either process, a key is to spot the good potential cluster leaders since its so helpful to get the first clusters really strong. It can be that reviewing the really good missional cell/home group leaders may be a helpful first indicator of possible cluster leaders. Those leading stagnant home groups will probably not produce dynamic clusters.

j) Love people more than the vision. People can tell.

CHANGE OF CULTURE

One of the biggest challenges that comes with introducing clusters is that there needs to be a shift in culture – all the way from the church leaders to the whole church body – and that shift needs to come in the attitude towards control. We introduced this fundamental change in the opening chapter and developed it in detail in chapter four, but it is really important to revisit this principle now, as it is one of the key changes of culture required for healthy clusters to form and grow.

Whether we subscribe to the "top down" structure of leadership (Anglican, Catholic, Lutheran, etc) or the "bottom up" structure (Baptist, free church, etc), we need to recognise that both are based on control… either the vicar/bishop/PCC keeping the laity in check – or the laity keeping the minister/area minister in check.

The primary function of both structures is to make sure that all is in control (finances, programmes, use of time, teaching, pastoral care, etc) and that everything passes through formal channels. So whenever any of these areas are tested, the default position of both systems is to maintain the status quo. This will hardly bring the freedom for genuine and significant change in the way we do church! What is needed is a change of culture based on release, where the attitude of the church is more "why not?" rather than "why?"

The church needs to be prepared to look for the people with vision, to release them to turn the vision into reality, and to resource them to grow the reality. This change will mean that visions are not stunted because the finances don't appear to be in place, or because the leader doesn't think it's a good idea. People should be freed up to explore where they feel God is leading them, regardless of these factors.

This low control releasing environment has to work right down to the small groups/cells, so that cell leaders don't try to hold on to their members, but are able to send them out into new vision. And it also needs to work right to the overall church leaders so that as they bring in clusters they don't fall into social engineering, but instead allow the natural groups of people to gather together around their own mission visions... even if this takes time. This change will also mean that the church knows they have the permission to "fail." It is OK for clusters to not be very successful, or to close at any time. This should be clearly seen as a basic principle of release... so that the lay leaders of the church in turn feel free to be adventurous, and give anything a try. After all, if it goes wrong... you can always come back!

Low control, however, does not mean that people can go off and do whatever they want without the church knowing what's going on. Instead, there needs to be the principle of low control/high accountability, that we explained earlier. If someone is going to enter into leadership of a cluster, or a cell, they should be ready to be accountable for their leadership. Low control means that anyone can develop a mission vision. But high accountability means that they will be held accountable as to how they are developing that vision.

This does not mean that their leaders can steer their path, because that would be control. But it does mean that they build a relationship based on regular support and prayer, and regular discussion of what's being done and why. This should establish a clear channel of communication between the clusters and the church. It also enables good discipleship practice between church leaders and cluster leaders (and then cluster leaders to cell leaders), based on pointing to Jesus and giving dedicated time to discerning where God is leading.

At St Thomas', as well as in other cluster churches, this is done in what are often called "huddles"… a gathering of leaders around their most natural leader for the purpose of personal discipleship. Again, these principles are discussed elsewhere, but it is key that they are flagged up here as we think about implementation. It is easier to bring in as the DNA of an emerging cluster system, rather than to try and fit it into an already ongoing structure that is based on other systems of leadership. If it is not low control/high accountability, then there is an increased danger that clusters would be little more than a restructuring of the church… when what is needed is to bring in new life and freedom.

SPOT THE EMERGING LEADERS AND MAKE SPACE FOR THEM TO GATHER PEOPLE

As you share the vision and values for creative mid-sized missional communities you will need to spot who are the folk who catch it. It's as though they begin to "pop up out of the pool." You will notice them responding as you share the principles; they will catch you after a service with an idea, or you may overhear them enthusiastically sharing with others. Invest time in them at this early stage and check your discernment. If they seem to be getting a call to initiate a cluster, encourage them to find a team and offer support and mentoring. This may mean drawing them into an emerging leaders huddle process. These early leaders may be leaders of existing small groups or other programs, or they may not.

As well as identifying the emerging cluster leaders and helping them form their team, you will need to begin to make space and opportunity in the regular life of the church, for them to gather folk to their vision. This may mean providing slots in the services for them to share and including their items in notice sheets or the church website – all as recruiting opportunities. Mike Breen issued "Fishing Licences" to his emerging cluster leaders in the introduction phase at St Thomas'. He let it be known that they had his permission and active encouragement to recruit to the vision of their new cluster.

Some creative ideas have emerged at several cluster-based churches to help these mid-sized communities draw in existing church members and to attract visitors. At the church building or celebration venue, the walls have become notice boards with all sorts of eye-catching tableaus for each cluster. These may include write-ups, diagrams, photos and artwork to communicate the vision and vibrancy of the community. At Sunday services and whole church gatherings, the central role of clusters is regularly emphasised. This can be illustrated with cluster testimonies and a time of welcoming visitors can be followed by asking cluster leaders to stand and encouraging those unattached to speak to them afterwards.

These principles need to become part of the ongoing life of a cluster-based church. And recently, at Sheffield, Philadelphia, one Sunday morning whole church gathering was largely given over to what they humorously billed as "Cluster Speed-dating!" The venue was laid out with round tables, one for each cluster, and on each were refreshments provided by cluster members and literature about the cluster. Those unattached to any cluster were encouraged to circulate and meet different cluster members and grill them with all their questions about cluster life.

WHAT HAPPENS TO EXISTING SMALL GROUPS?

A key factor for leaders to assess in deciding how clusters are implemented is the extent and state of existing small groups.

Extent of small groups: There are three broad situations so far as the extent of existing home group/small group life in the church goes. A church considering clusters is likely to have either a) no current small groups; or b) a proportion between one third and two thirds of attenders in small groups; or c) most or all their people in cells/small groups. At one level the easiest is when there is a clean sheet and no current groups. The field is clear, nothing has to be unpicked or closed down and prevailing ideas and values don't have to be challenged.

If there are a proportion of folk in small groups then this opens the possibility either to use those more committed people to resource the new vision or to find potential leaders with no existing group assumptions to pioneer the new model. And there is room for these to grow alongside the old small groups for a time if this is best. Lastly, the situation where most or all are already in groups can present the greatest challenge. Everyone has unlearning to do and embracing of new patterns, so skilled leadership is required. In this case the health and vitality of the groups will be particularly influential in implementation strategy.

Health of small groups: Here again there are three or four possible scenarios. The church may have either a) home groups that are stagnant, probably very inward-looking with no dynamic of mission and growth. Alternatively b) it may have quite lively small groups showing creativity, growth and change. Or c) the church may have serious cell-type groups that are vital, growing and multiplying. Finally, d) there can be a mixture of two or all three of these types.

In the first case there is no question of any of the home groups providing the breeding ground for Clusters and their leaders won't be suitable to lead clusters either. But the more inward-looking small groups are, the harder their members may hang on since the groups have evolved around their needs and comfort. Clusters have to develop separately and eventually swallow them up. In the second case with quite lively small groups with a desire for growth, it may be easier for them to let go and take a step further into more effective mid-sized missional clusters.

Then in the third case of dynamic cell-type groups, on the one hand some cells might already be made up of those with a common mission focus and they could grasp a vision to multiply into a cluster. However, most cells will only have individual evangelism goals rather than a shared mission sector. Some if they have been going a while may be happy to die and reform with people of the same vision to build a cluster.

However, the more recently cells have formed, the harder it may be to dismantle the membership and belonging in order to form viable single vision clusters. There is no easy answer here and time may be needed and different approaches for different cells. St Marks, Haydock's story in the introduction illustrated this situation when the unusual strategy adopted was to leave the recently formed cells with high commitment and gradually introduce clusters as mission teams unrelated to cell membership – the two structures co-existing at least for a few years.

Issues and options with small groups: We have already begun to explore some of these. But it is important to be clear that many existing leaders of small groups don't make the best cluster leaders... they find it hard to change, at least quickly. The exception will be those who have led outward-looking groups or cells. It is also rare for existing small groups or cells to stay intact and combine together to form a healthy cluster. It's too unlikely that they all share common vision and values. Occasionally one cell or group could be the seed of a cluster where they already share one purpose. We have told how this worked for most of the cells in Threshold church since the cells were already formed around a mission vision.

As explained at the start of this chapter there are two processes to introduce clusters – either transformation (revolution) or evolution. If the transformation process is adopted with existing small groups or cells, then this probably means that all would be closed for a fallow season and then clusters launched (there could be an exception of a few cells spawning clusters). Alternatively if the church evolves into clusters, then there is much more flexibility to keep some or all existing small groups for a transitional period. They may get absorbed into clusters at different rates as the number of these mid-sized groups increases.

DISPERSED PASTORAL CARE

An effective small group or cell system will already have spread the pastoral care away from one or two specialists at the centre, to the everyday life of small communities. Where this is already effective, the introduction of a mid-sized level merely extends these practices.

The watchword should be that most pastoral support of members is fulfilled by the loving and caring responses of the small group/cell. Issues that are more serious or demanding are then referred by cell leaders to cluster leaders. Their job is not as specialists, they may give some one-off input and advice, but perhaps organise wider support from others within the cluster or decide to refer the matter to overall leaders or outside specialists.

Hence the overall leaders only get involved in the more serious cases, and even here lessons are that many situations may be helped best with outside specialist medical or counselling services.

There are three vital principles here that have emerged from the cell church movement[2]. First, pastoral support should be based on **dispersed care** rather than focused on a few. Loving community is God's best first line of support. Second, it should work on a **reduced span of care** so that no one (especially lay) person is overburdened. Six people is a maximum guideline – half what Jesus took on! Then thirdly, as we have emphasised, there needs to be **ready reference to outside expertise**.

SHIFT IN CHURCH LEADERS ROLE

We have already highlighted that a crucial part of introducing clusters to a church, is the change in the role and function of the overall leader or leaders. First and most important, developing the last point, is the shift to a more releasing model from inherited patterns of control. This requires much more inner security if the leader is going to let go.

---

[2] Steve Croft develops these principles throughout his Transforming Communities, DLT, 2002

This deep-rooted confidence in the gospel rather than status or performance is the only way to the authentic liberating of others to their full potential – rejoicing whenever they do more or better than we can. It also sets us free from having to keep tabs on everything. The leader being in their own discipleship huddle is the best place to address these personal issues and grow in Gospel confidence.

The second shift is also challenging. This is a gradual change in activities and re-ordered priorities. In the church where everything is about the mini-cathedral Sunday Service, the leader spends most time and priority in preparation and up front presentations. However, as clusters become more the centre of how we do church, leaders have to give much more priority to equipping, supporting and releasing others. There may also be less frequent large celebrations for which to prepare. These changes become more marked as some clusters begin to meet on Sundays and consequently celebrations may become more periodic (i.e. fortnightly, monthly).

Associated with these changes for the overall leader, is a reduction in prominence. There is also the likelihood that more traditional church members won't understand these changes. The leaders' reduced visibility combined with the evident increase in ministry roles of cluster leaders, can lead to murmurings or even outright criticism... "why isn't the vicar/pastor doing what he/she is paid to do!" or, "Who do they think they are... that's the vicar's job!"

In fact the senior leader(s) priorities will shift much more to the planning and delivery of training and equipping the cluster leaders. They will give more attention to really high quality input at the periodic all cluster celebrations. They will "ride the range" of the cluster meetings, bringing a word of encouragement and vision as they act as connector of the dispersed networked church.

There is also a challenge for the leader to model mission as the identity of cluster church embraces much more intentional mission. The overall leader(s) have to discover how to lead from both the centre and the edge. Especially if a church begins to have significant numbers of clusters meeting out on Sunday.

Not only will leaders "ride the range" but they need to set up new management structures to provide communication to dispersed clusters. They will also need to ensure that there is financial provision for them and resourcing for youth and children's work. More than one church with clusters out on Sunday has invested in large plastic cluster boxes for collection each week as they are filled with notice sheets, the process for offerings, children's material, etc.

Part of the equipping and supporting role to cluster leaders will be the regular meeting with them in groups of 4 to 8 in the sort of "huddle" described earlier. Here there is a sort of group mentoring and coaching as they are apprenticed in their own life as well as their developing role. The church leader will need to develop processes of addressing character, skills of cluster leading, faith development and spirituality.

And finally, a big focus of leadership as Jesus modelled it, is to raise up the leaders who will follow in your footsteps, as well as releasing others into their leadership potential and letting them go to wherever God calls them. Essentially the intention of a good leader ought to be to do themselves out of a job, and to do this they need to be aware of the seasons of leadership that God takes them through.

These are the same four stages that cluster leaders themselves have to go through to grow and multiply their mid-sized missional community (described more fully in the next chapter).

They are principles that are developed much more in Mike Breen & Walt Kallestad's book, "The Passionate Church", and forms the basis of the square in LifeShapes.

So, as Jesus did, when bringing new vision it is good to clearly state your vision and invite people to follow. Not too many details are necessarily needed, just clear vision and motivation... and as people follow, the leader can adopt an "I do, you watch" approach.

However, gradually this season runs itself out and the team of emerging cluster leaders will become more aware that they have not yet developed the skills for the vision. This can be a very difficult time, and requires more of a coaching approach by the overall leader, and where they draw more alongside the team – getting a closer view of how the clusters are being led, etc. This phase is classically expressed as more "I do, you help."

As this continues gradually the third phase develops as skills and confidence increase, and the cluster leaders begin to own the vision more and gain more ownership. This is a time for the church leader to begin to release the up-coming leaders more into practical leadership, and there is now a shift into "You do, I help." And then finally the time comes when the leaders that have been raised are fully capable of doing the work and the overall leader can begin to fully delegate the running of the clusters to them. This fits into the "You do, I watch" description and now the church leaders(s) are looking for those who they can draw into a new huddle of those to whom they will pass on the supervising and supporting of the cluster leaders.

TRANSITIONAL OPTIONS FOR OUR SUNDAY SERVICES

As we observed in chapter six, despite our traditional version of Sunday events being more akin to biblical temple/celebration, we usually can't make hasty changes here. We have made repeated reference to the possibility of clusters possibly meeting on Sunday, but where does this leave the "Sunday church service?"

We have honestly admitted that most churches so far have adopted an implementation strategy that introduces clusters midweek and only very occasionally changes Sunday in the church building. This approach responds to the realisation that we need to recover the lost dynamic of biblical congregation, but defers any full return to biblical celebration as only a periodic very special occasion linked to seasonal festivals.

It is interesting to us that two of the churches that have begun to break the expectation of a weekly celebration-style gathering were forced to lose their special building, at least for a time. In Sheffield, St Thomas' lost the big Roxy nightclub venue at five weeks notice. In Chorleywood, St Andrew's were forced to the decision that their building refurbishment plans meant at least six months evacuation. In both cases without the celebration venue, clusters were forced to meet out three Sundays per month and a much deeper embedding of clusters and MSCs resulted.

Chapter fourteen describes the patterns of "riding the range" and "Pony Express", which evolved at both churches to resource and connect the dispersed clusters/MSCs.

Significantly again, St George's, Deal has struggled to get first one and then two clusters over two years. But as building refurbishment again means exile, a dozen clusters have come together. And reports of the first Sunday with them all "out" is that everyone is buzzing and one not-yet-Christian who came along to one of the clusters came to faith!

So far we know of only two examples where implementation has voluntarily shifted Sunday to a once a month celebration pattern, allowing regular clusters on the other Sundays. One is Threshold rural network of churches and the other the very small North London Vineyard.

Then again, as we recounted in the Introduction, St Marks, Haydock have some of their clusters out of the building on Sunday once a month. This has partly been to relieve pressure on a full building and partly as a strategy for mission engagement.

We shall have to wait and see whether some other churches adopting mid-sized communities begin to grasp the nettle of reducing weekly traditional Sunday celebration style. As pointers in this direction, St Thomas', Sheffield and St Andrew's, Chorleywood, provide an interesting contrast in their pattern of implementation once they recovered a central building after exile (St Thomas' acquiring the ex-industrial Philadelphia Campus and St Andrew's completing their rebuilding project).

In both St Thomas' and St Andrew's there was about a year without use of their own building, and during that time both initiated a once a month whole church celebration in a large rented venue.

However, at Sheffield, although for two years after occupying the Philadelphia site, clusters continued on three Sundays and celebrations on one Sunday a month, thereafter with a new leader, for two years now, all clusters have been required to return to midweek only and weekly Sunday celebrations (although this may be allowed to revert in a future season).

By contrast, in Chorleywood on re-occupying their "State of the Art" building – MSCs were given the choice whether to come back to a Sunday celebration service weekly, fortnightly or monthly. Whilst a few opted to cease Sunday MSC, roughly half of the seventeen MSCs opted for only fortnightly or monthly membership of the services (which was fortunate, since the growth through MSC development to over 1000 people couldn't have been accommodated if they all came every week!).

So far our observation is that the Chorleywood pattern of continuing MSCs on two or three Sundays a month may be producing a much healthier more missional mid-sized life than having ceased Sunday clusters at Sheffield. It may also be significant that the overall leadership at St Andrew's was more in line with the principle of low control as they released cluster leaders to make the decision as to their frequency of returning to the church building for Sundays.

IT TAKES TIME

It is important to go into this having right expectations, and so being prepared for the long haul. Clusters are not a short-term solution to church growth and structure. They are about becoming community-in-mission and take time to fully introduce, and for them to be effective they then need time to mature, grow, die, and be reborn. Clusters are a dynamic and organic way of doing church, and as such they need commitment for the long haul.

At St Thomas' it has taken ten years to fully bring the city-based missionary site (Philadelphia) into mature clusters. At the Crookes parish church, it had gone through the same cycle as Philadelphia for a number of years, but then in 2001 they observed that they had begun to lose some of their parish vision, and spent a further four years getting back to basics, gathering the church together, re-envisioning and then sending out again. The current Rector, Mick Woodhead, highlights a process they had to go through as they looked to re-implement clusters at Crookes.

In 2001 there were five clusters, 15 cells across a church membership of around 230 people. In praying through a focus for new vision, the church leadership felt challenged by the biblical principle that "unless a grain of wheat falls to the ground and dies, it remains only a single seed. But if it dies, it produces many seeds" (John 12:24).

They could see that they needed to let the clusters all die in order to see new life. So they closed everything down and gathered the whole church together across two Sunday morning services and began the long process of retrieving the church identity and vision. This involved laying a foundation of healthy cell principles and raising new leaders for cluster and cell mission focuses. Getting to this stage of seeing the challenge clearly took nearly two years!

The process they went through was a three stage process:

1. Time to think: Between April 2003 and August 2003 time was given for each cell and individual to pray and consider what their purpose was, what their calling was within the church. As they did this they were invited to join one of the two morning services according to their sense of calling… there was either the 9am (more prayerful, contemplative, servant focused) or the 11am (Community outreach focused).

2. Time to Act: Between October 2003 and Easter 2004 the two Sunday gatherings were launched, and a whole church evening meeting was also launched once a month, which was an opportunity for people to share their vision for new cells and clusters.

3. Time to Build: From Easter 2004 the new cells and clusters were launched, as were the huddles between the church leaders and cluster leaders, and between cluster leaders and cell leaders. Initially there was hardly any growth from the time when the clusters had shut down, and as they re-launched with five clusters and 16 cells.

However, the old had been allowed to die, and the new clusters and cells had been birthed into fresh vision. At the turning of 2005 to 2006, the immediate effects of this could already be seen, as there were now nine clusters and 23 cells across around 400 people. This should serve as an encouragement that clusters, if invested in for the long term, will bring health and growth.

AN ENCOURAGEMENT: JOINING A GROWING MOMENTUM

As we look at the implementation of clusters there will inevitably be all sorts of questions that arise out of your specific church context. And you may wonder quietly to yourself whether it will be worth the effort: what if this only works in two or three big churches? Well, fear not! We have referenced a few times in this book that there is an ever growing number of churches implementing clusters, and the momentum is building.

In this chapter we have given more detailed information on the very different implementation of processes of some eight widely contrasting churches and contexts. Beyond these we know of over twenty churches in the UK developing such creative mid-sized missional communities. And there are many more cluster-based churches across Europe, and many more that are seriously evaluating the road towards implementation.

It is a big shift in any church, but it is working. Clusters are being started in all sizes of churches – from a church big enough to have just two clusters – to churches with upwards of twenty.

We have also illustrated that these clusters are also proving effective in at least two rural contexts as well as suburban and city churches and a coastal market town. This is a multipliable model, and as the network of cluster churches continues to grow, the value in cross communication and resourcing one another and sharing testimonies grows as well. Below is a list of some of the churches that have joined the adventure so far!

SOME OF THE CHURCHES IMPLEMENTING CLUSTER

- St Thomas', Sheffield
- Holy Trinity, Cheltenham
- St Andrew's, Chorleywood (MSCs)
- St Barnabas', Kensington
- St Mary Bredin, Canterbury
- St George's, Deal
- St Paul's, Hammersmith
- Fountain of Life, Norfolk
- Emmanuel & St James, Didsbury
- North London Vineyard
- St Mark's, Haydock
- St Barnabas', Cambridge
- Hillsong, London (pub-sized groups)
- St John's Westwood, Coventry
- Highgrove & Woodlands, Bristol
- Good Shepherd, Romford
- St John's, Harbourne, Birmingham

CHAPTER TEN

Launching or Planting: Growing and Multiplying Clusters

STARTING A NEW CLUSTER – LAUNCHING OR PLANTING?

Among the many subtle variations on how new clusters can be started, I think it is helpful to distinguish at the start two broad categories. So let's explain the difference between launching a new cluster or planting a cluster from scratch.

Launching Clusters: Generally launching a new cluster involves quite a significant proportion of folks already in the church. Some may be attracted to become founder members of the new cluster from the pool of those who have not previously been in any cluster.

Others may be drawn from existing clusters. These folk will sense that they identify more with the vision of the new cluster and/or have stronger relationships there, and so will be released or sent out from their existing cluster. Alternatively, new clusters that are launched within the church, can plan to gain significant numbers to start from those completing some process evangelism course, such as Alpha, Y course or Essence.

Another characteristic of what I term launching a new cluster, is that it is likely to focus on a mission context and culture in which there are already significant numbers of existing church members. In other words this is not so much a cross-cultural mission engagement. For example, existing young adult creatives in the church launch a cluster to reach their friends and folk like them.

Planting Clusters: In contrast we can speak of planting a cluster when the process is more focused well beyond the existing church. Using the term this way, planting a cluster is likely to involve only a small number of existing church members. The initial core group will feel much more like a pioneer team.

This sense of team will be heightened because not only are they few in numbers, but they share a common call to a cultural context or neighbourhood well beyond the fringes of the existing church. So their experience is as a cross-cultural mission band. For example the team of existing members may be called to a deprived inner-urban estate, or to addicts and the homeless or to a residential home for the elderly.

PRINCIPLES OF THE LAUNCHING OR PLANTING PROCESSES – LUKE 10: 1 – 9

Although the dynamics of launching or planting may feel and be quite different, both need to involve most of the same processes. Jesus' commissioning and directions as he sends out the 72 in Luke 10 (and the 12 in Matthew 10, Mark 6 and Luke 9) are a helpful framework for all such mission ventures. We see six clear principles for clusters here.

1. It starts with "Go!" Being sent. To start a new cluster there has to be a change of direction – from an IN to an OUT emphasis. If clusters are defined by mission, this is especially true in the letting go of the old allegiances to

embrace something new. A real impetus and motivation is needed to press through the inertia to let things stay as they are.

2. Then the "2 by 2" speaks of the importance of Team. Clusters are launched or planted with a committed team that works and relates well together. It's a really significant task and the work is hard... so lots of prayer is needed for workers and the work. Team provides the mutual support and encouragement as well as the range of gifts.

3. "To every town and place" where Jesus was to go, makes the point about the need for a clear mission focus. In Matthew 10:6 Jesus speaks of sending to "the lost sheep of the house of Israel." Clusters that are healthy know who they are trying to reach and what social or geographic context they seek to engage and transform. Discerning the state of the harvest involves skills of listening and careful exploration to read the culture and recognise points of gospel connection.

4. Jesus exhorts his mission teams to be single minded, free from hindrance and distractions. This is so true for clusters, which require concentrated effort to bring something from nothing and to persevere in the face of inevitable difficulty and discouragement. Not taking two of anything underlines that Clusters need to be lightweight and low maintenance. A key characteristic that we emphasise throughout.

5. Then the key to unlock a mission context Jesus says is a "Person of Peace." Cluster launching or planting teams need to be encouraged with the faith that there are open receptive people who will give them a welcome. This should liberate everyone to be involved in evangelistic relationships into the chosen culture. This principle needs to be understood by all in the team and to shape how they and all who join the cluster, prioritise their time and activity.

6. Lastly Jesus exhorts his teams to stay with this person and to lodge in their house, sharing meals together. This emphasises the importance of building community and indicates that those links made by the cluster to people of peace, will open up all sorts of other networks of relationship. But even more important, we believe, in the principle of staying in their house rather than our house, is that they will set the culture and social tone of the cluster so that it is truly indigenous.

A ROUGH GUIDE TO LAUNCHING OR PLANTING

This biblical process of mission applies so well to starting clusters. We can expand on it by highlighting the following step-wise guide. It's important though to realise that some steps will happen concurrently and even in a different order. The list is more of a check to the things that need to happen rather than a pre-programmed sequence.

Pray and get initial vision: If clusters are defined by mission they are birthed in prayer and shaped and motivated by vision. This sort of prayer involves lots of listening and reflecting together to get a clear call from God. The emerging vision will include the values that will be the foundation of the new community. In an atmosphere in which faith and vision is encouraged and pioneers know they will be released, lots of ideas for clusters will spring up.

Recognise and appoint leader(s): Cluster vision is embodied in a leader and leaders. They need to be personally affirmed and the vision sharpened as clarifying questions are asked. Then they need to be released with the support of the wider leadership. This connecting to the rest of the church should involve identifying who will relate to the leaders for accountability and encouragement (e.g: which huddle group they join).

Select and call the core: Emerging cluster leaders need a core group or team to rely on and share the burden of creating a new mid-sized community. This core team should be passionate about the shared vision and have good relationships together. A range of five-fold ministry roles, gifts and personalities is also helpful.[1] It's also good to have a mix of the more mature and new Christians – often the recently converted take to clusters fastest as well as having lots of not-yet-Christian contacts.

Build community: Since clusters are communities in mission gathered around Jesus, it's clear in everything we have said that real quality community has to be built. We highlighted that special skills are involved in creating this bonded, interactive, caring and supportive environment. This is so important that we expand on it in a later section here as well as in chapter eleven.

Engage in mission and evangelism to gather a crowd: Leaders who launch or plant new clusters preferably need to have some experience or local training in mission engagement and appropriate evangelism strategies. The principles drawn from Jesus' commissioning as set out above, are the foundation here.

---

[1] Biblical roles Eph 4:7 & 11-13 and gifts 1 Cor 12 and Rom 12 – See Mike Breen & Walt Kallestad, A Passionate Life, Nexgen, 2005, Ch 15-17

With prayer goes listening and discerning the culture[2]. And expecting and looking for the welcome of the person of peace, all play their part.[3]

If a cluster is launched rather than planted, some of the initial crowd gathering may be from within the existing church, as we have described, but beware lest this substitutes for the harder and much more important task of sowing into the chosen mission field beyond the church[4]. So leaders who launch a new cluster must be just as focused and encouraging of mission engagement and evangelism as leaders who plant clusters with a pioneer team.

Develop Plans: Leaders of a new cluster need to know how to develop plans. As described in chapter two, these will unpack the mission vision (purpose); the community values (philosophy) and vocabulary for communication (name and story). It will lead on to the adoption of gathering patterns, spiritual rhythms, pastoral care and social and mission programs.

Once again, this planning process will be shaped throughout by prayer, the context and the people gathered, taking into account their five-fold ministry roles, their personalities and their gifts.

Enabling Ownership: It is vital for mission momentum and community cohesion that the vision and planning process is

---

[2] Community Research and Mission audit skills and resources are helpful here. E.g: Steven Croft, Freddy Hedley & Bob Hopkins, Listening for Mission: Mission Audit for Fresh Expressions of Church, CHP, 2006.

[3] A Passionate Church, Mike Breen & Walt Kallestad, Nexgen, 2005, Chapters 23 & 24

[4] Jesus says sowing is harder than reaping – John 4: 35-38.

owned by the growing cluster. All sorts of processes of corporate prayer, communication, involvement and brainstorming exercises or games are important here. This, together with two previous steps involving vision, values and plans, are developed in more detail in the next sector of this chapter.

Small Group Mobilisation, Pastoral Care & Discipleship: Most clusters are composed of small groups, although this is not essential. Such sub-structures increase the intimacy and belonging as well as being one key part of the discipleship that runs through everything. The new leaders decide whether these sub-units are to be part of the initial structure or only emerge later.

Some clusters start with one small group and grow to a mid-sized community while others may grow a mid-sized community first and only later consider breaking down into small groups/cells. The small groups are likely to have slightly distinct mission plans although all under the wider umbrella mission vision of the cluster. Really important here are choosing the right small group leaders, supporting them adequately and deciding on the pattern of life of small groups (which can be more or less prescriptive).

Whether these mid-sized communities have small groups or not, cluster leaders need to work out how pastoral care and support will be developed. The principles will be based on those explained in the previous chapter of dispersed care, reduced span of care and ready reference to outside specialisms.

Managing Cluster Seasons & Meetings: These are the skills that good cluster leaders develop. They are all about community development. As new clusters begin to take shape and bed down, the leaders in prayer, reflection and discussion need to discern the weekly and monthly pattern of meetings and the rhythm of seasons.

The pattern of meetings deals with the variation in how often cells meet and how often cluster. It involves encouraging cluster members to relate inside and outside meetings as well as developing opportunities for special cluster events and outings or even a weekend away together. The seasonal rhythm will involve the shifting emphasis from UP to IN to OUT.

GAINING AND SHARING CLUSTER VISION & VALUES

In chapter two we explained how Purpose, Values and agreed language (PVa) provided the glue for clusters and how it was leadership that was responsible to develop those key ingredients of missional community. So much leadership today is reactive. It starts with action and ends up in crisis management. In contrast, leadership should be pro-active starting with vision which leads to action and this certainly applies to clusters.

A helpful framework for gaining and sharing vision can be built around an adapted version of the LifeShapes learning circle[5]. The overall direction is that vision should come from God and work out as his kingdom rule in the world. So often God seeks to bring about his Kingdom rule through communities he calls into covenant to express his life and mission vision. The sort of steps for this process in a missional community are illustrated in the diagram opposite.

The right hand side is the part for leaders. First comes

---

[5] Mike Breen & Walt Kallestad, A Passionate Life, Nexgen, 2005, ch.3-5

listening and there is no substitute for listening to God to get vision and values for your community. This is followed by discerning what the leaders hear. This will include weighing direct revelation from God with the voice of the people and with circumstances and opportunities.

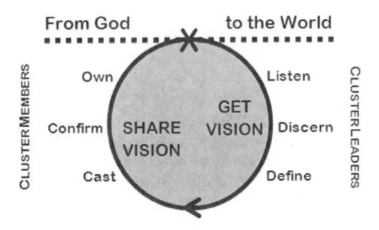

Moses started by just listening to the people and it ended in murder. Then he listened to God, the circumstances and the people and got the Exodus call and the ten commandments. Aaron listened only to the people and got the golden calf. From this process of listening and discernment leaders will define what they sense the cluster vision to be.

Then on the left hand side the cluster members are fully involved. First the leaders cast the vision. This should involve referring to the ways that God has spoken and given faith and allowing prayer and reflection by everyone. This leads to the confirming of the vision which involves a two stage sifting. As the vision is cast it becomes clear who has a real call and identifies with the cluster vision. Leaders launching or planting a cluster need the confidence to let some early adopters go.

However, at the same time there will be feedback from those fully committed to the vision that sifts and refines the vision itself. Again it's important that cluster leaders are secure in who they are and their call, and can allow some re-shaping of the vision detail at this later stage. The result of this process is that real ownership has come through involvement and God's confirmation.

PLANNING FRAMEWORKS FOR DEVELOPING CLUSTER/MSC LIFE

Some leaders are intuitive and naturally operate a sound planning and communication process. And God often seems to honour the rather unplanned efforts of pioneers initiating a new missional community. Precisely because clusters aim to be low maintenance and lightweight, many lay leaders will prefer a fairly loose process combining action with discernment in context. Certainly prayerful listening to God and the mission culture will play an important part in shaping the evolving community.

However, there are proven planning processes that can be very helpful for clusters/MSCs. Even if they prove too involved for some to apply in detail, they are helpful to have in mind as a rough sort of "check list." We first met them in John Wimber's Vineyard Church Planter's Manual. This scheme helped the leader plan answers to the key questions as they moved from Vision (Principles) to the desired future. The steps are summarised below. They are fully illustrated with the actual planning exercises that were carried out by the leaders of Wacky and Airborne clusters in Appendix 2.

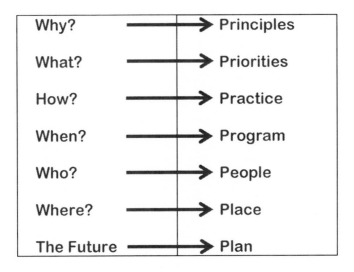

Why? ⟶ Principles
What? ⟶ Priorities
How? ⟶ Practice
When? ⟶ Program
Who? ⟶ People
Where? ⟶ Place
The Future ⟶ Plan

With their passion for "vocab" with alliteration, Wacky coined this planning exercise "Processed P's." To gain ownership they first used icons to communicate their priorities. They called these the "12 Pillars of Wacky". Then second, they got all cluster members to engage with the exercise with groups brainstorming, feedback and writing them in the "cans" of Processed P's. Again, the actual icons and group sheets are reproduced in Appendix 2.

SUSTAINING A VIBRANT CLUSTER COMMUNITY

We have seen that cluster leadership, especially in the early phase, must start with vision and lead to action. The heart of it is "seeing it clear, then working it out." Earlier Chapters have also stressed the identity of clusters around mission purpose and community values. A related pair of leadership processes are vision (here including purpose and values) and empowerment. Some have summed up leadership in these two elements (L = V+E). In other words, the heart of this leadership helps the cluster to be clear about where it is going (its aims and objectives) and fully enabled, supported and equipped to get there.

The matrix below is helpful for clusters and cluster leaders to review. Step one is to explain these principles of leadership and how the matrix shows the possibilities of being in a community (church or cluster) which is a) low on vision and empowerment (bottom left); b) high on vision but low on empowerment; c) low on vision but high on empowerment, or d) high on both.

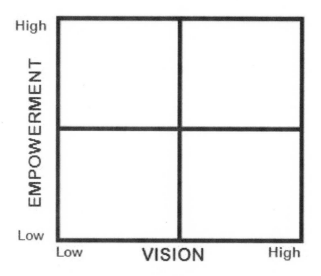

Step two is to brainstorm as a core team or emerging cluster, what it would feel like to be in each of these different quadrants. This next diagram suggests the sort of answers.

		Low VISION High	
High	Power struggle Boring **COSY** Holy huddle Static	Motivating Alive **DYNAMIC** Satisfying Challenging	
EMPOWERMENT	Stagnant Frustrating **DEAD** Reactive Apathy	Confusing Fear/Anger **BURN OUT** Soul Destroying Disillusioned	
Low	Low	High	

The final step is to get people's assessment of where we are in our particular cluster community. This can then help determine whether more attention is needed on the vision and values side or the empowerment side. This review is helpful to get healthy cluster development from launching or planting right through each phase... although the responses and action required will vary at each stage.

FOUR PHASES OF A CLUSTER'S LIFE

Much analysis has confirmed that most groups that are small enough to experience real community, go through four phrases of a life cycle. Cell church describes healthy cells going through Forming, Storming, Norming and Performing! Team building theory has tracked development through the phases of Dependence, Counter-dependence, Independence to Inter-dependence.

179

Mike Breen's version of the discipleship and leadership square laid the foundations for initiating cluster principles and so obviously is most helpful for understanding and leading cluster growth and development[1].

We briefly introduced this framework for overall church leaders in the last chapter. This is leadership based on a seasonal framework, and is geared towards raising new leaders, releasing gifts, doing yourself out of a job and allowing the spread of the kingdom. As we have said before, for St Thomas' Church, this forms the underlying principles of how clusters work and is therefore a central feature of cluster leadership. This draws on the phases of the building of the disciples' missional community in the Gospels and the four different leadership styles adopted by Jesus for each phase.

The square can be applied to clusters in the sort of way illustrated in the diagram opposite.

The L1/C1 (Leadership 1/Community 1) phase is exciting and motivating as the leader(s) set out the vision and folk feel called and chosen to join the core/team. This is characterised by high confidence and enthusiasm but low competence and experience. The leader needs to continue to be directive, strongly casting the vision through this phase, knowing (as we saw in the last section) that the vision sifts those who are called and those not called. The leader needs the confidence to see the core/team reduce during this phase as the vision sifts folk. This is the apostolic phase.

This follows on to the L2/C2 phase when inevitably things get difficult. People are thrown together and their differences naturally cause tensions. The reality of the vision and mission

[1] Mike Breen & Walt Kallestad, The Passionate Church, Nexgen, 2005, Chapters 13 & 14

engagement is now shown to be really hard and without God, it's not going to happen. Morale plummets as the honeymoon wears off and the cluster phase is characterised by low confidence and enthusiasm as well as low competence and experience. The leader(s) need to inspire by demonstrating real faith in the vision and to encourage by getting really close to people (high accessibility) in a coaching mode.

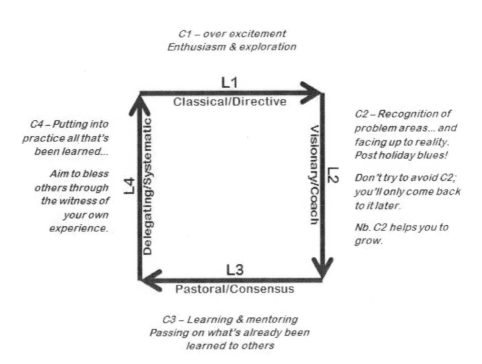

The third cluster phase C3/L3 emerges as the cluster begins to see growth, breakthrough in mission engagement and increasing quality of community. It is therefore characterised by increasing confidence and enthusiasm flowing from growing competence and experience. Cluster leadership now shifts to a collaborative style with lots of involvement and discussion of plans and ideas. This is a time for the leader(s) to begin to

181

release the upcoming leaders more into practical leadership of parts of cluster life, and to begin to see the whole cluster being released into where their gifts are calling them.

The fourth and last phase is C4/L4 when the maturing cluster moves into real fruitfulness. Here the vision is really seeing results and now apprenticed leadership is emerging and lots of gifts and ministry are flowering. This phase is characterised by high confidence and enthusiasm based on the high competence and experience obtained. The appropriate style for cluster leaders needs to shift to a delegating style as the leaders multiply themselves. But it is not the time to settle down! The square is not a closed system. Towards the end of this phase Jesus said "now you will see me no more... and its good that I go away..." So as apprentice/assistant cluster leaders take over more, the original leader(s) at the same time is looking for and expecting to find new vision from God for the next frontier.

So the process starts over again as the mature cluster prepares to multiply in C4/L4. This is often the hardest part, so we deal with this next.

CLUSTER MULTIPLICATION

Just as there are many ways to skin a cat... so there are different approaches to cluster multiplication. But all of them can be characterised by apprehension and preceded by avoidance! This is not surprising because none of us like change and a good cluster that has the qualities to grow to the point of multiplication will inevitably want to hold onto those good qualities. So we need to understand both the possible models and the processes well if we are to successfully negotiate the natural outcome of health and growth.

50:50: The most obvious model of multiplication is to take roughly two halves of the large cluster and launch two new ones. Some clusters have grown so fast that they have reached 90 or even 120 or so before it was clear how to multiply and who should lead... and so three equal emerging clusters were formed.

This is a process rather like fission and it's really important to get two strong nuclei... represented by new leadership teams and new visions. Preserving key relationships and coherence can most easily be achieved by whole small groups/cells going one way or the other – although cluster multiplication isn't always that easy!

Budding off: A second process is where multiplication is achieved by keeping much of the cluster intact but one small group (perhaps one that has grown to the point of multiplying itself) is launched as the seed for the new cluster. It may not be quite as neat as this. The small group budded off to form the new core to launch or plant a cluster may draw a few extra folk to itself from some of the other cluster small groups.

Clearly the distinctive vision and values will determine which small group forms this new cluster core and who is drawn to enlarge this small group. In rare circumstances sufficient critical mass for the core of the new cluster can be drawn from two small groups coming from two different clusters.

Sending out Pioneers: This is the third model of cluster multiplication. It particularly fits with a cluster planting rather than a cluster launch as we described them earlier. Thus emerging leaders within a cluster embrace a new vision that is distinct and feel the call and confidence to pioneer a new cluster from scratch. Clearly their apostolic ministry and cross-cultural gifts will be proved through the experience of this approach.

If these are the different models for cluster multiplication, what are some of the key processes to seek to ensure that this vulnerable stage is negotiated with the best outcome?

Process – Prepare: Implement: Celebrate: There are these three stages in multiplying clusters. First there is a time for careful preparation and planning. This will involve judging the right timing; choosing the best new leaders/teams; clarifying the two new visions/mission focus; carefully sharing the new visions so that folk can choose where they commit; managing the expected makeup of the new clusters – members and small groups.

Once the best has been done to plan and prepare, the second stage is that these plans have to be implemented with strong support from the overall church leaders and clear communication throughout. People need to be prepared for some inevitable bereavement as some relationships are loosened.

Finally, once the multiplication has been implemented it should be celebrated. This both emphasises that growth is good and also gives opportunity to link up with old friends and be encouraged by God's faithfulness. So the two new clusters can come together to celebrate their family relationships and share testimony of what God is doing in each of their new lives.

Key Issues to Manage: Whichever model of cluster multiplication, there are common keys to a healthy process through planning, implementation and celebration. Some of these have already been referred to. The apprenticing of strong assistant leaders paves the way for them taking on more responsibility as the cluster multiplies.

As far as possible the new clusters should each have new vision and values that are as distinct as possible from one another. This helps members to decide where to go and to make strong new commitments. It also ensures greatest strength and cohesion after dividing. Each new cluster has enough clear and separate identity from the other to thrive and to avoid confusion or a sense of weak motivation (there's not much reason to be separate).

The timing of the multiplication is also critical. On the one hand, if it's a 50:50 sub-division, there needs to be sufficient critical mass developed to sustain the two new halves. However, on the other hand experience has shown that the apprehension that tends to delay multiplication, can all too easily lead to a loss of momentum and the growth dynamics that led to the need to multiply can dissipate. Don't delay too long or you can lose it!

Lastly, it is of course most helpful for overall church leadership to play a significant part in helping and guiding the multiplication process as well as giving extra support through the vulnerable time of implementation and the early steps of new cluster life.

SUMMARY – THE CLUSTER LEADERS "JOB SPEC"

Clearly the processes that we have described here from launching a new cluster, to building the community around shared vision, growing the cluster through effective evangelism and releasing of ministry through the body, right on to multiplying the cluster, all have to be enabled by the cluster leader(s) and their team. So we have provided an outline of the goals for a typical cluster leader in Appendix 5. The list may look long and could be daunting but it must not be read with inherited congregational assumptions. These are lightweight, low maintenance communities-in-mission, remember!

So all the aspects of the cluster life are to be simple, released and shared through its members. Also we have emphasised that an emerging cluster is a fantastic place to grow in leadership character and skills from small group to mid-sized community. So the list represents a journey not a starting requirement.

CHAPTER ELEVEN

Cluster Meetings – So What Happens at these Non-Meetings?!

We have said that clusters are seven-day-a-week community. So something called a cluster meeting isn't the only expression of its life and may not be the most important. Whilst clusters will normally have gatherings when everyone comes together, they do normally also meet in small groups or cells, and there are likely to be accountability partners or triplets planning their own get-togethers. In addition other sections of the cluster may link up from time to time.

For example, several clusters have football teams. These are usually made up of Christians and not-yet-Christians. These will also draw folk from different small groups and certainly won't be the whole cluster. The same may be true of other areas of common interest across the cluster, such as walking, climbing, parenting, running an Alpha course, etc. Activities, planned and spontaneous allow the natural friendships within and outside the cluster, to grow and develop.

These broad principles of cluster as mid-sized community with a varied life, are crucial but clusters do have meetings all together and it's also important to understand these. What is their frequency and pattern? What is the style of gathering? What are their venue requirements and expressions of leadership? So here we shall explore the nature of cluster gatherings, looking at all these aspects and more!

FREQUENCY

It is obviously an important general principle for clusters to meet all together with some pattern of regularity. This cements cluster identity and belonging and enables the vision to keep sharp.

The interval between whole cluster gatherings will vary according to the type of cluster and its community values. They will also be influenced by the pattern of larger meetings across the wider church or the whole church. The pattern of alternation between cluster meetings and small groups also varies.

Cluster leaders manage the frequency of meetings in the light of these wider factors and also the internal issues of where the developing life and vision of the cluster is up to. This may mean that leaders discern that the cluster level needs emphasising and so the frequency of this expression increases. At another time it may be judged that the small groups need more space and the pattern reverses.

When cluster meetings all together are only midweek, then typically they may be once a month and small groups three times monthly. However, they may have an equal frequency with small groups, each happening twice a month if there is a week when there isn't a large gathering (no celebration or whole church) then clusters may gather on Sundays.

But again cluster leaders need to be free to think outside previous norms and stereotypes – maybe sometimes it will be better to meet in small groups on such a Sunday and clusters stay on the weekday. Or maybe the Sunday opens up the opportunity for quite a different type of gathering such as a cluster brunch, family party or an outing all together.

NOT A SUNDAY SERVICE!

No please, not a mini-Sunday service! It's death to a cluster because it's actually a presentational celebration-style and certainly not lightweight! Because the model of a Sunday service is so strong in the minds of those who have been Christians for any length of time, this mental model has to be broken. Our experience is that it dies hard.

Even when years of cluster meetings mid-week appear to have broken this association and real interactive community-building times have become the norm, you just have to say that cluster meeting(s) is on a Sunday and back it comes like a flood.

Clusters start thinking they have to have seats in rows, worship bands, sermons, liturgy and formal structures. Those things may be necessary and appropriate for larger meetings but clusters are precisely to escape from that straight-jacket and explore creativity and imagination as we build community interactively together.

This can't be stressed enough. Our sense is that not only does habit and association push towards the Sunday Service, but in the short term it can be the easy option... to settle for what we know. But it only seems the easy option in the short term to avoid the challenge of exploring the unfamiliar. Over time, it is anything but lightweight and low maintenance.

Clusters that try to ape a "service" get worn out with the burden of coming up with the goods over and over. Remember that cluster leaders are people with families and jobs and no bible college training.

Even more important is the fact that others who might rise to pioneer a new cluster instinctively see the presentational style and sophisticated gifts required for a 'mini-service' as unattainable and would never offer themselves.

Furthermore, as we explained in Chapter Six when we explored what's wrong with inherited congregation, a cluster as a Sunday Service is a contradiction. It's trying to be a mini-celebration, it will be naff and it will lose the distinctive cluster power to gather – extended family community.

1 CORINTHIANS 11-14 TYPE MEETINGS

These four chapters of Paul's first letter to the Corinthians could be seen as the text-book for cluster get-togethers. In fact they have only fully come to make sense to me since encountering the community dynamics of these mid-sized community groups.

Throughout these chapters Paul is addressing issues relating to the gatherings of Corinthian Christians. He may be issuing correctives or answering questions, but over and over it's **"when you meet together…"** (1 Cor 11: 17,18,20,33, 1 Cor 14: 23, 26).

The table opposite gives the different aspects or components of these early church gatherings that Paul is commenting on. Let's look at each as they build mid-sized community.

MEALS TOGETHER

First, what is clear is that most of their meetings involved food. The Acts account refers to this habitual practice more than once[1] and here Paul addresses the issue of inclusivity as they meet around a meal. Clearly they regularly ate together. This obviously sets a limit on the size of the gathering. Although Paul at one point says it would be better to eat at home rather than create disunity by selfish overeating or being insensitive to

---

[1] Acts 2:46; 20:7&11

others, this certainly doesn't mean don't eat together (1 Cor 11:33-34). It just emphasises how strongly he is exhorting against selfishness and divisive practices.

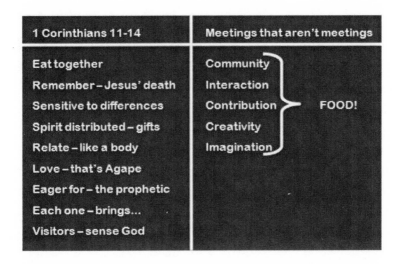

1 Corinthians 11-14	Meetings that aren't meetings	
Eat together	Community	
Remember – Jesus' death	Interaction	
Sensitive to differences	Contribution	FOOD!
Spirit distributed – gifts	Creativity	
Relate – like a body	Imagination	
Love – that's Agape		
Eager for – the prophetic		
Each one – brings...		
Visitors – sense God		

So we find it no coincidence that the most common thing that our clusters love to do is eat together. Whether it's a sit down meal; an outdoor BBQ; a bring and share, a family cluster shared Sunday lunch; an ethnic meal thrown open to outsiders; the cluster regularly meeting at Pizza Express; an early morning mission week cluster prayer breakfast at a Tapas Bar; or... the list goes on.

It has been noted that "not all clusters that grow eat together, but all clusters that do eat together seem to grow!" Sharing food together and table fellowship was so common to Jesus in the Gospels and it is our overwhelming experience that it's one of the best ways to build community at the mid-size.

The small community setting of the cluster can include an Agape meal. Here breaking of bread and sharing a cup can appropriately happen in an informal but ordered setting (1 Cor

11:17-26). Furthermore Paul's exhortation that such table fellowship should be shared in holiness of life (1 Cor 11:23) can be even more effective than a liturgical confession, when the cluster breaks down into accountability pairings and they can challenge one another on the areas in their lives that God is reforming.

INTERACTIVE SPIRITUAL GIFTS

The range of spiritual gifts that Paul expounds (1 Cor 12:1-11) and that he encourages in such meetings (1 Cor 14), can only be expressed most fully in cluster size. Small group is ideal for the immature to explore and learn, large Celebration events may permit one or two to exercise such gifts from the platform by "coming to the front." However, only the cluster/mid-sized group allows everyone, learners and mature, to build <u>one another</u> up as each one shares a song, a word, a revelation, a tongue or interpretation (1 Cor 12:7 & 14:26) or as all prophecy (1 Cor 14:24-25).

Such exhortations of Paul that all should be involved includes just the sort of interactive, extended family social dynamics, where everyone is a contributor. His descriptions and instructions couldn't be clearer. This is exactly cluster community dynamics that we have experienced at their best. When one starts, the previous person ceases (1 Cor 14:30); when one brings a tongue, another interprets (1 Cor 14:27) not everyone does the same thing (1 Cor 12:30) but all do contribute, one after the other (1 Cor 14:27 & 31). This works all together, although occasionally the prayer and application may be best facilitated in little sub-groups.

This extended family ownership of the whole, as all play their part is also where spiritual gifts can be a sign for the unbeliever that may be welcome in such cluster gatherings (1 Cor

14:24&25). One cluster outdoor barbeque we attended included a time to say farewell and pray for a family that was moving away. After food, fun and fellowship, different members prayed for the couple and their child and little baby. Some shared scriptures and others "prophetic" words or pictures. Then from the back of the gathering a visitor spoke up... "I'm not sure what all this means, but I sure hope that the love I can feel here goes with these folks wherever they are going!" (an example of a not-yet-Christian's prayer!?).

When this dynamic works well with the majority as contributors (rather than spectators at the celebration event) we can most fully see the corporate expression of the church as Body (1 Cor 12:12-30). As we all fulfil different active roles we truly and practically express that we are all members of the one body – eyes, ears, arms, legs all honouring one another and being blessed and built up by each other[2]. Only in groups of around 20 to 60 can this "every member a contributor" dynamic most fully be worked out.

LOVE – THE ULTIMATE INGREDIENT

But whatever gifts are shared at the meeting, whatever faith exercised, however good the meal shared, flowing through all of it must be the sort of love that Jesus demonstrated and desires to pour into our hearts through his Holy Spirit (1 Cor 13). This means that the distinctive quality of this extended family relating will be the sort of serving of one another, forgiving one another, being kind to each other, honouring each other, and having the same mind, as was in Christ Jesus (Phil 2: 1-16).

---

[2] This description of Christ's body in 1 Cor 12:12-27 clearly refers to the dynamics of a local meeting rather than a city church (Romans 12:5-6) or universal church (Eph 1:23; 4:25; 5:30).

ESSENTIAL ELEMENTS – UP:IN:OUT

It helps to know what elements make a rounded community and build up Clusters in their shared life together. In chapter three we developed the three relationships of UP:IN:OUT that give biblical balance to the whole life and essence of clusters. Now these same three dimensions provide a framework for the gatherings of mid-sized groups. Lay leaders are set free to grow in leading cluster community events as they have such a simple guideline. And this is where the LifeShape of the Triangle is so helpful. Cluster leaders know that their group has to develop its relationships UP to God, IN to one another and OUT to their mission focus and the world.

However creative and interactive the cluster community experience, this simple UP:IN:OUT framework helps keep things on track and maintain a healthy balance. Sometimes a meeting will express all three elements equally, whereas at other times there may be an emphasis on two, or even just one. But the leaders are conscious of this and in the flow of gatherings make sure that this is compensated next time and the balance maintained.

Thus a cluster brunch with a walk in the park that draws in friends and social contacts might be IN and OUT. This might be followed by a cluster gathering exploring how together we can grow in engaging with the majesty of God... an UP and IN meeting. Even if the focus of a get-together is prayer, whilst it will have a strong UP dimension throughout, it can also enhance IN, as community prayer life is built spending part of the gathering in pairs, part in small groups and some together as the whole cluster.

Such a gathering might also incorporate OUT as time is given to pray for forthcoming outreach events or for specific not-yet-Christian friends and contacts. The OUTward dimension of a meeting can further be expressed by a community activity carried out in partnership with not-yet-Christians or by planning and preparing for some involvement in social justice, the environment or evangelism.

As we explained in chapter three, each dimension of the life of the mid-sized cluster serves its specific mission purpose and community values. This obviously works out in the focus and detail of cluster gatherings.

For example, a cluster that is reaching professional young families and values intergenerational community will build its meetings around activities that facilitate the involvement of any and every age, both within and beyond the group. Similarly young adults engaged with the creative arts network will express their UPward prayer and worship life involving such creative media. These things will also characterise the style and character of their building relationship together as well as their outreach.

Again if the context has a strong sports and outdoor emphasis, this will colour all aspects of the cluster life. Whereas an inner-urban estate's community meals building the IN dimension may be "pie and peas" rather than "wine and cheese" and building relationships OUT may be a neighbourhood litter-pick and pub pool and dominoes rather than pub quiz. By contrast, community (IN) may still be built round food in nothing vaguely resembling a "meeting" with a drop-in cafe for the homeless and a mobile soup and hot drinks van amongst prostitutes.

VENUES FOR CLUSTER MEETINGS – WHERE?

Clearly the issues here are practical and pragmatic. Decisions will depend on what is available, affordable and what serves the culture and values of the cluster and the sort of meeting that's planned on any given occasion. In this sense, venues are secondary. The primary issue being about creating real participative community and engaging with the chosen context.

When clusters are first being explored by a church, sometimes they will settle for using a facility on the site of the church building – a meeting room, lounge, Sunday school room or the like. This is free and familiar, representing the minimum challenge for new leaders who aren't confident and want to take one step at a time.

However, it will be clear from everything we've said that this is likely to increase the tendency to be conformed to churchy patterns of meeting and works against the mission priority of clusters building relationships with those in their mission focus and therefore creating an appropriate, welcoming context for visitors when invited.

So clusters meet in every sort of venue and none... even the big outdoors! The mission focus of the cluster may mean that a local pub is ideal, or a function room of an Italian restaurant with the best cappuccino coffee served (which has changed the view of church for many!). A cluster working with addicts has chosen a very spartan meeting place – very basic bare boards and plastic tables for drinks and sandwiches and immediately across the road from the 24-hour pharmacy where methadone is obtained.

Clusters seeking to be church for young families or all ages may use their homes, especially in areas with large houses. For parts of their gathering they may use different rooms or spaces in the house - conservatory or patio for fine weather socials. Youth clusters have found this same pattern very effective meeting in homes, jammed in several rooms and splitting down into cells for part of the time.

Although these examples illustrate the mission priority of cluster by choosing venues highly suitable to invite not-yet-Christians from our target communities, this is still in "come to us" mode. Some other clusters are more fully into "go to where they are" mode. For example, school based clusters are engaging the pupils, teaching staff and support staff of a school and becoming church on site.

The same principle applies for clusters planted in residential homes for the elderly. When it comes to workplace clusters, these also seek to create church in the workplace. However, depending on the size of the company or complex, this may either be appropriate for all meetings and activities to be in the actual work premises, or it may be that some events will seek to draw together folk from one or several workplaces into an appropriate venue off-site.

LEADERSHIP ROLES IN CLUSTER MEETINGS

From what we have said already, it should be abundantly clear that the leadership of cluster meetings is very different from leading in a worship service in a traditional church building. We've made the point that cluster is about extended family, community building and the watchwords are *lightweight* and *low maintenance*. Reflecting on the exploding wave of lay people rising up to lead clusters where these principles are being adopted, it's clear that these are gifts and skills we have not looked for or developed before in inherited mode church.

Community building skills are the heart of it. And our guess is that most theological colleges and seminaries preparing vicars and pastors, have little or no training in community building. There may be sessions on liturgy and conducting a front-led presentational style service of many kinds and occasions, from Sunday morning Eucharists, to weddings to funerals to family services (and these latter may be the closest they get to building community and interaction) but they still aren't releasing the whole gathering to a contributing and fully participatory experience.

Just as networked or <u>dispersed</u> church for a missionary movement is <u>releasing</u> rather than <u>controlling</u>, so this is the essence of leading a cluster meeting. The cluster leader or leadership team need to know and understand the dynamics of community building that they are seeking to achieve in their meetings. But they don't have to provide all the ideas or lead through all the activities.

They seek to identify and release many within the cluster to contribute in different ways on different occasions. The cluster leader(s) will keep a steering hand on proceedings and their authority will be recognised – more or less in the background. Normally they will play a more visible part, at least at the opening and conclusion. Their leadership style in meetings to create community is very much as facilitators and catalysts. On the other hand, this is different from their leadership style when sharing vision and direction.

So who are the cluster leaders seeking to identify and release to create the meeting? There are those who are naturally gifted at community and have an instinct and feel for it. They may be creative types with well developed imaginative processes. These people are key to break the Sunday Service mould and get things started on a different track.

However, once the whole cluster have experienced several gatherings with a range of community creating ways of operating, lots of others of us can catch the idea and develop skills in this area that we have never had a chance to discover before. This then is a process of enlarging the pool of contributing leaders that begins to reinforce itself.

WHAT'S DONE BEST AT WHAT SIZE?

As cluster leaders consistently seek to avoid the Sunday Service phenomenon, it can help to think through what's done best at what size or level. We have majored in this book on recovering biblical congregation as distinct from the inherited mini-cathedral dynamics. But it is also important to think through what works best in a small group community of 8-12 people, as distinct from what's best at a mid-sized cluster community of 30 plus. More subtle can be the difference between a midweek cluster gathering and cluster done on Sunday.

As part of our cluster leader training we have got leader teams from different clusters to brainstorm their experience and their ideas of what is best at each size/level. This will involve exploring all three relationships of UP:IN:OUT at small group, cluster (and cluster Sunday), and celebration. And by contrast, they need to think through what doesn't work best at each level. These are things to avoid! The diagrams on the next few pages when produced in A4 format, provide scope for them to cover the sheet of paper with their thoughts and ideas. This exercise creates real cross-fertilisation from one cluster to another, as well as sharpening understanding.

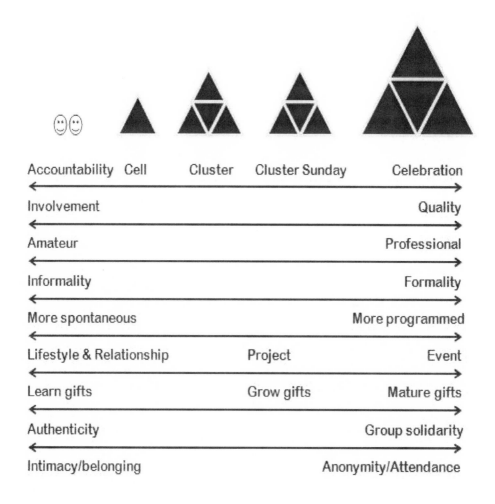

Accountability   Cell   Cluster   Cluster Sunday   Celebration
←——→
Involvement   Quality
←——→
Amateur   Professional
←——→
Informality   Formality
←——→
More spontaneous   More programmed
←——→
Lifestyle & Relationship   Project   Event
←——→
Learn gifts   Grow gifts   Mature gifts
←——→
Authenticity   Group solidarity
←——→
Intimacy/belonging   Anonymity/Attendance

The sorts of issues that are addressed include quite churchy questions like, at what level(s) to break bread/share communion, do baptisms, weddings and funerals and where to take offerings. They also range over every sort of social activity such as BBQs, walks in the country, weekends away, safari suppers, pub quiz nights, treasure hunts, bonfires and video discussions. They explore the place of children and youth as well as creativity in worship, community and outreach.

The general principles that underlie the ideas that emerge follow the trends illustrated in the first table. For example, we quickly recognise that you can't aim for highest quality and at the same time involve everyone or achieve intimacy. The spontaneous and informal become increasingly possible with reducing size of gathering, whereas large celebrations are chaos without programming and detailed planning.

One other helpful realisation that emerges relates to reality and consistency. At larger celebration gatherings we don't necessarily do or mean everything that we say (technical term is cognitive dissonance!). We may sing or say things that are not true at that time for everyone... from "I fall down on my knees"... to faith statements... to expressions of surrender or commitment... "I count all as loss!" This is OK in such large settings where everyone is at different stages and moods. But in cluster size or less, we need to break bonds of inconsistency and step out of integrity mismatch. The smaller more intimate gatherings give the opportunity for each to do and to say what is authentic to them at the time.

WHAT DOESN'T WORK BEST AT WHAT LEVEL...??

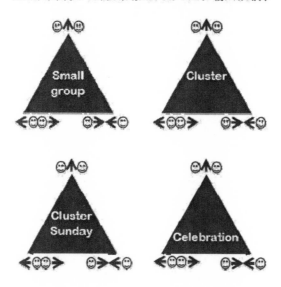

WHAT WORKS BEST AT WHAT LEVEL???

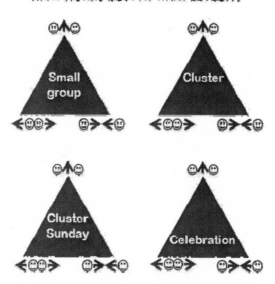

202

SO WHAT IS A CLUSTER GET-TOGETHER REALLY LIKE?

Although clusters aren't all about meetings, at one level the very best way to understand what they are all about and to actually get the difference, is to experience one when it meets together. There is no substitute for being part of one. All the writing here of explanation, analysis and description of clusters can't be as good as the real thing in its most accessible expression – the cluster meeting.

So even though a cluster seeks to be a seven day a week way of life and a whole new lifestyle of being church, the meeting if it's really an extended family community experience, can significantly change our mindset and open our eyes to a lot of what we are talking about here. Visitors and leaders from other churches have often commented after attending their first cluster meeting, that they have really "got it" and seen the vital difference from Sunday service.

So the next best thing to experiencing a cluster meeting is to be able to follow a number of examples of real life meetings that have happened in different clusters and that have worked. Appendix 3, therefore, has a range of write-ups and simple outlines of different cluster meetings. Because the cluster vision and values, and its mission focus, are all crucial to the essence of the cluster and should shape its gatherings, these are stated at the beginning of each illustration.

If you were to try any of these for a similar social context we believe they should give a quality experience. But that is really not the point. The aim is that these few examples illustrate the principles that we have been explaining and that they open your mind to the possibilities. So we strongly recommend that you now browse these cluster meeting outlines in the Appendix to bring to life all that we have tried to explain in this chapter. It's our hope that as you read through them you will have reactions like, "Oh! So that's what it looks like;" "That's what they've been on about;" "Oh! I reckon I could do even better than that!"

CHAPTER TWELVE

Youth and Clusters

So far we have examined the essence of clusters with the principle focus on adults. Sometimes we have made specific reference to clusters for young adults and for the elderly. But what about youth and children? Do the principles that we have developed about these mid-sized communities in mission work for teenagers? As it happens, experience with cluster-type groups in youth ministry is proving our arguments almost more than in any other situation.

TRADITIONAL YOUTH GROUPS NO LONGER WORK

For over fifteen years now it has been clear that conventional youth groups don't gather and grow teens anymore, like they used to. In the 70s and 80s with good youth leaders and a varied program it was possible to regularly attract over 100 youngsters... but those days have gone. Programmes provided for teenagers are now rarely effective.

Again it was Mike Breen as long ago as the 80's, who exposed the fundamental flaw of youth ministry based on a "provider-client" model[1]. In fact he exposed this as a fundamentally unbiblical pattern for any ministry. And with the development of his "A-Teams" based on peer ownership, he pioneered a whole new approach that underlies all recent detached youth work.

---

[1] Mike Breen, Outside In, Scripture Union, 1993

Involvement, interaction, participation, ownership and developing peer leadership are now the watchwords. This is true whether it's "A-Teams" based on a detached youth model, or Peer led youth cells. In fact, in common with both these models, some sort of smaller group is now almost indispensable for work amongst teens.

YOUTH CELLS AND CELEBRATIONS ARE WORKING

As the traditional youth group declined in effectiveness, so insights from the cell church movement began to prove particularly effective amongst teenagers[2]. These small groups of teenagers seemed to provide the place of intimacy and belonging where they could find their identity. With the loss of Christendom and the vacuum of biblical knowledge these cells also enable in depth discipleship as Jesus' principles are applied to young lives. Also, the dynamics and reduced demands of such small units released the discovery of "peer-led youth cells." With the support of adult facilitators or mentors (younger or older), later teens thrived on leading groups with younger teens.

At the other end of the size range, youth also thrive on large, high quality, celebration gatherings… the bigger the better. It will be their music style and their musicians and their choices influencing most aspects. And for high quality in their style it will almost certainly involve a lot of quite costly "technical gear." All this means that periodic youth celebrations are usually most effective across a district or region. Only very large churches have the resources to equip such "happenings" on their own. Such culturally geared large events tie into the "gig"

---

[2] Bob Hopkins (ed), Cell Stories as Signs of Mission, Grove Ev51, 2000, ch.3 and Paul Hopkins, Youth Cell Outlines, Cell UK, 2002

scene and are very much what not-yet-Christian teens can be easily invited to. These such large gatherings with a presentational format also have a degree of anonymity. Teens like the crowd, but also like not to be noticed in the crowd. When led well and sensitively, youth celebrations can provide a very safe place for young people to begin to explore a spiritual dimension to their lives.

So considerable evidence has been building up to show that youth cells and celebration are vital parts of the way forward for teenage ministry. The principles for both are tying in with the biblical and sociological understandings that we developed for these large and small groups in chapter five. Even the fact that large celebrations tend to be periodic rather than weekly corresponds more to the biblical pattern of festivals.

But what about a mid-sized cluster group for teens? If cells and celebration are working, is this surplus to requirements? Let's look at the experience of one church that introduced mid-size groups and see whether, where and why they might fit for this age group.

ST ANDREW'S, CHORLEYWOOD DISCOVER YOUTH MSCS

St Andrew's, Chorleywood had had a successful youth work for years with cells as a foundational component. They have also linked up with other churches in the area for regular joint events including an annual inter-church youth camp called "Ignite." However, teens were expected to come every week to the adult evening service in church and this had only been of limited effect.

Then in November 2003, the whole church began the introduction of MSCs – Mid-Size Communities, based on the cluster principles we have examined here. Their youth leader

Pete Wynter describes the journey that this has led to, as a radical transformation. In fact, their experience has convinced them that youth mid-sized community is the key size and social unit that has released mission, youth leadership and growth.

At the start they launched two MSCs drawn from those in their previous youth work. They met in a hall near the church building and this was a reasonably good phase that already showed the new potential of youth cluster. Improved effectiveness in these two MSCs led to growth as other youth were drawn in. However, the venue didn't really encourage the essential dynamics of community and it also tended to attract street youth to hang around and cause problems with neighbours. This led to a rethink of the implementation strategy and the real breakthrough came when they multiplied the MSCs and moved into private houses!

Some houses in Chorleywood are large and MSCs of 15-30 began regularly meeting in four venues around Chorleywood each week. Parents were generous hosts and the youngsters could sometimes use several rooms to spread around.

The pattern that quickly developed was for an initial hour or so in activities all together (even if spread in different rooms!), including worship, testimony, theme and community building. This was then followed by breaking down into cells for the second period of some 45 minutes. Interestingly a few years before we had met with the fastest growing youth movement in Norway and they had developed similar mid-sized youth communities meeting in homes with the same pattern of half all together followed by half splitting into cells in different rooms. At St Andrews they also found that this arrangement rapidly released another level of effectiveness and growth.

It was now really clear how the hall venue had limited growth and hadn't given a context for "community in mission" that is the heart of MSC/Cluster. In fact Pete identifies the key difference between their previous work and the way youth MSCs are now developing, is that "It's missional!" These are communities for growth and multiplication. They generate such of the "buzz" of real community as 15-30 youth gather (or cram!) into a house and have a very varied rapidly changing program. Then there is the dispersed multiple nature of the groups – which can take on different areas, estates or social groupings as their mission focus.

The second new characteristic that Pete noticed, was that these MSCs are smaller than the youth celebration or Sunday service and immediately provides more belonging and more ownership. It's really attractive and makes it easy to invite friends.

Thirdly, Pete recounts how these mid-size communities have produced an explosion of youth leaders! Communities of 20 to 25 youth are proving a fantastic training ground. This is the exciting aspect of clusters that we have observed from chapter one onwards! Not only are the youth cells peer-led, so are the MSCs. The emerging leaders among the teenagers are released and supported with adult overseers and they grow in gifts and skills. They get opportunities to teach, lead, worship and give testimonies and it's just a fantastic training ground. Previously there was only the periodic youth service allowing just a few to be used. Now in the MSCs it is multiplied out to many fold gatherings and it is weekly.

Yet another unexpected spin-off has been that the youth cells now work much better. The pattern of teenage life means that attendance is always irregular. This meant that on a bad week a cell of six to eight could be down to two or three. This was a negative experience, making it hard work and draining momentum. However, in the new pattern as part of an MSC evening, if numbers are down in one cell, they can link up with another in the shared MSC venue. The mid-size also deals better with fluctuating numbers since their good community dynamics can be sustained with anywhere between 15 and 30.

The results of all this over just a couple of years is that the 14-18 age that used to be a single youth group called "Breakout", now has grown to three full MSCs and two emerging ones of ten to fifteen each. The younger group of 11-14's called "Acts" has morphed into another MSC. And there is a seventh emerging MSC called "Fluid," which is successfully working with kids off the streets who often hang around the church. It is very missional and beginning to function effectively with most being not-yet-Christians.

The pattern that has evolved is that MSCs meet weekly on a weekday evening. Then for the past 18 months they have "Th3D" celebration all together on a Friday night in the church building from 7.30 to 10pm. But this doesn't happen on the 4th week, since on "Fourth Sunday" the whole of St Andrew's comes together - there are no MSCs and the youth also join in on that Sunday celebration.

SO FOUR "SPACES" WORK BEST FOR YOUTH MINISTRY TOO

As we shall see, St Andrew's are not alone in finding that mid-sized youth clusters not only work, but release cell and celebration to be most effective. We could also have mentioned, that in common with many other church youth ministry, they also adopt accountability pairings or triplets as the smallest unit.

So in youth church as in all church, it seems that clusters confirm the sociological principles that human relational health is best with private space (accountability), intimate space (youth cell), social space (teens MSC/cluster) and public space (youth celebration... and inter-generational celebration)[3].

In this we have seen that mid-sized youth cluster particularly contributes to the range in a) building community; b) engaging with diverse mission fields (and there are lots of youth sub-cultures); c) developing lots of leaders and d) providing a special synergy with cells.

CLUSTERS CHALLENGE LEADERS OF YOUTH WORK

When we looked at the introduction of clusters to a church in chapter nine, we saw that one of the greatest challenges was to the role of the overall leader. The experience of introducing mid-sized communities into youth work presents the youth leader with exactly the same adjustment to a completely changed role. Pete Wynter at St Andrew's is typical when he explains that his job has changed massively.

Now his primary focus is investing in youth as leaders. One of the early pressures of implementation came because he had not realised the extent of the need to support the leaders of the emerging youth MSCs. Each household-based MSC has three or four later teenagers who shape and lead the community. They have to sort out who and how they will do worship, a rota for speakers, a team of helpers and how and when to divide into cells.

So implementing youth clusters means spotting the teenagers who are beginning to show the gifts of leadership for these interactive communities. Then it requires working out a pattern of support for these emerging leaders. Again Chorleywood gives one example. They have MSC leader's meetings (huddle

---

[3] Joseph Meyer, The Search to Belong, Zondervan, 2003.

style) twice a term, one at the beginning and one in the middle (coinciding with a week with no cell). Once or twice a year they have a full retreat day with a combination of input and space, focusing on both strategy and character development.

What used to be an annual February half-term three days away, has now become a national teenage leader conference, which all the local MSC leaders attend and get input on speaking, leading community, worship and character. Over and over Pete finds himself saying to his teenage leaders that they are now doing what he used to do – and in fact what lots of UK churches employ youth workers to do!

OTHER CHURCHES' EXPERIENCE OF YOUTH CLUSTERS

In addition to the example of St Andrew's, which has been doing youth MSCs for three years, St Thomas' in Sheffield has for ten years based all its youth work on clusters combined with cells and "A-Teams." Similarly Holy Trinity, Cheltenham, which was the second UK church to implement cluster principles has proved from the start that they work particularly effectively for youth.

Although we shall draw some more illustrations from these two pioneering churches, the mid-size group has been adopted and adapted by other churches that are much smaller and are in varied contexts. This includes one youth cluster developed in the Threshold rural network in Lincolnshire and one in the Fountain of Life in Norfolk.

With such rapid decline in youth involved in UK churches, Bob Jackson has ably demonstrated from the statistics[4] that one of the best or only ways forward for appropriate mission in this

---

[4] Bob Jackson, Hope for the Church, CHP, 2002, chapter 13

age group, is cooperative across local churches. He cites the advantages, and often the necessity of Deaneries, Towns, groupings of parishes, working together in youth ministry. Not only is it logic, but it is working in many places. Especially where many villages may only have one or two Christian churched teenagers, cells can still work by combining two or three villages together and clusters by linking villages and a small town.

St Thomas', Sheffield: The experience of ten years working with youth clusters confirms that the same principles apply as for adult clusters and for youth MSCs at Chorleywood. John Mansergh emphasised the strength of youth clusters in building community and creating ownership. They enable the emergence of a culture of reaching, discipling and adding in not-yet-Christians more easily than any other size.

John also points to their mission effectiveness as vehicles to adapt and reach out to the ever increasing range of youth sub-cultures represented by sports, music, arts, etc. Clusters are a way to speak the language of emerging youth culture, which moves so quickly that it requires the lightweight low-maintenance nature of cluster.

A particular experience in St Thomas' growth with the cluster-sized community has been how easily the gifts of the Spirit are released and explored. There seems to be enough youth for people to feel comfortable and as if they aren't the centre of attention, but few enough to see everyone drawn in and ministering to one another. Teenagers have grown in prophetic gifts and in learning to pray and minister the healing of Jesus.

As with adult clusters, a key to starting has been to lay foundational values of youth leading their own stuff and serving. As they serve and add into it they have a stake in the whole and this gradually integrates them deeper into the work. They then get a vision/values carrier who expresses that actively through the three dimensions of UP:IN:OUT. The youth often plan and lead their cluster God times together. The social dynamic is also great as this size whether they get to eat together, go to the cinema together, have girls' days, boys' retreats, weekends away, etc.

Although they have found that cluster membership needs to be more fluid than with adults (youth moving from one to another), they have found it good to have at least one cluster specially focused on appealing to not-yet-Christians and at least one emphasising serious discipleship. Cluster size has none of the high maintenance of celebration or the cells need for stability. Throughout it all John again observes that it's not about providing for the youth, but about youth producing their own youth work.

The Path, Cheltenham: "The Path," centred on Cheltenham, is perhaps the best illustration we know in the UK of the effectiveness and flexibility of cell, cluster and celebration working for youth co-operatively across a region. Originally and still primarily, the youth work of Holy Trinity, Cheltenham, this has now multiplied to link up towns and villages across parts of Gloucestershire and Worcestershire.

Because Holy Trinity already had youth cells and youth clusters, when they came to launch a regional celebration event monthly called "The Path," things were perfectly structured for drawing in, supporting and resourcing other youth works of any size and in any location. What began with an invitation to regional youth to come and join in their monthly high quality celebration "happening" – was followed by helping them form youth cells wherever they were, and then by linking these up into sub-regional youth clusters.

With their minster model and servant mindset, The Path has now developed an integrated regional system for training and supporting the cell and cluster leaders. They have also used their increasing "clout" to open doors for very significant mission engagement in the needs of youth in the region – including working with excluded youth and young offenders. All this has so impressed business and society leaders in the area that the network has been able to obtain a host of sponsorships from household names.

Many of the community engagement projects require the sort of commitment and numbers that they couldn't be taken on by a single youth cell. Again, it is the mid-size that has great missional significance. Their OUT activities have also highlighted the effectiveness of working within schools as the most appropriate mission engagement for youth (as for children). So as they relate and work with teens in school catchments they have planted cells. These then are also grouped into clusters.

Furthermore, whilst the periodic big event celebrations give high profile visibility, the mid-sized clusters give cohesion – especially where cells may be scattered across a few tiny Cotswold villages.

The diagram illustrating the make up and functioning of this three level missional community and resourcing network among youth is overleaf. The outer triangle represents this whole inter-church youth movement. You will remember that in the Foreword we showed our dream for church as a multiplying mission movement! Then the sub-divided triangles inside represent all the clusters and each has a list of their constituent youth cells.

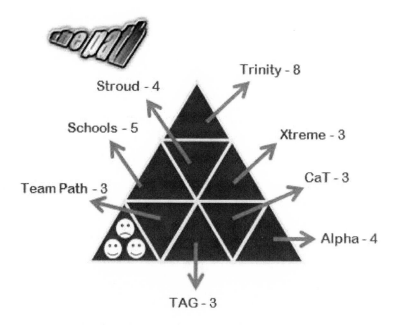

Trinity - 8

Stroud - 4

Schools - 5

Xtreme - 3

CaT - 3

Team Path - 3

Alpha - 4

TAG - 3

**33 TRASH groups in eight clusters
making one celebration!**

The cells are called "Trash groups" – (as you will have picked up by now "vocab" is part of the glue that holds together a movement beyond church walls). Holy Trinity has lots of youth and so they have eight cells in their clusters. On the other hand, across the town of Stroud they are four cells networked to form one town wide youth cluster.

The cluster that joins together cells emerging in secondary schools has five trash groups. Some of the other clusters group together cells from rural villages. It is also significant that the central team leading The Path movement with its events, training and resourcing, is made up of late teens and early twenties, many of whom have grown through the system. Since cells and clusters is healthy community for youth, its also how the team do community and support one another in a cluster of three cells.

SOME QUESTIONS AND CONCLUSIONS

We hope that these further examples illustrate how the three biblical levels of small, medium and large communities, each with their own particular dynamics, works excellently for youth. In fact, since there is the highest proportion of non-churched among youth, with little Christendom memory, this organic movement of mission is most easily embraced. The example also shows that clusters of youth cells provides such a good way to network teens across both rural, urban and city.

This truly is so flexible once inherited mode relinquishes its control. Our observation is that clusters applied to youth ministry confirms every principle and rationale that we have developed in the rest of the book.

Now there are some questions that "youth church" of this sort raises. Issues like, "Surely having such generation specific communities is wrong. We want teenagers in our congregation!" Or even, "we have relied on our few teenagers helping with our children's Sunday school, you can't take them away!"

In addressing these issues, first we have to recognise that expecting teens to join in inherited church is what has led to us losing most of them. The priority issue is whether we will hold onto them from 12-13 age onwards. Secondly, we have to recognise that cultural change is now so fast in the West that each generation represents a distinct sub-culture. So the question about homogenous groups addressed in the final chapter is also the answer here.

Some have used Bob Jackson's statistics, which show the most growth among churches that have all ages present, to prove that we should be principally doing all age church. We believe that rightly examining the statistics behind Bob Jackson's research shows that its precisely those churches that have significant **separate** youth community that have the full range of ages present in their returns!

Certainly most youth aren't at their most lively on Sunday morning when most inherited mode church happens. A few may be encouraged to do so to help with children's work, but in the next chapter we show how clusters also produce a different approach to children and church. But the really important principle is to recognise that once we move away from one day per week church event to whole life discipleship in community, there is room for bridging between generation-specific elements. Youth love to go to tea with oldies and hear the stories of their faith. Youth can play a part in inter-generational clusters, as well as have their own mid week cells and clusters. In fact, it tends to be when the major part of regular cluster life shifts to Sunday that these issues become hardest to resolve. But from the excitement of highly effective missional mid-sized youth communities – let's move to children.

CHAPTER THIRTEEN

Children, Clusters and Inter-generational Community

Before going into the specifics of how children's ministry works in cluster-based church we need to repeat a general point. One of the biggest issues affecting the implementation and working of clusters, is whether they happen on a Sunday. When introducing clusters to most existing churches, they will have a six day a week life with Sunday services staying largely unchanged. But if clusters start to meet at all regularly on Sunday, then they replace the expectations of existing church folk about how these Sunday services have all sorts of specialist provision for children of different ages. This has potential for great conflict of priorities, but we shall deal with this less usual situation, later in the chapter.

SUNDAY SERVICES CONTINUE UNCHANGED

In the more usual initial phases of implementation clusters only have their life midweek. In this situation children will continue to have either their separate provision in age-related Sunday school or be integrated in some sort of family service. There are then three main possibilities for children's involvement in clusters. Firstly, all the clusters can be for adults, students and youth in which case children don't experience full cluster dynamics until their teens. Secondly, some clusters are specifically inter-generational and the children are as fully involved in the leading, interaction and community as any other generation. The third alternative is that a church could launch clusters exclusively for children, with a few facilitating adults. Many "Kidz Clubs" based on Bill Wilson's principles[1] have elements in common with clusters and are of cluster size.

However to date, unlike youth ministry, we are not aware of St Thomas' or any other church implementing clusters exclusively for children. However, St Thomas' have run children's cells quite widely and successfully as have other churches.

Furthermore, St Thomas' have, over the past ten years, used a wide range of activities and gathering sizes with their children's work. When these groups/gatherings are cluster size then they would use the interactive/participative principles of clusters explained here, but they have not been an ongoing community for children. Similarly they apply celebration dynamics when they have periodically gathered large numbers of children.

It is important to note that in the first scenario in which there are neither inter-generational nor specialised children's clusters, this does not preclude the children from partial involvement in the life of the predominantly adult cluster. In fact there are a range of intermediate implementations between adult cluster and fully inter-generational ones.

For example, a step is taken when an adult cluster has an occasional event on weekend or holiday period. This could be a Saturday morning or afternoon involving the whole family. Or it could be a cluster family lunch after church service, followed by an outing. Some clusters have residential weekends away and this would obviously involve all ages.

A cluster called Kernal developed its strong family values without being completely inter-generational in all its activities.

---

[1] Bill Wilson, Whose Child Is This, Charisma House, 1994

Mid-week evening meetings started at 5pm with a tea for children and a parent. Later, when another parent returned from work the children would be taken home to bed and an evening adult only time followed. This cluster also had regular Sunday family bring and share lunches in church after the service.

INTERGENERATIONAL CLUSTERS

Since the essence of clusters is "extended family" community, these mid-sized groups are perfectly suited to embracing all ages and involving everyone. And this is the key... inter-generational clusters **involve** all the ages. Once children experience these interactive, everyone contributing gatherings, they get it quicker than any other age group.

Children down to the youngest ages can participate and even down to five or six year olds can lead certain parts. Also whole families can share together in participating or planning an inter-generational cluster meeting with children having some of the most effective and creative ideas. Some daytime clusters have been inter-generational without involving all the family. They are made up of a parent at home plus pre-school children. This is rather like transforming a parent and toddler group into a mid-sized missional community!

We love the case when a whole family was brainstorming at teatime about what to do at a cluster and each one coming up with an idea that they could lead. The youngest, a six year old boy, wanted to invite anyone who wanted prayer and he would pray for them. And so he did, with a line of folk including some visiting vicars coming up for him to pray for their needs! We also love the report of a seven year-old who was part of an intergenerational cluster who woke his parents up at 5am to tell them "I can't wait to go to Paul and Louise's for cluster this morning!"... "Great Joe... go back to bed!"

Another story we love happens to be from this same inter-generational family cluster, Generator. They had involved the children in participating and leading all parts of their life together over a few years. This had led to all sorts of children's gifts growing significantly. One ten year old boy began composing his own worship songs as well as playing his guitar. The overall church worship leader heard one of his songs and at the next celebration with over 500 present, the ten year old led on the platform as the whole church learnt his song!

It is not our purpose to go into all the excellent skills, ideas and resources for developing healthy intergenerational community. There are experts here such as Daphne Kirk[1].

So when do intergenerational clusters involving children meet? This is hard on a weekday. We have outlined above some creative ways in the daytime; or a rolling evening program starts with shared tea, followed by different activities as some come, some go and the interactions change as the age make-up shifts.

Other all age clusters will meet at the weekend to avoid work. There are plenty of options on a Saturday if family cluster is a priority. If there are still weekly Sunday services, then such clusters have met either for combined family breakfast before the service, for all age Sunday lunch or for afternoon tea. I so liked the inter-generational cluster we visited for Sunday lunch where the top consultant surgeon carved the joint with all ages milling round the kitchen table and into the dining room and living room.

---

[1] Daphne Kirk, Intergenerational Cell Resources, Kingsgate, 1999

FACING A MUCH MORE FUNDAMENTAL CHANGE

Before we look at the issues that arise when clusters start to meet on Sundays, we need to face up to a serious underlying issue. We have come to recognise a fundamental weakness of typical western church life that seems on the surface to be one of its great strengths. This is a picture of parents bringing their children to the church building on Sundays where there will be specialist groups tailored to narrow age-ranges and led by gifted children's workers.

It was when one of St Thomas' leaders was visiting Denmark that they brought back a report of a very different picture. They encountered a church that was daring enough to suggest that this was just the church colluding with our dependency culture. Their analysis was that the church was slotting into the "provider/client" relationship to fulfil parents' highly refined expectations to provide for the Christian education of their kids.

Put the other way round, the church had assumed the parental responsibility to disciple their own children in the faith. It is argued that this is not only the wrong way round, but much less effective long-term. Faced with this St Thomas' and some other cluster-based churches are on a journey to shift the whole philosophy here.

This philosophy would start with recognising the primary God-given responsibility for discipling children as belonging to the parents in their everyday family lives. Hence church redirects its energies in some or all of four new directions. Gifted children's workers don't become redundant – far from it. They just find a redirected role, just like overall church leaders and youth workers in a church based on mid-sized communities in mission.

First the children's specialists prepare high quality material to support parents in this vital work – providing them with

223

resources to build spirituality and learning together into the whole daily rhythm and routines. Then secondly, instead of providing a highly developed and refined program for churched kids every Sunday, the children's workers concentrate on a periodic (i.e. monthly) whole church celebration when high quality children's work can be incorporated.

Thirdly, the central church team can prepare lightweight resources to equip adults in the clusters to develop and deliver appropriate children's work for cluster get-togethers. Then fourthly, the gifted children's team are freed up to also function as children's missionaries and start providing outreach-oriented programs in schools and after-school clubs, where churched kids can invite their non-churched friends with confidence. This is another case of rethinking our resourcing from all inward focus to a priority on the outward! The church recovering its identity as "community in mission."

This philosophy embraces the dual principles that whilst parents are responsible for their children "it takes a whole village to raise healthy children." This is where inter-generational clusters can perfectly provide this wider support for this new vision of family-based children's discipleship.

Linked to these new insights is the acceptance that it is possible that the highly developed Sunday school approach can collude with culture to place an over emphasis on academic and conceptual truth at the expense of holistic discipleship of children, which also addresses social development and emotional intelligence.

On one occasion we were sharing these ideas with one parent and children's worker who had been rather critical. Not only did she come to see things in this new way, but recognised the same principle that we described in chapter five of wanting to copy festivals and celebration dynamics to the local congregation (the congregation aping the cathedral principle).

She realised that New Wine summer camps had developed more and more sophisticated children's programs, taking them off their parents' hands for a week of holiday which is fabulous... but then she and other parents wanted to raise the provider/client standard still further to reproduce the same program, back at local church every week!

It may be that the more highly professional parents will find this shift most difficult. They may transfer their high expectations for their children's education by schools, to expecting the church to make and keep their children walking as Christians! But whatever your culture or context, if you begin to do clusters regularly on a Sunday, this is likely to require this sort of major change in thinking and practice. And we have emphasised earlier that changing values has to come first and takes time, sensitive communication and lots of repetition.

THE CHALLENGE WHEN CLUSTERS START TO REPLACE SUNDAY SERVICES

When this is just a very occasional practice such as a once a term "Cluster Sunday," there is little problem. For the one-off everyone adapts and clusters that don't normally meet with children will involve all ages of their members' children. However, when cluster gatherings shift from mid-week to Sunday more regularly (once a month or fortnightly), or as the norm (often with monthly celebrations), then children's experience of church changes radically and we have to re-think the whole philosophy.

As it happens, the examples of St Andrew's, Chorleywood and St Thomas', Sheffield provide the best examples of how children's work was transformed to resource families discipling their own children at home and mid-sized communities involving and caring for their own children in their meetings. Once these supporting structures reinforce the underlying change in values and philosophy described above, a gradual shift in expectation and practice has begun to emerge.

In this case, Sheffield may provide the best example of resourcing parents to introduce discipleship into normal seven days a week family life. The central children's team have for some years now, produced easy to use leaflets for parents to use at meal times, other family times or night time reading and prayers. These have often covered a term at a time or focused on special seasons like Advent, Lent and Pentecost. They contain simple suggestions every day from things to pray for, to bible verses to learn, to simple exercises, crafts or games, all with a spiritual significance. Resources like these that enable family discipleship already begin to take the pressure off the cluster (or church) to deliver everything in this area.

On the other hand, Chorleywood are currently providing the best example of resourcing cluster members for the child discipling element of their community life. When in September 2004, we did the first training weekend at St Andrew's to introduce mid-size community principles, it was the leaders of the children's work who seemed most uncertain. Remember that the church was facing evacuation from their building for refurbishment in January 2005 and everyone doing MSCs three Sundays a month for six to nine months!

And as it happened Todd Nightingale and Dave Hill had invested so much in developing a centralised program for children based on Willow Creek resources. They had worked up state of the art range of activities to teach and entertain large numbers of children on a Sunday morning. These involved very creative child friendly age-appropriate teaching that was high energy and big input; and they had recruited and trained lots of leaders into lots of groups. This had taken a long time to build with high presentational and dramatic input (Dave is an actor who had had experience with TV).

However, all credit to them, they grasped the new MSC vision and the quite different underlying values and philosophy that we explained. They accepted the new challenge to dismantle all that they had built and redirected this skill and experience to equip ordinary MSC members – so that people who had never done children's work could grow into effective but lightweight child discipling.

At first they continued to use the Willow Creek material and themes, but moved from a "script format" for them and their specialists to perform, to an "outline format" to give to the untrained. Suddenly as they visited the MSCs on Sundays, they saw huge numbers of folk enabled to do what they had never done before. They saw mums and dads leading children and before long this kid that hadn't known this adult, now having a relationship.

Dave admits that there are obviously some children who like to be with larger numbers and some thrive with fewer. But Dave also shares how it is just lovely to observe how kids now had lots of adult friends rather than a special children's worker. MSCs truly were becoming more like extended family and he noticed a year six girl helping a year one girl and having a little relationship.

It has been a huge gear change. From building Sunday groups of children they now help MSCs have all sorts of groups, but with lots of life. And as children's workers, Todd and Dave have learnt lots of new skills.

Having started with adapting Willow Creek scripts into outlines they have learnt how to read a lesson, understand the content so they can live and breathe it – in order to provide just enough for a lay person to get the story across and involve others. So now they are able to write their own outlines from scratch (samples of which could be made available to help other churches on this journey). They develop a little worksheet with the aid of readily available web resources they have discovered so that every MSC child can have a theme related game or colouring picture.

Now that the church building is available and there are weekly Sunday services, lots of clusters have chosen to be meeting out on a rota. Some once, some twice and some three times a month. So the children's team, now under Dave, still produce their three times a month MSC resources – but now they and their central team will be giving exactly the same input to Sunday school groups in the church building. These simplified outlines work for both.

Lastly, the gear change for the children's team has also allowed the development of more missional activity in all the four primary schools, and they are now known by kids in every school. They do assemblies, classes and after-school clubs. They work with other churches in Chorleywood and are reaching hundreds of children beyond church. Outreach also includes a week's holiday club in a local school called "Detonate" with some 350 kids and they now link this with Pre-Detonate and Re-Detonate events with over 100. There is also a monthly outreach club called Friday Night Live with non-churched children. In time all this should build a mission synergy with the family MSCs that are growing in confidence in working with their children of all ages.

So from this chapter we have identified all sorts of ways that children are not just included in cluster life, but are playing a full part as all are discipled together in the way of Jesus. As clusters become more central to the new way of doing church, the responsibility of discipling children poses some of the biggest challenges to change both our thinking and our practice.

CLUSTERS

PART FOUR

CLUSTER ROOTS, SWOT'S AND FAQ'S

Origins can enlighten outcomes – as can facing the upsides, downsides and frequent questions

CLUSTERS

CHAPTER FOURTEEN

Tracing Cluster Roots

In this chapter we dig back a bit to identify some of the developments and changes that ultimately crystallised in the principles and practice of mid-sized missional communities or clusters. We think it's important to identify these, both to honour those pioneering developments that paved the way, but also because it sheds more light on the essence and missionary rationale of clusters.

TWO STRATEGIES TO BEAT THE BUILDING BARRIER

Over the past 20-30yrs, a number of churches in the UK that have experienced growth and outgrown their buildings at a single service, have opted to continue growth through a second event in the same building. Sometimes this practice was stimulated by the research findings of the church growth movement, which identified that once a building is 80% full, then further growth is highly unlikely.

The explanation of these findings is that once this level of capacity is reached, there are few available seats for latecomers and newcomers and these aren't easy to find being dispersed through the building, and often at the front. The difficulty and disruption of seeking these out, combined with the sense that the building is sufficiently full and that ones presence wouldn't be missed, is thought to explain the observed phenomenon. The problem is often described as reaching the point when you lose people out of the back door as fast as you seek to draw them in through the front door.

It was back in 1991 in their report entitled "Get up and Grow"[1] that Administry identified this doubling up of events in a single building, as a type of church planting. In their research, they identified two broad categories of approach to beating the building barrier. The first, they described as a **duplicate service** and the second, as **multiple congregations**.

In essence the duplicate service simply aimed to process more people through the same space. At its simplest, the vicar might preach the same sermon, the organist play the same hymns, the sides persons give out the same books and each service repeats the same pattern for the same kind of people. By contrast, the multiple congregation, typically will have different people leading, the service will have a different style and will be aimed at significantly different people.

The essential difference in philosophy here, is that the first model continues to see itself as a single community of faith that merely requires the timetabling of two Sunday services to enable the growing numbers all to be accommodated within the fixed building. The multiple congregation on the other hand, is founded on the principle that growth involves multiplication and is to be continued through the formation of two new communities of faith, in the place of one.

The fullest expression of this second approach is therefore when each community of faith has its own leadership, its own pastoral care, its own worship team, its own mission focus and worship style. Perhaps most significant of all, it is when any small groups and midweek life are also associated with the

---

[1] Get up and Grow – An analysis of Church Growth & Church Planting, Administry, Aug 1991

distinct community of faith. In other words, the two new faith communities are each **places of belonging** in a way that need not be true in the case of the duplicate service model.

If, week by week, members' social patterns change, with Granny visiting this week, and Johnny playing football next week, then in the case of the duplicate service, it will be fine for the family to switch their attendance between one service and the other, according to convenience. They will not be missed as they would in the multiple congregation model, where commitment to belong to one or other congregation would be the basic assumption. We need to stress that the fundamental difference distinguishing these two models is the shift from seeing a Sunday service as an event to seeing it as a unifying expression of the life of a community of faith.

As well as describing these two distinct models of growth, the Administry Report identified a very significant finding from their survey. This was, that of the cases where the duplicate service was tried, it was found that over 50% gave up the endeavour within the first five years.

By contrast, of the churches that adopted the multiple congregation approach, none were found to give up during the first five years. The Administry Report did not identify the causes for this discrepancy nor make recommendations for strategy. It simply alerted readers to the much higher failure rate of the duplicate service so that they could be forewarned in any planning for the future.

Anyone who has been involved in either of these approaches, will readily be aware of plenty of pressures that build up, which could lead to a decision to abandon the experiment. In the early stages of any new venture aimed at growth and further effective evangelism, there is a lot of enthusiasm generated that can carry one a long way.

However, processing two groups through the same building on the same Sunday morning inevitably gives rise to all sorts of pressures and difficulties. These range from getting the people in and out through limited access points, to how one arranges coffee and tea and fellowship after one gathering whilst trying to welcome those arriving for the second. Then there are the pressures on parking and getting people's cars in and out at the same time. These challenges are in addition to the demands on those who open and shut the building, now over a much wider time frame, together with all sorts of extra demands of preparation and resourcing of the two events.

Although the reasons for the very different success rates were not clear, the results made a sufficient impact on us that whenever we were sharing vision for mission, growth and church planting, we would often quote the statistics and merely leave them to speak for themselves as a warning to take seriously the costs and vulnerability associated with growth through duplicate services. It has taken more than ten years of working with all sorts of different church projects and especially the first hand experience of St Thomas' in Sheffield where clusters have been developed, to enable us to arrive at a more in depth understanding of the background principles and dynamics underlying this phenomenon.

Nonetheless, from our description so far, you should already be making links with all we have been discovering about clusters/MSCs. It is clear that the multiple congregation approach has the seeds of the cluster vision. It is multiplication at the congregation level. It is recognising the importance of maintaining a place of belonging at the mid-size. And it links a congregational community with its own clear mission objective.

Now let's see how these foundations took their next development towards cluster.

STORY OF GROWTH & DEVELOPMENT AT ST THOMAS' SHEFFIELD UP TO 1994

Robert Warren was Rector of St Thomas, Crookes for some twenty-eight years up until 1993. He built on the strong foundations that had been laid by predecessors, developing effective mission, evangelism and growth. This led to the common problem that we described above, of no further room in the full parish building on Sundays at Nairn Street. Through the 70's and 80's this problem was addressed in part by two major rebuilding programs to enlarge the building capacity.

However, continued growth and combining with the local Baptist congregation to become an LEP (Local Ecumenical Project) all meant that the extra space still wasn't sufficient to cope. So Robert Warren and his leadership team were one of the early examples of responding by doubling up services. In implementing this, they became one of the classic examples of the **multiple congregation** model identified by Administry.

And over time, this intentional strategy led to the multiplication first into two, then three and finally four distinct congregations. Each gathered in the enlarged parish church building at a different time on Sunday and each was seen as a faith community in its own right.

The story and strategy were written up by Robert in his first book "On the Anvil"[2]. In particular the matrix arrangement that they developed to support and reinforce this multiple structure, was illustrated on page 50, and is reproduced overleaf. This shows how each of the four congregations that emerged and grew had its own team leader, worship team, administration, ministry and pastoral teams.

The matrix also shows how in order to provide cohesion and

---

[2] Robert Warren, On the Anvil, Highland, 1990, p50

the best equipping and resourcing of these teams, their leaders were combined at a whole church level. This was therefore one of the most fully developed expressions of a multiple congregation approach to mission and growth, at that time.

CONGREGATIONAL LEADERSHIP TEAMS					WHOLE CHURCH TEAMS
TEAM LEADER	X	X	X	X	STAFF TEAM
PASTORAL LEADER	X	X	X	X	PASTORAL TEAM
ORGANISER	X	X	X	X	ORGANISER'S TEAM
MINISTRY LEADER	X	X	X	X	MINISTRY TEAM
WORSHIP LEADER	X	X	X	X	WORSHIP TEAM

One of the congregations was the Nine O' Clock Service (NOS) which, subsequent to moving out of St Thomas' building in 1991 and rejecting its accountability, developed its sad and disastrous deviations. However, the fact that it was able to move to an alternative venue powerfully illustrated the point that each congregation was fully self supporting and had its own identity and was very much a place of belonging.

This well developed model of multiplying communities of faith, each relating to different worship services in St Thomas' on a Sunday, proved itself extremely effective for continuing ministry, mission and attendant growth. At its height with the four congregations it had reached at least 1000 members. Even after the Nine O' Clock Service moved out prior to the tragic failure of its leader, it still involved at least 700 people.

Now on Robert Warren's departure in 1993, Mike Breen was appointed as successor and arrived in 1994. However, to understand how Robert's multiple congregations in one building led to Mike's vision of multiplying mid-size clusters across the city, we have to look where Mike had come from.

MIKE BREEN'S EXPERIMENTATION WITH DIFFERENT MODELS OF CHURCH AT BRIXTON

Mike Breen came to Brixton in 1988 having worked in poor deprived communities both in Kingsmead in East London and at St Martin's in Cambridge. These had led him to pioneer new approaches to detached youth work, which involved releasing young people to develop their own varied program of activity and community[3]. He had also studied new expressions of church that were emerging around the world including the cell movement of Yongi Cho in Korea[4] and the Base Community movement of Latin America.

At All Saints Brixton Hill, he took over a parish with a patchwork of inner urban cultural and ethnic communities. It is significant that as well as this diverse mission field, developments would be influenced by a new building that had intentionally been built quite small, assuming only small congregations in inner urban areas. It could comfortably accommodate with good sight lines, only about seventy five people. These factors were crucial in shaping the mission and growth model that Mike subsequently developed[5].

Engaging in mission with the plural social context led him to develop different communities of faith which grew into at least three services in the small church building on Sunday. The evening was more focussed on youth culture, one morning

---

[3] Mike Breen, Outside In, Scripture Union, 1993
[4] Paul Yongi Cho, Successful Home Cell Groups, Bridge, 1981
[5] Mike Breen, Growing the Smaller Church, Harper Collins, 1992

service more on young families and another more for those who had moved into parts of the parish experiencing gentrification. For the latter context, with memories of school chapel, a more traditional style of service was appropriate. Mike came to understand these multiplying services in the church building, more as celebrations than biblical congregation.

Alongside these services on Sunday were midweek mission-focused smaller groups which he called pastoral bases[6]. These pastoral bases again drew together a combination of principles from church growth and from base community insights. In this process, Mike Breen was looking to rediscover authentic biblical expressions of missional church at different social sizes. The pastoral bases with between six and 40 members were lay led, highly interactive and participative. He saw them as re-discovering authentic biblical congregation [7].

MIKE BREEN SUCCEEDS ROBERT WARREN AND LEADS IN FURTHER MISSION & GROWTH

Mike Breen is a strong visionary leader with a track record of pioneering new things. Certainly Mike's arrival as rector in the Spring of 1994 did lead to significant changes. It was not long before Mike introduced a new level of community of faith in the life of St Thomas', which he called "Clusters."

Although there was an initial dip in membership, the introduction and development of these mid-sized communities then led to a further period of concerted growth. Some three years after the introduction of clusters, I was talking to a member of the previous leadership team, who commented that he gathered that Mike Breen had proceeded to dismantle

---

[6] Bob Hopkins (ed), Planting New Churches, Eagle, 1992, ch.10
[7] ibid, esp. p134-137

everything that Robert Warren had built up at St Thomas'! My response was with full conviction, "Oh! no, I think rightly understood, what Mike has done at St Thomas' has precisely continued and extended the foundational principles that Robert laid in place!"

What Mike had done was what he does instinctively at each new place to which he comes to lead. In his first weeks and months he had reviewed the mission opportunities and the existing mission structures of the church at St Thomas'. He recognised that the multiple congregation model that Robert had established was based on broadly the same principles on which he had established multiple congregations in and beyond the much smaller building at All Saint's, Brixton Hill.

However, he very perceptively discerned that even with the much larger building at St Thomas', they had once again hit the ceiling limiting any further growth. This ceiling was represented by the size of the building (even though it had been substantially enlarged) and by the number of social hours on Sunday at which people were likely to turn out and attend church.

In the second half of the 90's in Mike Breen's early years at St Thomas', there were services at 9:15am, 11:15am, 5:15pm and 7:15pm. All except the 5:15pm were at the 80% full limitation level. With no possibility to extend the building any further, many leaders would have seen these as insuperable barriers and resigned themselves to no further growth potential and focused on other areas of church life. However, Mike's conviction was that the size of building and the number of sociable hours on Sunday are purely arbitrary limitations and in no way should be accepted as hindering further growth in the Kingdom of God.

He stuck with the model that both Robert and he had proved effective, namely multiplying new communities of faith at the congregational level. If this couldn't happen in the parish church building or on Sunday, then congregation-type expressions of church had to be re-invented that were free from the building and from Sunday. And that led to the creation of **clusters**.

From his experience at Brixton with Pastoral Bases, these missional communities would probably be significantly smaller than most people thought of congregations. And once clusters were launched and working, it was only a matter of a couple of years before St Thomas' had reached 13 clusters where only four congregations were possible when they met in the building on Sunday. Growth had been freed up from the arbitrary limitation of Sunday services in a special building.

It is particularly interesting that the basis on which Mike shared the vision for clusters with the members of St Thomas' was as a strategy of "Building Missionary Congregations" across the city of Sheffield. Building missionary congregations was of course the central theme and passion, which Robert Warren developed after leaving St Thomas' and his seminal booklet with that title has played such a major part in reshaping national thinking about the church[8].

KEY TO MULTIPLE CONGREGATIONS COMES CLEAR

A careful reflection upon these developments, enables us to identify the key difference between Duplicate Services and Multiple Congregations, which neither we nor Administry had picked up. Once the multiplication of missionary congregations was shifted from Sunday services in the parish church to clusters, it wasn't long before we suddenly realised why the

---

[8] Robert Warren, Building Missionary Congregations, Church House Publishing, 1995

duplicate service approach to growth in a church building had a high failure rate relative to multiplying congregations.

Now that we were in clusters, our primary experience of church was not in a special building or a Sunday religious event. When people asked us what church we belonged to, for the first time in our Christian lives, we couldn't use these reference points. Rather we had to answer by describing the faith community that was our place of belonging.

We found ourselves describing the mission focus of our cluster and its community values. For decades we had said church was not a building but the Body of Christ. Now for the first time in over 30 years, we realised that this had become true in our experience in a new way. We had to describe our church involvement in terms of the people we were part of and what we held in common.

These were the things that held us together when we had lost the normal Christendom core shared experience of building and Sunday service. And the key concept that hit us was the sense of "what held us together"... GLUE!

This was revelation to me. When a congregation getting its identity from one Sunday service, divided into two duplicate services in order to grow... it lost its coherence. No glue! This was why so many attempts at growth of this model, failed within five years. The glue of that faith community had been taken away and not replaced.

In duplicate services, folk vary which one they go to according to their social engagements that week, so it's no longer a place of belonging. Also there is not an ownership of a distinct mission vision. The loss of these two vital components of "glue" or coherence was highlighted by the key role that these play in clusters (as we expanded in chapter two).

LATER DEVELOPMENT HIGHLIGHTS AT ST THOMAS'

We have made reference throughout the other chapters of this book to the evolving St Thomas' story. This has included lots of aspects of how clusters developed and grew, and how structures of resourcing and support changed. To conclude this chapter perhaps we will highlight a few of these and add one or two others.

Clusters in the first phase at St Thomas' were all midweek expressions of mid-sized community. But Mike wanted to increase the sense that they were fully church and to gradually emphasise that they were the core of how we were going to be missional church in the future. So a once a term "Cluster Sunday" was introduced. On this Sunday there were no services in the Parish Church and clusters were encouraged to find venues, inside or out, and be creative.

During this first phase, with mid-week cluster meetings and small groups, the four Sunday services that continued at the parish church had effectively changed. Under Robert Warren they had been specifically structured to be congregations, places of belonging and membership, each with distinct style and leadership.

Now that belonging and identity was in clusters, people were once again free to attend whichever service on Sunday fitted their social life that week. And the same preacher spoke at all four services and the same worship group led. With the understanding from chapter five of biblical/celebration, these had now become in effect duplicate **celebrations**.

Also in the early phase, clusters tended to be weak on a clear unified mission focus. This gradually changed and it became clear that the healthy ones gained identity and momentum from commitment to engage with a specific neighbourhood or social/cultural network. This led to the next phase in which it was clear that some cluster mission was to the parish of Crookes and some to networks or areas across the city. To build on this widening mission reality Mike then introduced a whole church celebration event in the city centre. For this the enormous venue of Ponds Forge was rented – first once a term, then later monthly. When it was unavailable the Lyceum Theatre or famous Crucible were used.

Later this distinction between city and parish mission crystallised and all clusters had to clearly associate with one or the other. This was facilitated by the taking over of the redundant Roxy nightclub as a rented home in the city centre. From four services in the parish church to choose from, now it was only one – for parish based clusters – and two celebration-style services in the Roxy, morning and evening, for city-focused clusters.

Two years later it was more all change again for the city clusters, as the Roxy was condemned by Health & Safety at six weeks notice. So it was "Out of the nest" for sixteen clusters in February 2002. They all had to develop Sunday activities and find Sunday venues "at the drop of a hat." Mid-sized missional communities they surely were – and on a pilgrim journey! At this stage in fully dispersed mode in the city, it was important to develop patterns to hold it all together.

The first thing to be implemented was what we called the "Pony Express" and "Riding the Range." Each week the central administrative staff produced material to keep all the clusters in touch and also to resource them for things like their children's work. Twenty large plastic boxes were purchased like those that parents would use to clear away children's toys and these were stacked at the parish church to be collected on Sunday morning by a member of each cluster and taken to their meeting.

This would contain the week's notice sheet as well as any other centrally produced church publicity. The question of Sunday collections came to senior staff minds fairly quickly and forcefully! Financial reps were appointed in each cluster, collection plates put in their cluster boxes and when the box was returned it would come back with cluster members tithes and offerings.

If this was the "Pony Express," then "Riding the Range" applied to the new pattern of life for the staff on Sunday. They would meet at the parish church at 9:30am for prayers and sharing any items of importance for clusters and then they would head off to put in an appearance at the different cluster meetings. In the early days because of the importance of keeping Mike as the leader in touch with this dispersed church of many clusters, he might visit three clusters in two hours on a Sunday morning. Staff visiting the clusters would give special notices and share encouragements from other clusters to keep folk in touch and to encourage and stimulate morale. They might also from time to time share a biblical word.

Another innovation that had been introduced shortly before the end of our time at the Roxy came even more into it's own. To keep the whole church together, both parish and city work and two city celebrations, a whole church gathering had been begun called "Second Sunday." To begin with this had used facilities both at the Roxy and the Cathedral. The idea was a varied programme through the afternoon and evening of one Sunday a month to be more like a festival. It aimed to respond to the needs of all the ages from the youngest through students and young adults to the young families and to the oldest.

It began with a choice of seminars at 3pm in the afternoon on a range of topics in parallel with children's work, was followed by tea and sandwiches all together and then led on to an evening with substantial worship, teaching and ministry. With the clusters dispersed and having no united Sunday celebrations for all the city clusters, this "Second Sunday" with the whole church became even more important. Without the Roxy the largest venue we could find we could hire was the university Octagon that holds between a thousand and fifteen hundred.

This "Second Sunday" whole church happened almost every month and was key to keep a sense of cohesion and for Mike to share in depth teaching and the ongoing direction or vision for the church.

Major change has continued to be the norm for St Thomas' for both the city and Crookes parish clusters. For the city clusters a new permanent home became available in early 2003 at a redundant engineering works – now the Philadelphia Campus.

Then a year later Mike left for the USA and Paul Maconochie took over. Soon afterwards it was "all clusters back to the central venue every Sunday" for him to establish his leadership relationships and to communicate his new vision across the church. Paul presented a simple visual summary of the ten year journey of folk at St Thomas', Philadelphia Campus, included here in Appendix 6.

For the Crookes clusters, their new leader Mick Woodhead, took them through a transition to Cell Church foundations that involved closing all clusters for a year and then re-launching clusters (see chapter nine).

The one consistent feature of these developments at St Thomas' that has been repeated is... regular change. Some has been planned and some forced upon us. Some is just the consequence of being the first church to pioneer this pattern of mid-sized mission communities... and "never having been this way before!"

However, the overwhelming conclusion is that this ability to cope with change way beyond any experience of a traditional church, reinforces the great strength of focusing the essential life of the church on lay-led, lightweight communities. The extent and frequency of change has been beyond what one would want or certainly recommend. It has had a negative effect on eroding some of the identity and belonging of clusters and also of disrupting some of their mission engagement (recognised in chapter fifteen).

However, the continuing overall health of what is now "two separate churches in covenant" is fantastic testimony to the effectiveness and resilience of clusters in our rapidly changing world.

Most Frequently Asked Questions & The Homogenous Hot Potato!

ALWAYS THE SAME ANSWER!

It depends! In most question and answer sessions I now start by warning that my first answer will almost always be... "it depends!" And that is a very important and genuine answer.

On the one hand the contexts of church and cultural setting are so varied that these are bound to influence any answer. Furthermore, we have repeatedly argued and explained that clusters are highly flexible and adaptable. Mid-sized communities are not a blueprint or single model concept. They are based on a number of foundational principles so any answer will have to seek to refer back to those principles and to explore how they may apply to a range of possible scenarios. So you see, it really does depend!

FREQUENT QUESTIONS

Clusters that challenge how we do congregation and Sunday Service, certainly generate masses of questions. As we have led cluster conferences and helped introduce the concept to churches and train their leaders, we have encountered most! Hence, the contents of this book have already been largely shaped by these questions and our efforts to answer them. So we hope that we have already covered most questions like...

- Describe a cluster in simple layman's language. (Chapter 1 and Summary before Contents)
- What's a cluster meeting like and how is it different? (Chapter 11)
- How often do clusters meet and do they meet on a Sunday? (Chapters 10 & 11)
- Isn't it all just more work for already busy people? (Chapter 10)
- What's the biblical basis for this mid-sized group? (Chapter 5)
- What about Children and Youth? (Chapters 12 & 13)
- Are clusters what people are calling emerging church? (Chapter 8)
- Give us more ideas for how to build community in cluster gatherings. (Chapter 11 & Appendix 3)
- What's wrong with how we've been doing it? (Chapter 6)
- Why should we change? (Chapter 7)
- Where did these ideas come from and have they been fully tested? (Chapters 9 & 14)
- How do we start to implement these principles in our church? (Chapter 9)
- What happens to our existing small groups if we adopt clusters? (Chapter 9)
- Could I start a cluster? (Chapter 10)
- What makes a cluster tick? (Chapters 2 & 3)
- Are clusters really so different? (Chapter 4)
- So what happens about baptisms, weddings and funerals? (Chapter 3)

So, quite seriously, we are not going to try to do any further work on answering all the above frequent questions. We really do think that if you still have any of those listed above, we should encourage you to go back to the chapters we have referenced.

But there is one other frequent question that isn't listed above. And although we have touched on it at various points, we think it's so important that we give the rest of this chapter to it. So perhaps the most frequently asked question of all is "Surely we shouldn't have single culture or single generation homogenous groups? The gospel makes us all one!"

Before getting into the detail of answering this thorny question, we need to make a couple of points clear. First, we should face the challenge that most inherited congregations at Sunday services have for decades been among the most homogenous groups anywhere in the UK. We have lived quite happily with 8am, 9.30am, Family service... and now perhaps the 6.30, which is now "younger style," where half a century ago it was "below stairs."

So whilst this is a valid and important question, we need to honestly ask why we have been comfortable not to address it to our long-standing homogenous church congregations/services. At worst we may have to recognise a hidden attitude that we haven't wanted people in our congregation who aren't like us. Or at best we need to admit "the plank in our own eye." But most of all we need a new clarity of understanding about the biblical principles here and therefore the biblical answer to the question.

THE HOMOGENEOUS CONUNDRUM OR HUP

This question relates to the Homogenous Unit Principle (or so called HUP)[1] and is one of the most complex and controversial

---

[1] See C.P. Wagner, Your Church Can Grow, Regal, 1995, chapter 8

in the field of Christian mission. Expressed at its simplest, it runs… "Is it or isn't it acceptable (or desirable) to have Christian communities made up of only one homogenous culture or social group?" The most learned church leaders, theologians, and missiologists around the world strenuously disagree with one another. So it can't be easy to resolve. We have even heard the same eminent Christian leader express the opposite view depending on how the issue is presented.

In our one year church planting training programs we take the best part of a weekend to address this question and seek to present a resolution. So we are so bold as to believe that there is a resolution. A resolution that holds that homogenous groups are right and not right… but not at the same time or in the same community structure.

So there, I have already given you some clues! So if one key to resolving the apparent conflict is community structure, then it shouldn't surprise us that different sized expressions of church like mid-sized clusters (especially if they are made up of a cluster of smaller cells!) can have a key role in resolving the question… rather than creating the dilemma.

But if it's so hard to explain and get a resolution, it certainly can't get a quick answer and it's not going to be easy to answer even in a few pages. However, we will try and go some of the way and give a summary of the answers[2].

Another clue we have just given is that it's a paradox. And our weakness at coming up with the resolution in the West, is that our thought processes are Greek-style, which are linear and all has to agree. Biblical Hebraic thinking on the other hand deals

---

[2] Some of the insights are drawn from Lausane Occasional Paper No1: The Passadena Consultation – Homogenous Unit Principles, 1978

with a relational God and humanity made for community. And that means holding apparent opposites in tension. So the HUP can be right and not right... but in different situations!

First lets take a step back and think about social and cultural differences by remembering what sort of differences we may expect when we go abroad. Maybe think of a country, like Spain or Turkey or Thailand. We expect a different language, different food, different temperatures, as well as climate! Then there are customs, currency, clothing, family patterns, and so much more that we take for granted. The list on the next page still doesn't exhaust the extent and complexity of cultural variations.

Now we need to see that this cultural diversity is God's doing. The whole of creation is a kaleidoscope of variety and God's creative variety extends equally to human culture. Hence to form faith communities that express this diversity honours God the creator and respects humanity made in His image. Even in heaven every tribe and tongue will be represented and distinguishable – not made one bland mixture (Rev 5:9).

If we are planting a church to reach an ethnic group, for example amongst Asians, Hispanics or Afro-Caribbeans our first thought is the need to be appropriate to the culture. Furthermore, we probably realise we don't understand these ethnic cultures very well and so the best people to interpret them and decide what sort of church is contextual are Asians, Hispanics and Afro-Caribbeans themselves!

Furthermore, we readily recognise the failures of our mission efforts in other continents during the colonial era of earlier centuries. It seems obvious now that to export hymns ancient and modern, robed choirs and stained glass windows to Africa, was unhelpful cultural imperialism. As was declaring drums the devil's music.

SOME CULTURAL VARIATIONS

Dialect   Food/drink
                                    Music

Family Relationships   FESTIVALS   Climate
Hygiene   Customs/Traditions   Etiquette

Body Language   EDUCATION   Class
                    Structure

Temperament   Currency   LAWS

PEOPLE'S APPEARANCE   Humour
                    Literature
Recreation/sports   Values   Personal
                    space
Media (TV, paper)   Employment
                Shopping
Transport   Politics   Clothing   Morality

Fashion   Authority structures
                    Money

However, a problem for many white British Christians is that we expect cultural differences abroad or among other ethnic groups here, but we are blind to them within our own ethnic grouping. This is very serious for our mission engagement and developing church beyond the fringe, since in fact the cultural differences between professional, middle class and the urban poor may be more challenging than moving from a professional English culture to a professional Spanish one. This blindness may be a primary reason why the church has so often been weak and ineffective amongst the urban poor. The only church we offer is of an alien culture and there is rarely a church of the poor for the poor.

With our culture getting more diverse and pluralistic, cultural blindness like this gets even more serious. So, in developing church today, culture affects a whole range of things. It's not just the style of worship and type of music, important though it is for these to be contextual. There are also things like the patterns and places of social community life (at a superficial level "wine & cheese" or "pie & peas"!); the values and priorities we hold (for instance between people/relationships relative to time/task/performance); the size of group within which people sustain relationships and most important, the models and styles of leadership practised in the community (middle class managerial leadership is almost universal in our churches but not in all our cultures!).

Not only are we white Anglo Christians often blind to culture in our own ethnic group, we even resent the talk of differences, using "us & them," thinking it "snobbish" or un-Christian. We then tend to seal the matter by adding theological argument that different sorts of congregation are divisive and contradict the unity of the Gospel. With such arguments we go on justifying imposing our culture and preferences on others in our mission and church practice.

I say imposing because as sociology and anthropology prove, when two cultures meet, you don't so much get a hybrid mixture, rather one will dominate the other. And the really important insight is that the culture which ends up dominant is not necessarily that of the larger group, but rather the one with higher educational and financial power – certainly not gospel values!

Greater understanding of how evangelism works has also opened our eyes to the corporate dimension. A not-yet

Christian on a journey to Christ encounters the Gospel lived out both in a messenger but also in a gospel community. If that gospel community is of a different social or cultural group, then it is made much more difficult for the not-yet Christian to respond. In addition to the barrier of the cost of the gospel, there is now also the twin barriers of the community expression of the gospel failing to communicate in his/her culture/language and then this presents the need to become part of a "foreign faith community."

The conclusion is that we need to put no extra barriers and the not-yet Christian should not only hear the gospel in their dialect, but see it lived by a group in their culture and be able to join a gospel community of their culture[3].

Put in everyday terms, we or our teenagers, or our homeless, or our art community, need to be able to say to any friends... "Come and see, come and spend time with us, we are a group of folk just like you... except Jesus is transforming us!"

This principle of creating churches that are appropriate to the culture is based on the mission model of Jesus, which is incarnation. Jesus left heaven, laid it all aside and becomes one of us. Whilst never turning anyone away, his clear mission focus was to "the lost sheep of the house of Israel" and so he commissioned his disciples (Matt 10 v 5).

Each new church needs as far as possible, to be born out of the culture in which it is set to be authentic. This means that cross-cultural mission church planters have to learn Paul's lesson "become a Jew to reach Jews and a Greek to reach Greeks... all

---

[3] The classic expressions of this are Vincent Donovan, Christianity Rediscovered, Orbis, 1978 and Bruce E. Olsen, Bruchko, Creation House, 1973

things to all men... in order to win some"[4]. It's not just a matter of planting a church to *reach* them, so much as a church *arising among* them.

Now, so far all these arguments and biblical principles have supported the formation of clusters and mid-sized communities that are specific to each culture and context. These principles that we have explored are all foundational to the approach of this book. Clusters need to arise in different contexts, whether social, ethnic, cultural or generational (where these now represent distinct sub-cultures). These mid-sized communities are to be indigenous, contextual... inculturated – to use the technical mission term.

These principles are also those expressed more fully in Mission-Shaped Church. This incarnational pattern of mission to create church of each context is likened to a seed (the gospel embedded in a small mission team) falling into the ground and dying, so that it may become many new seeds (fresh expressions of church) - John 12 v 24.

However, this frequently asked question is not just plain wrong or misguided. It too is founded on sound biblical principle. So, before you think that we are only putting all the arguments on one side, let us look at the main argument on the other side.

In the last hundred years we have learnt so much about the evils of cultural prejudice and segregation. The promoting of homogenous church groups sounds to be rather like this... so isn't it wrong too? Not only has Jesus made us all one in a new humanity, he has done it by tearing down the dividing wall that separated mankind based on cultures (especially Jew & Gentile) and by ending the hostility and enmity that separated us

---

[4] 1 Corinthians 9:20

(Ephesians 2 v1-8). Paul even seals the argument that there is now neither Jew nor Greek, slave nor free, male nor female (Galatians 3:28). I'm sure he would have added today, neither old nor young!

This seems so clear cut that it appears to end the argument as conclusively as seemed our reasoning on the other side. But when confronted by apparently contradictory biblical principles we can't just jump one side of the fence or the other. That would be to embrace one truth and deny others. Nor can we jump from one side of the argument to the other depending on how the question is put (which I have heard some theologians do). That's what Greek linear thought does to us. Hebrew thought on the other hand holds them together for resolution. In fact, there are four foundational Christian truths that relate to the homogenous/heterogenous question. We have in fact already referred to all four.

Four Christian Theologies relating Gospel:Church

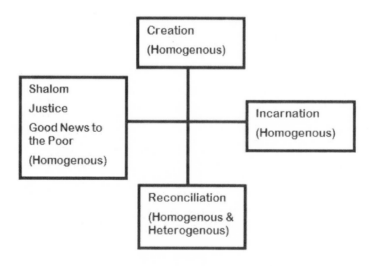

Of the four, three clearly support homogenous expressions of church whilst one challenges us to go beyond that. The table below sets out these four theologies. And we hope that you can recognise that we have drawn on all three of the theologies of creation, incarnation and justice for the poor to support homogenous, inculturated expressions of church or clusters/MSCs. But we have also identified that reconciliation requires something more.

RESOLUTION OF HOMOGENOUS AND HETEROGENOUS

If you have followed with us so far... now we find the resolution of the apparent conflict that we hinted at, at the beginning. We have to find ways that in Time & Space all four truths can be worked out and held together in the life of mission and church.

Time: With the imperative for mission and evangelism, we have established that not-yet-Christians should preferably be able to start by hearing the gospel in their language; seeing it lived by a group of Christians of their culture and being able to join such a community to be discipled without crossing a culture gap. However, as they continue in discipleship, it is most important that new Christians are exposed to Christians from other cultures and social groups.

It is an invaluable part of any Christians growth to experience Christian community that is different from their culture. In fact this is itself a most powerful witness to the reconciling work of the Cross of Christ... that the world may know (John 17:23). It also is the proof against our developing a relative gospel that is actually justification based on our culture rather than grace. And this is no gospel at all... it's just being "bewitched!"

(Galatians 1:6-7 & 3:1). We all need exposure to the "Global Christ" to keep us rooted in grace.

So time is the first dimension that opens up the possibility to have homogenous communities as starting points from which Christians move on and out to engage with different Christian cultures to grow in their discipleship.

Structure: This is the second element... that of space and size... proving a context to reconcile homogenous and heterogenous communities' expressions of church. Church is not a single static structure or unit, nor was it ever intended to be. Once again we have been trapped into a false position by accepting the lie that church is a one day a week religious event in a special building.

Once we recover church as seven days a week lifestyle community, forming and reforming in lots of gatherings of different styles and sizes... then we are liberated to express both the homogenous and the heterogenous in a way that all of us can be fully involved in both. The contradiction evaporates, the conflict is emptied and no longer do we have to fight one corner or the other!

So how may this structural resolution work out in practice? Here we shall see that far from posing a problem, clusters provide a much greater opportunity to resolve the one type only or mixed type question.

First we have cell-sized groups. And these don't have to be a fixed set of always the same 8-12 people always meeting on the same day. That may often be appropriate, but church is relationship, not a rigid structure. Some household size groups meet in different combinations at different times and places through the week... they mirror the natural way that people link up in their neighbourhood.

Then we have groups of extended family size and style which we call clusters or mid-sized groups. Here we open up another level of variety and flexibility. So we may have cell-sized groupings that are relatively homogenous in social, cultural or generational makeup... but a clustering of these at the mid-sized level. This is bound to introduce some greater diversity. Maybe they become inter-generational where there have been youth cells and children's cells.

However, it can still be that at the mid-sized cluster level there is fairly similar cultural make up, such as all young adult, students, oppressed poor, professional families etc. But this is still not the only level at which the church expresses its corporate life. Clusters of very different social or cultural make-up can do things together. At the larger celebration level there is even more diversity as clusters gather together. And as things get larger, depending on the setting – rural, suburban, urban or city, there is scope for periodic whole church or inter-church get-together for festivals, special events and missions.

So once community is not static and is also multi-layers of different sizes, there is every scope for mixing up Christians of as great a diversity as is present in the region. And that doesn't begin to include the cross-cultural experiences possible through short-term teams that are sent and received nationally and internationally.

MAKING THE MOST TO MIX UP SPACE AND TIME

We hope that we have now resolved the apparent conflict and provided an understanding of how we can hold together both homogenous and heterogenous church experiences. We have also tried to show that clusters, far from presenting the problem, provide greater opportunities to resolve it. Now lets see some further practical ideas for ensuring that relatively same type clusters or cells always have significant cross-cultural experiences.

First let's recognise that among the many different elements of culture that we put in the table at the beginning of this chapter, some present greater barriers than others. Some on the other hand can even build bridges rather than divide. Clearly language has the greatest potential to divide and exclude... It truly is a fairly impossible barrier to cross if the group size is intended to promote any real relationship to happen. However, large celebration gatherings can be inspiring with all singing in their own language and with various options for translation of what's spoken.

In today's multi-media multi-shaped world, music style is one of the strongest culture carriers. Hence, gatherings that bridge between different cultures and generations are often best to minimise the music. Shared worship without music can be fine although worship styles in general can often be hard to bridge. On the one hand, cross-cultural cuisine is a positive attraction - everyone loves a foreign dish! So once again eating together is one of the best forms to integrate folk from different homogenous cells of clusters.

In fact all forms of social interaction tend to be the easiest at bridge building. Doing practical projects together with a fresh focus also takes attention off differences. This is also true of doing mission together. This can be both unifying and provide the creative challenge of encountering the gospel in different stories and metaphors.

We can illustrate these principles with the experience of the Emmaus cluster at St Thomas'. This is a cluster of predominately professional families of all ages. In 2002 one young adult member had a job teaching English to asylum seekers. Many were from Iran and as she built friendship with her pupils, she suggested that the best way to learn English was to be immersed in a social context with Brits. When asked where this could be, the first answer she thought of was that her cluster was a possibility. One Iranian came and the extended family dynamics was a cultural bridge to his experience in Iran. Soon he had invited other Iranians to cluster and it wasn't long before bible readings were in English and Farsi. By 2004 it was clear that the number of Iranians could best grow and invite other Iranians if they began their own small group. Integration and outreach continued as this small group put on an Iranian meal and Brits & Iranians all invited new folk from both communities!

By early 2005 after a series of baptisms, periodically the Iranians met as a cluster size of their own. However they still came to some Emmaus cluster gatherings and were regular at larger celebrations. Interestingly, the relatively modern western music style of these gatherings was only a minor hurdle for them as these Iranians had no history of Christian music at all and their media experience in the UK had been of modern Western music. Their teenagers would be seen from time to time but the best cultural connection for them would seem to be with British teens of their own age.

Later that year they attended a national gathering specifically for Iranian Christians over a few days. They came back inspired... one said to me, "We are grateful that you English introduced us to Jesus, but now that we have experienced him amongst our own people, we really know him!"

Another illustration we refer to elsewhere, is of the children in an intergenerational middle class cluster who asked if they could meet and bless those in the homeless cluster. So arose a termly joint gathering of the two clusters with the children coming up with ideas such as baking cakes to take and share.

THE FULLEST EXPRESSION OF RECONCILIATION REQUIRES HOMOGENOUS UNITS!

This also highlights a principle that most people seem not to have recognised. Namely, that for the full measure of reconciliation to be worked out, you need the **corporate** meeting of different social, cultural and generational groups. When the two meet, we are not looking for a mixing of the two cultures – a sort of mayonnaise! Each has to experience the cultural community of the other, for culture is relational. The corporate Christ in one culture has to engage with the corporate Christ in the other. When Gentile cluster eats kosher Sabbath meal with Jewish cluster and as Jewish group shares bacon prayer breakfast with Gentile group – then His kingdom comes on earth...

So surprise, surprise! The theology of reconciliation does point us to heterogenous engagement. But it's not complete unless we also have authentic homogenous, corporate cultural expressions of each... building bridges collectively to one another. So even our fourth theology requires the homogenous in order to open up the full measure of the heterogenous reconciliation in Jesus!

This is an appropriate point to conclude this chapter. We can now begin to see the answer to this question, that the fullest expression of the reconciling and unifying power of the gospel is only experienced when indigenous, homogenous groups do exist and they come together to experience one another's different gospel communities.

When one or two individuals from one culture join a large Christian group of a different culture this is good, but the exchange is largely one way. The "outsiders" experience the "insiders" culture. One culture still predominates. On the other hand, both cultural expressions of church experience the fullest challenge and unity when the two corporate expressions meet together and accept one another. This inter-relationship honours and respects the integrity of each... each is challenged by the other... neither being submerged by the other! This is the Kingdom of God!

And this also gives us a right perspective on a fifth key theology – the truth which tells us where it is all leading – the end times or eschatology. Some have argued that at the end it is all heterogenous as all barriers are completely removed and we are fully one. Every tribe, tongue and nation united around their God (Rev 5:9-10; 15:4 & 22:26). But this again misses the point. Culture only exists as it is socially expressed. So every tribe and tongue will be present and preserved in its cultural identity whilst also being perfectly at one with all the others. Heterogenous doesn't replace homogenous... it will be both together... we shall experience perfect hetergenously homogenous communities!!!

CHAPTER SIXTEEN

SWOT Analysis –
An Honest Appraisal

Something called a SWOT analysis is often used to assess the value of something, and whether it is appropriate for a given situation. SWOT stands for Strengths, Weaknesses, Opportunities and Threats. This book has obviously focused largely on the positives of the cluster model, highlighting its strengths and the opportunities it can open up. It will be good to summarise these here. But even more important is to take a good hard look at the weaknesses and the threats.

For some these will lead them to decide that clusters are not for them in their situation. Not for now at any rate. For others they will help a balanced, realistic adoption of the principles, and also allow an implementation that minimises or avoids the threats. So from every perspective this is a very healthy honest appraisal.

Now as it happens, Mark Stibbe, the senior leader of St Andrew's, Chorleywood, presented his SWOT analysis to their Mid-Size Community (MSC or cluster) leaders in June 2005. This was some 20 months after MSCs had first been talked about and 14 months after the first MSCs were launched. This period had also included nearly nine months of being without a building in which the whole church met in MSCs/clusters three Sundays out of four. So the principles had had quite a thorough testing time. Whilst we list our review of the main SWOT's for clusters, the diagrams are from the PowerPoints presented by

Mark. There is, as you might expect, a very high degree of overlap. Although naturally some of Mark's are the more specific results of the implementation at St Andrew's, such as their experience of "God's favour on the project."

STRENGTHS

Biblical Congregation: If our thesis is correct that the underlying principles of cluster represent a recovery of true biblical congregation, then this is the principal strength. Furthermore, we should expect these biblical principles of a mid-sized, extended family community to be able to express themselves in any culture, context and church situation.

Mission Dynamics: This includes the challenge for each cluster to own a mission focus and to develop real mission engagement. It's also the "We'll come to you" model Mark identifies, changing the direction of church. The mid-sized community is a very natural context for evangelism, providing both an outlet for people's passion and a clear focus for supporting each cluster's mission endeavour. We have emphasised our experience that healthy clusters are defined by mission and both leaders and members constantly speak of and discuss their mission. Part of the new missionary effectiveness of clusters is the ability to have a whole diversity of communities in mission, engaging with and reflecting the diversity of our society. And whilst each cluster takes on a different sub-culture, their inter-relationship in forms of networked church enables the other missionary dimension of reconciliation between cultures.

Strength of Community: Mid-sized clusters create strong and healthy community in which there is a wide pool of relationships which is still small enough to enable getting to know everyone and a real sense of belonging. This quality of community is particularly enriched by the recovery of biblical congregation and the interactive, participative nature of meetings based on 1 Corinthians 11-14. The sense of adventure that Mark noted not only provides momentum but draws folk together. These open, strong, functioning relationships, make a very attractive community to non-churched people. Hence it becomes a point of gathering. The possibility of networking to central resources can also strengthen cluster life.

St Andrew's, Spring 05

Release Growth within the Body: Here again there are a range of strong aspects to clusters. There is the context of people maturing in their gifts. Andrew Williams, Associate Vicar of St Andrew's, sums up this new mobilisation of lay people in his lovely expression "Unlocking the gold reserve!" It's a model which addresses "Consumer faith" which tends to be fostered by inherited congregation as a service you attend that's led by professionals and you judge whether it meets your need. Cluster is the sum of its parts and fosters contribution in everything. All this makes clusters an excellent complement to cells/small group, as a context for discipleship "as you go." The cluster life of UP:IN:OUT provides the context for holistic lifestyle discipleship.

Leadership Development: Clusters give lay leaders a step beyond cell/small group leadership. It's an attainable next step for many for whom leading a Sunday service would be a step too far. Not only is the group size smaller, but the whole context is less presentational, less emphasis on professionally trained quality and much more on facilitating interaction and involvement. The lightweight/low maintenance character plays a big part here in encouraging lay leaders. The cluster also fosters an apprenticeship culture which is so fruitful and effective for developing community and missional skills.

Flexible, Adaptable Principles: Whilst we speak of a cluster model... it's not a blueprint or fixed package. Not only are clusters highly variable in style and character, but they can be launched or planted in different ways. Also, there is variation in how they are linked within the same church or across a number of churches. They can work in any size church and in contexts from urban to rural. A somewhat unusual or even ironical strength, is that if clusters are weak and stagnate, there is opportunity to bring them to a healthy end without losing people. So often in church we only know how to start things.

Coping With Change: We may see later that a threat from operating with clusters can be excessive change. However, it is also true that in our social context of diversity and rapid change, clusters provide a model that enables people to embrace a much higher level of change than inherited church.

WEAKNESSES

We have made a strong case for clusters recovering biblical congregation. If we are anywhere near the mark on this, then we should expect there to be far fewer weaknesses than where we have ended up in this list. Some of the weaknesses cited here do therefore relate a lot to the challenge of replacing inherited congregation with its deeply rooted assumptions.

Unfamiliarity: Perhaps the greatest weakness of these re-imagined mid-sized communities, is that they are completely new to leaders and people alike. This is highlighted by the fact that unlike the introduction of small groups 40 years ago, they don't fill a vacuum. Rather they challenge and replace a very familiar model that is deep in the experience and therefore expectation of church folk. This means that there may be more potential or latent resistance to this change than usual, in inherited church.

However biblical and logical it may be, people's instinctive reaction will be to resist or find fault. Even when the change is willingly embraced, people's natural tendencies will be to revert. It can also be perceived as complex because it's new and different. Certainly a weakness that can be associated with this, is the use of too much jargon to introduce or explain the new ways (sorry if you have found this book has too much jargon!).

Opens Up a Host of Real Threats: If it is biblical and may have fewer inherent weaknesses… its difference and unfamiliarity means that the range of threats that we list in the next section is long. This in itself can be seen as a weakness.

New and Harder Leadership Challenges: As this book should have made clear, leading a cluster based, dispersed church requires a different sort of leader and style (especially see chapter nine). It's not the sort of leadership most in inherited mode were selected or trained for. Overall leaders have to have more inner security in order to release control. It's also more demanding, more varied and much less visible. To set alongside this, is the fact that leaders who successfully change gear and become equippers, say that it's realised what they were made for.

Clashes with Western Trends: The common western trend is that folk have become more and more busy in the past decades. Work demands more of those with jobs and parents have to ferry and/or accompany children to all sorts of distant events. There is therefore intense pressure on spare time. Hence, although clusters seek to be lightweight/low maintenance, and although they should replace not add extra meetings – nonetheless a movement from lay spectators to lay participators must present challenges if not problems. The positives should create more motivation and rewards – but we can't escape the problem of time. Of course at root there may be a challenge to the pressures of consumerist employment expectations... and a gospel imperative to be counter-cultural.

Some Practical Difficulties: This dispersed way of these mid-sized groups presents different difficulties in different social contexts. But one common one is the finding of suitable venues for gatherings of over 25 people. There are only a few neighbourhoods with houses this big! Having venues can add cost when the church still owns a large costly building never used seven days a week. There can be a vulnerability to lose the cluster venue. This pilgrim experience can have a positive side. However, equipment can be an associated extra cost and hassle. Especially when clusters start meeting out on Sunday, then all sorts of new challenges emerge such as managing financial giving… and communication weaknesses usually increase.

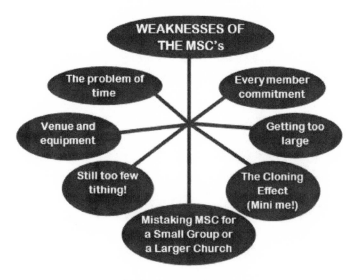

St Andrew's, Spring 05

OPPORTUNITIES

Most of the strengths we have highlighted earlier are opportunities to be realised when first introducing clusters. But in a more general sense we see the following wide open opportunities for the application of the principles behind clusters.

New Sort of Planting: As a rediscovery of biblical congregation, which we have largely lost, it is clearly an enormous opportunity. This full recovery of the dynamic described through 1 Corinthians 11-14 can happen either by transitioning all or part of an existing church or by planting cluster and clusters from scratch. This is a new sort of planting that frees us up from just repeating the building and event centred model.

A Mission-shaped Church: In all these ways it is truly an opportunity to implement the principles of the Mission-shaped Church report. A host of different communities in mission can arise authentically within our multi-cultural plural society. Clusters can emerge from neighbourhoods and non-geographic social networks. In this way they can fit with the patchwork of cities, suburbs or rural villages of the UK and Europe. This can go beyond providing visibility in multiple contexts, to bridging the gap between church and culture. In fact clusters have a potential to take mission-shaped principles to a new level. Because they are based on extended family patterns, mid-sized communities have a real potential to contribute to rebuilding this lost element of western culture and restoring community cohesion.

Restoring Discipleship: In conjunction with cells, clusters are disciple-making communities. We have argued in chapter seven that one of the greatest weaknesses of the western church in post-Christendom, is that we have lost discipling communities, which is the central function of the church. So here again clusters share with some other models of emerging church, the chance to recover discipleship as a lifestyle and the whole basis of following Christ – not just a course.

Creativity in Community and Outreach: Once congregation is no longer trapped in a formal building with tightly structured expectations of an event, mid-sized clusters have the opportunity to release all our God-given creativity both in building community and engaging in mission and evangelism.

Growth and Multiplication: With this creative mission engagement and highly attractive quality of extended family community, clusters can also be a real point of growth in numbers. With this growth comes the opportunity for kingdom multiplication at this mid-sized level as well as cells. This opportunity to multiply is described in chapter ten, but is only possible if we follow the principle of keeping clusters lightweight and low maintenance. With the practice of leadership teams and apprentice leaders, this multiplication also has the potential to release a leadership explosion.

Coping with Change: If the glue is really well worked out in clusters (chapter two), then its amazing how folk can cope with levels of change that created trauma and division in inherited church. In our rapidly changing society this is a strength of healthy clusters. However, the rate of change must be kept within reasonable limits or this becomes a threat!

Transforming Children's and Youth Experience of Church: In chapters 12 and 13 we have explored the opportunity here. This is not only the opportunities presented by intergenerational clusters with full children's contribution. It is also the release of youth cells to gather in very fruitful and evangelistic youth clusters and see all the opportunities we have identified here.

Deal with stuck Home Groups: So many churches have Home Groups that were introduced over the past 30-40 years, that are now stagnant and stuck. Shifting them to cell church principles is an excellent strategy. But many churches have found this too hard or confrontational a route. Some have even tried and failed more than once. However, introducing and developing clusters is a real opportunity to "swallow the problem whole!" You don't have to hit people's security zone in their longstanding home groups. Rather, once folk from old-style home groups have experienced the healthy mission engagement and growth of mid-sized clusters... they just gradually let go!

New Appreciation of Gathered: This is a slightly indirect opportunity. But the repetitive experience of mini-cathedral event week after week obviously can lose its appeal even to those brought up in it. Once cluster is the dynamic centre of discipleship and belonging, folk can gain a new appreciation of the larger celebration gatherings. This can be the more so as energy is released to improve and enrich the quality of these larger (now sometimes more occasional) gatherings.

St Andrew's, Spring 05

THREATS

When exploring weaknesses of moving to clusters, we recognised that this change in how we do church opened up a considerable number of threats. Whilst not in themselves providing reasons not to embrace mid-sized communities, these threats need careful recognition and require able leadership to guard against. This is therefore one of the most important practical sections of the book for those seriously considering going this route.

Fail to embrace mission: We have emphasised the mission dimension of clusters throughout. It's the core rationale for clusters and should be the defining feature and identity of these communities. But it's all too easy to share the vision and initiate the process and just have folk reorganise themselves into mid-sized groupings. This is what Mark Stibbe aptly calls *the illustration of radicalism*! Mission means changed priorities and changed life patterns and a new church model won't achieve it on its own... even if it makes it easier and puts you slap in the mission context!

This threat is really about hiding our light under a bushel! Because with the introduction of clusters we have recovered really attractive community... but folk outside have to discover it's there and for them! Take careful note that this threat is principally when starting clusters for the first time, unless you are planting out new cluster(s). Transitioning existing church means you can have the illusion of growth through absorbing church members not yet in clusters... then you even multiply and have a further illusion of effectiveness!

In common with transitioning to cell, it's imperative to get the desired DNA at the start. Injecting mission into already formed clusters that haven't got it – it's hard! Better to dissolve and reform the cluster in our experience.

Just Duplicate Sunday Service Identity: This is the second major hurdle you can fall at. Cluster leaders who have been in inherited church have deeply conditioned patterns based on what's familiar. These first two threats are what Laurence Singlehurst calls the "swerve to rot" tendency in us all. It's all too easy for clusters to be just too "churchy." The cluster leaders fall back on what they know and do a mini-sermon, get a worship band and devise a liturgy. Interaction, contribution and extended family community never gets off the ground. You are back where you started... only one step worse. Lay cluster leaders are trying to be mini-vicars, and so...

Cluster Leaders Burn-Out: It's a major threat if you don't rigorously pursue a lightweight, low maintenance principle. Lay leaders of mid-sized communities with day jobs and families and a new priority of mission engagement can't sustain it if they are expected to be more than facilitators and enablers. Running a performance oriented Sunday service-type gathering requires too much preparation and is too high stress.

Very important here too, is that cluster leaders aren't mini-pastors either. Cell and cluster health depend on the three principles of a) dispersed pastoral care combined with b) reduced span of care (six people max – as explained in chapters nine & ten) and c) referring all significant pastoral problems to overall leaders or outside specialists. Of course spreading the load is also crucial within the cluster with leadership teams and apprentice leaders sharing the responsibilities.

Failure to Develop Leader Support and Accountability: We have made it clear that when this model is expressed in a dispersed church, a matrix of resourcing and support is its strength and proof against this threat. But churches that haven't been used to giving a high priority to supporting small group leaders will often struggle to recognise the importance of support as cluster leaders take on mid-sized communities.

It was some four years after the beginning of clusters at St Thomas', Sheffield, before huddles were introduced to give regular support to cluster leader teams. As outlined in chapter nine, it is a major change of role for overall leaders with reallocation of priorities and time. The flipside of support is accountability. If attention is not given to this then this dispersed releasing environment could allow independence to develop with an immature cluster leader.

St Andrew's, Spring 05

Loss of All Age Church: Before exploring this threat, we need to recognise that sadly, most UK churches are not at all all-age and they haven't been for decades. In fact, it's getting worse as congregations age and young adults, youth and children are being lost at a disastrously high rate. So the main positive as we recognised in chapters 12 and 13 (and the opportunities) is that clusters can be a fantastic way to recover all ages into church! The threat, therefore, is only relevant for the minority of churches who already have significant numbers among the emerging generation. For them, there is the danger that as these generations are brought into generation-specific clusters, they don't mix with adults and the elderly. Again, chapters 12 and 13 have explained that this is no reason to abandon youth and young adult clusters that may be the only way to bring lots and lots of not-yet-Christians among these generations into discipleship. Rather, we then need to build bridges across clusters to give opportunity for mixing the generations. Furthermore, we saw how many clusters are in fact intergenerational and this eliminates the threat at a stroke! Certainly love and encouragement is needed to avoid people settling into single-generational clusters as their only experience of church (or single social or cultural clusters). Everyone needs to work at relating to those in other clusters (as explained in the previous chapter on the Homogenous Unit question).

Package not Principles: We have highlighted the threat that is so common in western church circles – to copy a blueprint rather than create firm first principles. Our whole thrust and reason for writing this book has been to seek to avoid this danger. In describing clusters and giving frequent reference to their development at St Thomas', some might read it as a single model package. But, as well as giving three stories in the Introduction with very contrasting applications, we have littered the chapters with examples from other churches. These are intended to illustrate the flexibility and adaptability of clusters when working from the underlying principles.

Too Much Change: This is a threat that has proved real for certain clusters, and at certain times, at St Thomas'. So as can happen, an opportunity of coping with change can become a threat if taken too far. Managing this is not always easy. On the one hand some clusters have been so static that they have asked to die gracefully whilst others grow and multiply. So the positive opportunity of multiplication can threaten belonging and community quality, if it happens too often at this larger mid-sized level. Another tension that contributes here is that the apostolic pioneers are so helpful to initiate and give momentum to clusters, but left to themselves or as the guiding influence, they can cause "repetitive change stress!" Apostolic types need the opportunity to inject their strengths but to be able to move on without repeatedly inflicting their propensity for change on the community.

Control Mode Creeps In: We explained in chapters four and nine that dispersed cluster mode church requires a change of overall leader style to release rather than control. This is challenging and unfamiliar to most church leaders. So they can start a move to clusters seeking to release lay initiative and leadership, but instinctively revert back to type. This will threaten the enterprise with tension and division as there is conflict between message and reality. We've said that overall leaders need real inner security to give this high level of releasing... and if it's not present, they can even end up misreading the motives of lay people who take new levels of initiative as they respond to their encouragement to develop clusters.

Parents Misread Loss of Children's Work: Chapters 12 and 13 outlined the underlying shift in philosophy of the discipleship of children for cluster based church. For parents who over decades have become used to highly developed separate children's work, this can seem shocking. Their negative perception can really threaten this pattern of emerging or transitional church. We hope that careful explanation and then the positive fruit of this alternative approach for children can empty the threat and make it a strength, as in the implementation at St Andrews, Chorleywood. However, it is also important to note that when clusters are principally midweek and not Sunday, this is not a significant issue.

Weak on Biblical Teaching: This can be the cry of those reared on weekly extended biblical preaching when they encounter either cell church or clusters. The first answer is that the real threat is from this Christendom model that has filled Christians' minds with biblical truth with no discipling community to work it into their lifestyle. Nonetheless we acknowledge that whilst cells and clusters have the great strength of biblical application, they need to guard against the secondary threat that there is never any extended ("deeper") biblical exposition and that cluster leaders might be unlearned in biblical truth that they pass on.

The right correctives here are first, the periodic celebration gatherings of clusters where the highest quality biblical teaching can be concentrated. And second, the training of cluster leaders in biblical truth and the "trickle down" of applied biblical revelation through being regularly "huddled" by more experienced leaders. This is further strengthened in the St Andrew's model by the provision to MSC leaders of biblical teaching materials prepared by the overall church leaders.

Less Cohesion: A dispersed model is bound to risk reduced cohesion. The question is, have we been so cohesive we have never infiltrated the mission field of society (the ghetto problem!). So yet again the aim must be balance. Releasing clusters to much more effectively engage our multi-faceted culture, whilst finding appropriate inter-connectedness. As we have said the model can vary greatly here. At one end is the well developed matrix of larger churches like St Thomas', Holy Trinity or St Andrew's, at the other a loose link up of planted clusters.

A threat to clusters in large churches is that the centre or big church, tends to "Trump" the dispersed or small church expression. This is not intentional, it's just that the structure at the centre can inadvertently dominate or frustrate varied initiatives of individual mid-sized communities.

Poorer Communication: Churches are already renowned for poor communication and a dispersion into clusters could well aggravate this. However, it can be a chance to develop more creative and more effective channels of communication – written, spoken, electronic, visual. Chapters 9 and 14 have given some initial ideas to work on.

Financial Challenges: This is another very practical threat. On the one hand sticking to larger more formal Sunday service style fits with regular collections. On the other multiplying mid-sized dispersed communities can create new costs of equipment and buildings rental. There is also the possibility of confusion as to where financial processes and responsibility lie in a dispersed network. Threats these clearly are. But once again they may just be challenges to readjust how we do things to adapt to a new way of being church. Appointing a finance person in each cluster, taking cluster offerings, encouraging direct giving and saving costs on large venues, can all reduce or avoid these threats. On the other hand, applying the principles we have outlined through planting clusters will eliminate most of these threats.

Mirror Consumerist Society: As with the threat of not embracing mission, it is possible to take the cluster concept of mid-sized communities and just operate them to meet the needs of already Christians. So we must recognise a risk that the "pick and mix" consumerist values flowing from an individualistic free market worldview, can subtly subvert this Kingdom congregation. But this will be impossible if the mission imperative of the Gospel energises cluster leaders and members to lay down their lives in sacrificial love UP to God, IN to each other and OUT to the needy broken world.

CONCLUSION!

It doesn't seem right to end the book on a long list of threats posed by embarking upon mid-sized cluster church. However, we would remind you that a SWOT analysis is done in order to make oneself aware of the Strengths in order to build on them, and the Threats in order to avoid them. So why not go back and reread the strengths and opportunities. It is our conviction that if most churches undertook a timely honest SWOT analysis on their current activities, they would see clusters/MSCs as an invaluable way of addressing many of the issues it raised.

So we strongly urge you, that if you have got this far... well done indeed... but do go back and re-read the first few pages in the Introduction. These three very different stories should fire you again or pick an early chapter to remind you of the amazing potential of these biblical principles. We are shifting from church as **Event** to church as seven days lifestyle **Community in Mission**. Under God's hand, carried forward by the enabling wind of His Spirit, our vision and hope is still for the release of movements of community in mission! We pray that God will bless the efforts of all who work with Him to apply these principles.

CLUSTERS

Glossary –
Some Explanations of New Words

Cell (see chapter five)
This is a particular type of small group. It is typically a gathering of 6-12 people. It aims to be holistic – with wider life than just a prayer, fellowship or bible-study group. It aims to develop the cell life in relationship to God, one another and in mission outwards. It usually follows a simple structure to ensure these relationships – typically four W's of Welcome, Worship, Word and Witness. Cells seek to grow and multiply and therefore always should have leaders-in-training.

Cluster/Mid-Sized Community (see chapter five)
This is a term developed at St Thomas' and used by many other churches. It was originally used because the new mid-sized mission communities they pioneered, were made up of a cluster of small groups. But the term is now interchangeable with other descriptions like Mid-sized Community (MSC). The essence is an expression of church that is larger than cell and smaller than what people think of as a Sunday service gathering. The way it works is the main distinctive. It is whole life community of Christians united by a mission vision.

Celebration (see chapter 5)
This term is used in the specific sense, not just the general sense of a party. It refers, like cluster, to a size of Christian gathering, but more particularly to a type and style of gathering with a specific social dynamic. Celebration is the largest sort of Christian get-together. It is presentational in style, with clear representative leaders "up front" working to a pre-planned order/timetable and often with written liturgy to facilitate some

degree of participation. It aims for the highest quality in music, language and visuals, and hence uses specialists and the most trained/gifted. It is a "happening" more than community, as it tends to be anonymous.

Huddle (see chapter two)
This is a name given to a structure for support and apprenticeship. It usually gathers from 6 to 12 leaders and emerging leaders, and to develop them in character, skills and faith, through interaction and input. Typically there will be a huddle of leaders at one level led by a leader at the next level. For example, the church leader will huddle a group of cluster leaders, and in turn cluster leader(s) will huddle cell leaders. Such meetings are usually short and well focused, often using an outline or list of questions.

LifeShapes (Lifeskills)
Throughout the book, reference has been made to this framework for discipleship and leadership development. It is a whole life application of biblical principles based around light images or shapes. This is the foundation (or "rule of life"), which was developed at St Thomas' at the same time as clusters were introduced and adapted. These principles provide the core values for doing holistic mid-sized community in mission (cluster) and so are naturally related to many of the issues described in the book. It is our strong recommendation that some such foundation be employed if clusters are to be seriously implemented. For the first eight years the name was Lifeskills, until publication as LifeShapes in 2004. The LifeShapes principles have been published in two books – *The Passionate Church* and *A Passionate Life*, both published by Nexgen in 2005.

UPA - Urban Priority Area
This designation of UPA was coined in the Faith in the City report of 1985[1]. It refers to urban areas with a high index of deprivation across a range of indicators. It was recognised that the church is typically very weak in these contexts and offered a challenge for appropriate mission engagement.

---

[1] Faith in the City report, CHP, 1985

CLUSTERS

Appendices

Appendix 1:   Examples of Cluster Vision & Values in
Different Mission Fields
(expanding Chapter 2)

Appendix 2:   Examples of Planning Cluster Launch &
Development
(expanding chapters 2, 3 and 10)

Appendix 3:   Examples of Mid-sized Gatherings in
Different Contexts
(expanding chapter 11)

Appendix 4:   Comparing & Contrasting to Other
Smaller Expressions of Church
(expanding chapters 4 & 7)

Appendix 5:   An Illustrative Cluster Leader's
"Job Spec"

Appendix 6:   The 3 Phases of St Thomas' – Sheffield
Paul Maconochie's Summary of the
Changes
(expanding chapter 14)

Appendix 1

Examples of Cluster Vision & Values in Different Mission Fields.

These particularly illustrate Chapter 2.

1. Generator Cluster
2. Home Cluster
3. Rise Cluster

GENERATOR CLUSTER
Power for all generations

Vision
Reaching out to our family and friends to demonstrate God's love

Values

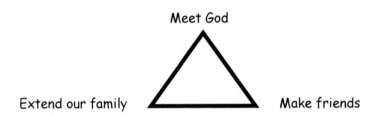

Meet God

Extend our family

Make friends

We aim to:

UP (Meet God)
- Participate in and explore different ways of meeting God so that both adults and children grow spiritually
- Learn how to worship as a family of all generations, with children rather than in spite of them
- Learn how to tap into God's powerhouse and develop ministry in the Holy Spirit

IN (Make friends)
- Make friends of all ages
- Develop community parenting
- Be an extended family, from babies to grandparents. Have older brothers and sisters for our children, to come alongside them and act as role models

OUT (Extend our family)

- Seek to draw others into our extended family
- See the kingdom of God break through into everyday life
- Demonstrate to all that our walk with Jesus is a natural part of our lives
- We see our mission field as our people of peace (both adults and children) and the children of our cluster

Style

Generator is a fully participatory cluster where all generations can grow spiritually. Both adults and children are involved in and responsible for gatherings, bringing words, pictures, interpretations and songs as we meet with God. Our structure is flexible, to help us work out Christian living and family life together, so that they are not in conflict.

HOME CLUSTER - Vision for a purpose (May 2004)

Experiment with worship and spirituality

- to worship God in spirit and truth, in breadth and depth
- to praise God for who He is, what He has done and what He will do
- to use gifts, abilities, sense and emotions
- to 'reframe' the secular as sacred
- to practise living lifestyles of worship
- to be equipped for our spiritual journey
- to receive God's love and give it away
- to express thankfulness as a community
- to try, fail and explore in worship
- to cut and paste past, present and future
- to follow traditions and create our own

UP

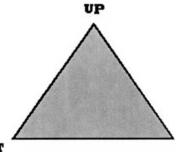

OUT

IN

Engage with the post-modern world

- to take God's love out in a relevant way
- to share the old stories in new ways
- to provide opportunities for new people to join our community
- to give small groups a focus for their energy and love of others
- to love mercy & act justly
- to contribute to 21st century culture
- to enter into open debate and conversation
- to admit when we are wrong and learn from mistakes

Experience God and community in creative ways

- to be open, caring, sharing, loving, praying community
- to be extended family
- to encourage vulnerability, openness and honesty
- to be accountable
- to commit to seeing each other grow in Christ
- to witness God as community
- to share each other's dreams and visions, highs and lows
- to encourage men and women into leadership
- to support those involved in arts and music
- to embrace diversity
- food, glorious food

St Thomas' Church @ Philadelphia Campus
Connect Celebration

Rise Cluster Vision
"accessible church"

"But for you who revere my name, the sun of righteousness will rise with healing in its wings.
And you will go out and leap like calves released from the stall."
Malachi 4 v 2

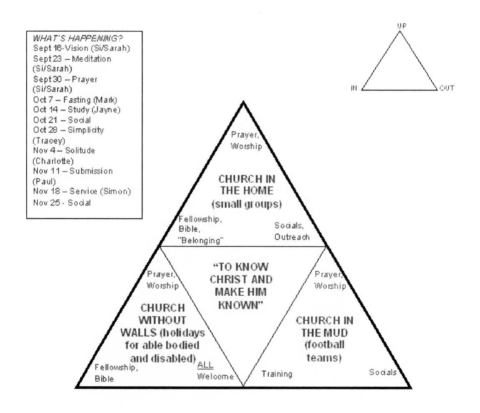

Tuesdays, 7.30pm   Please see overleaf

FOOTBALL TEAMS – CROOKES FC, DYNAMOS FC, ATHLETICO FC

Rise has 3 football teams which play on Saturday mornings in the Sheffield and District Fairplay League (sdfpl.co.uk). The aim is to give local churches an opportunity to serve their communities by providing regular, competitive football played in a spirit of fair play. In so doing to build relationships with our communities and to share in life and word the good news about Jesus. Each team has a squad of 22 players, and we meet to pray for all involved in the football on a Saturday morning at 9-9.30am in the Gilbert Room at St Thomas' Church in Crookes.

SUMMER CAMP FOR ABLE BODIED AND DISABLED YOUNG ADULTS

Here are the SU (scriptureunion.org.uk) holiday details for the camp we lead on each year. We (me and Sarah) have been asked to lead the camp overall from summer 2004 onwards for 3 years and if you would like to come as a leader you would be most welcome. Or if there are people you know who would be interested please feel free to pass this info on.

General details for 2004
Camp name: Rise
Dates: 30 July – 8 Aug 2004 (approx. Dates)
Age: 15-18, Price: £155
Approx. Numbers: 12 disabled young people, 20 able bodied young people, 20 leaders
Where: Lord Mayor Treloars School, Alton
Overall Leaders: Simon and Sarah Nicholson

The camp is mixed able bodied and disabled, and as such is unique among Scripture Union's holidays. Every disabled young person is cared for by 2 to 4 peers (depending on the nature of the disability), together with a leader. Training is provided on how to care for the needs of the disabled folk and use of hoists/moving and handling equipment, etc. All disabilities are physical i.e. there are no mentally disabled young people. There are many activities throughout the week: archery, sailing, day trips, swimming, bowling, sports, crafts, as well as bible discussion groups each morning and main meetings each evening. All young people should be physically fit. We have spare brochures and other info if there's anything else just ask!! We also always need able-bodied lads (aged 15-18) so if you know anyone who may be interested please let us know!

OTHER INFO (as of 2003)

Rise is a Cluster (of small groups) within Connect Celebration, which has a young adult focus. Connect is led by John and Liz Lovell, Gareth and Lizzie Robinson, and Phil and Mags Kelly (who will be leaving in January 2004). Connect meets on the first Saturday of every month at the Philadelphia Campus from 7-9pm. This is a time to meet up with the other Clusters and Small Groups in our Celebration, to encourage and pray for each other, to give and receive. Current dates: 4 October (vision), 1 November (harvest), 6 December.

Appendix 2

Examples of Planning Cluster Launch & Development

These particularly illustrate chapters two, three and ten.

1. The "12 Pillars of Wacky" defining their priorities as cluster.
2. The "Processed P's" planning by the Wacky Leaders.
3. The "Canned P's" sheets used for Wacky members feedback.
4. The "Processed P's" planning by the Airborne leaders and members.

The 12 Pillars of Wacky

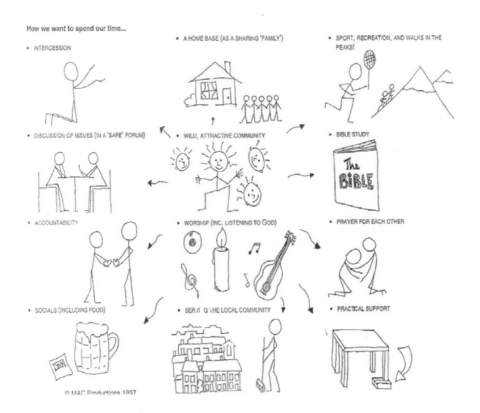

How we want to spend our time...

- INTERCESSION
- A HOME BASE (AS A SHARING 'FAMILY')
- SPORT, RECREATION, AND WALKS IN THE PEAKS!
- DISCUSSION OF ISSUES (IN A 'SAFE' FORUM)
- WILD, ATTRACTIVE COMMUNITY
- BIBLE STUDY
- ACCOUNTABILITY
- WORSHIP (INC. LISTENING TO GOD)
- PRAYER FOR EACH OTHER
- SOCIALS (INCLUDING FOOD)
- SERVING THE LOCAL COMMUNITY
- PRACTICAL SUPPORT

© MAC Productions 1997

298

Wacky Races Cluster – Processed P's

Wacky Races' Processed P's

	Principles (values) - Why -	Priorities - What -	Practice - How -	Programme - When -	People - Who -	Places - Where -	Plan - The Future! -
Wild (up)	"Exploring Christianity for our Generation"	**Doing:** Exploring	Meeting together as a large group (our primary identity) to grow up, in & out. The main environment for big worship, upfront teaching & big socials	Every third week meeting as one large group	Everyone (Planning Group responsible for organisation)	Large group meet where can (Methp.s?): preferably non-religious building?	Develop worship and sessions together that are appropriate to us as a group
		Experimenting	Small groups to encourage more experiental worship, prayer & 'safe' discussion f issues			Small groups meet in 'homes'- households that all members feel they can drop in when appropriate and be part of the household- extended family)	
		Enquiring (minds)	Home groups & Big meeting - God focused but accessible to others	Other two weeks meet in home group 'families'	Everyone (Home group hosts to co-ordinate)		
		Pushing Boundaries					
Attractive (out)	"Relevant Lifestyle"	**Having:** Having Faith	Serving others in wild above normal meetings ways	Special events over and above normal meetings e.g. Student lunches, Young Adults Conference, Lots of Parties!	Everyone (different work groups for different activities)	Wherever people are!	Consider major events: Summer / New Year Balls, Sports stuff etc
		Having a Heart	Committing time for other friends				
		Having Friends	Encourage friends to join in easy access activities- stuff they'd LIKE to do	also see 'Plan'	Everyone		Develop working groups to respond to developing issues eg re-cycling, homeless etc
		Having Fun					
Community (in)	"Committed Relationships"	**Being:** Being Family	Everyone being involved in a household based family group where if they aren't there, they are missed - sense of belonging	Meet 2 out of 3 weeks in home group 'families'	Everyone (Home groups facilitated by co-ordinators - normally the hosts, however everyone's role is vital)	Anywhere but with home group household as a focus	Consolidate & develop open, real, significant accountable relationships
		Being Real	Accountability groups in 2's &3's where reality rules	Meet once a week or whenever possible	Accountability groups organised by those involved		Look for 2 small groups to multiply, Easter '98

Wacky Races Cluster – Canned P's

Having reflected on the Wacky Races Processed P's your suggestions and comments would be much appreciated. Please put them in the tins of Processed P's below.

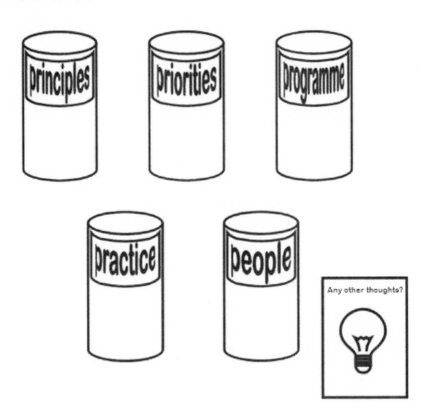

Airborne Cluster – Processed P's

AIRBORNE CLUSTER	Principles WHY?	Priorities WHAT?	Practice HOW?	Programme WHERE?	People WHO?	Places WHEN?	Plans FUTURE?	VISION 2000
UP	WORSHIP	INSPIRING WORSHIP (musical and non-musical)	Through praise and thanksgiving resulting in PASSIONATE SPIRITUALITY	Small groups / And / Cluster	All called to accountable lifestyles / Use of GIFT ORIENTATED LEADERS	SMALL GROUPS meet alternate weeks with CLUSTER	To multiply - EMPOWER- ING LEADERS - HOLISTIC SMALL GROUPS - Disciples rooted in Christian basics - Convert to Jesus	Give praise and thanks with GRATITUDE
IN	SERVE	Those in Cluster and Small group	FOOD at Cluster on Thursday / LOVING RELATION- SHIPS	Cluster / And Ministry resource / And Small groups	Small groups to prepare and clean up and facilitate	THURSDAY GAMES ROOM 6.45pm UPPER HALL 7.45pm ST TOMS AIRBORNE CLUSTER	FLEXIBLE STRUCTURE / To ensure quality and quantitative growth	Continue to serve with GRACE
OUT	WELCOME	The Stranger	Through NEEDS ORIENTATED EVANGELISM	Celebrations at Crookes and Ponds Forge on the streets through Networks and Neighbourhood	Any who are strangers to St Toms, small groups or Cluster life & strangers to God the Father, Jesus or the Holy Spirit	CROOKES 10.30am PONDS FORGE 10.30am 7.30pm	Life Worth Living / New Wine Conference / Airborne Alpha 2000 / Luis Palau.	Welcome the stranger with GENEROSITY

DON'T FLAP SOAR

Appendix 3

Examples of Mid-sized Gatherings in Different Contexts

These particularly illustrate chapter 11

1. Wacky Races Cluster – Young Adults
2. Intergen Cluster – Intergenerational
3. Grassroots Cluster – Inner City estate
4. Become – Emerging Student Cluster
5. Generator Cluster A, B & C – All age (a series of meetings)
6. A to B Cluster – Homeless and addicts
7. Divine Cluster – Professional middle-class estate
8. Home Cluster – Young Adults in Creative Arts
9. Walkabout Cluster – Social, Justice & Environment
10. Go Global Cluster – Reaching and integrating internationals

Wacky Races Cluster

Mission Focus: Young Adults
Core Value: Wild Attractive Community

Example of Weeknight Gathering

Preparation: Leader team agree roles and delegate one cluster member to buy & bring biscuits and another to bring edible decorating stuff.
Theme: CIRCLES OF INTIMACY

Outline:

1) Informal mingling over coffee as folk gather

2) Word of welcome and couple of community notices

3) Encouragement to focus on God with two songs led by single guitar

4) Reading by one member of leader team Mark 3: 13-19 & 31-35

5) Short explanation by another member of leader team that Jesus built community with at least three levels of intimacy

   a) His closest friends who shared his deepest thoughts and experiences... Peter, James & John.

   b) The twelve with whom he shared life and was team

   c) The 72 who were part of his wider circle and like his extended family (Luke 10: 1-21)

6) Instruction by another member of leader team that within the Cluster there are those like the 72, we know their faces, may not know all their names, certainly don't know what's going on in their lives. Go and get a biscuit, decorate it and

take it to someone you don't know that well. Find two things you share in common. Then pray giving thanks for one another.

7) Instruction by another member of leader team that you again get a biscuit and decorate it and take it to someone you know well, probably a member of your small group but not your most intimate friend. Share together some way that you have experienced God recently and one need to pray for. Pray together.

8) Lastly, instruct folk to find one of their intimate circle (Peter, James or John), again sharing a decorated biscuit together. This time share something that God is challenging you to change in your life, pray for his help and agree accountability.

9) Conclude by sharing in small groups how developments are going with not-yet-Christian friends. Have a short time of prayer for not-yet-Christian friends and a worship song. If appropriate an informal sharing of communion could be the climax of the time together.

Vision: To build inter-generational community and draw in those looking to belong in extended family

Values: Include... the single and elderly finding a place to belong in family; family dynamics as the place to learn discipleship; adults to model and support children growing in the UP:IN:OUT of faith and children to challenge adults with the freshness and naturalness of their faith.

Venue & Day: This was an occasion when the cluster met on Sunday morning in a public meeting place – a room in a museum.

Theme & Aim: Growing worship in the family. The meeting aimed to put everyone in a family group and to explore creative ways of bringing God into many of the key aspects of life.

Gathering: As people arrived they were offered tea, coffee, soft drinks with doughnuts and biscuits as they mingled together.

Explanation: The aim and pattern of the meeting was explained. We were going to explore different aspects of worship together in extended family groups. There were five stations and groups would move round from one to the next at roughly ten minute intervals as the leader directed. Any who were not part of a biological family were attached to one and adults and children were to help each other with the activities at each station. There was a short explanation of what they would find at each station and what to do.

Station 1: *Praise & Thanksgiving:* A TV screen had been set up with a video loop showing views of the natural world and God's creation. A card had written instructions to take the pens, colouring felt-tips and paper and as an extended family, put together an illustrated psalm. A bible was open at a thanksgiving psalm to stimulate more ideas. Conclude by reading/displaying the family psalm.

Station 2: *Sorry & Forgiveness:* At this station there was a plastic sheet on the floor, a box of coloured play dough and again a card of explanation. Each individual was (with help where appropriate) to think of something they were sorry for that week and model it or make some representation in the play dough. Then an adult was to share how God's forgiveness was free and complete in Jesus. A bible was open with an appropriate text to read if desired. Then the whole group were to squash flat their model or image to demonstrate that sins are not only forgiven but completely forgotten – gone for ever.

Station 3: *Prayers of intercession:* Here there were some Sunday newspapers and ones, twos or threes leafed through to find things that stimulated them to want to pray. They then had small sheets of paper to write or draw a prayer. There was then a washing line hung up with pegs and the family added their sheets to a growing array

	pegged to the line. They could also see and pray the prayers of groups that had gone before.
Station 4:	*Evangelism:* Moving to this station the group found strips of cut out stick figures of people (sometimes called origami). They were to think of someone they knew at school, work, neighbourhood, sports team, etc. that they wanted to come to know God... what they called a "person of peace." They wrote or were helped to write their name on one of the cut-out figures. They then prayed as a group for these people and for opportunities to share and care.
Station 5:	*Giving:* Here there were envelopes so that individuals and family members could make their usual gifts and offerings to the church. Then they were encouraged to think of people or situations known to them – close at hand or far away, where help was needed. This might be financial, practical or a card or letter writing. These were supplied for use if appropriate. They were encouraged to think of acts of kindness and make plans together – baking a cake, taking a meal round or just going and spending time.
Note:	a) We attended this meeting as visitors and were thrilled to be allocated as adoptive aunt and uncle to an extended family.
	b) There wouldn't have to be all these stations – less could be done with more time at each, others done on another occasion.

Grassroots Cluster

Mission Focus: Firth Park, Sheffield
(Inner City Geographical)

Venue: Upper room of local Pub in Firth Park –
Sunday starting between 10 and 10:30am!

1. Informal mingling and encourage people to grab a chair and gather round to start

2. WELCOME/TESTIMONIES Word of welcome from a cluster leader and invite people to come to the front to share fresh testimonies of what God is doing in their lives.

3. CREATIVE WORSHIP/CONFESSION
a) Start with saying words on screen (standing).
b) A moment of silence to invite the Holy Spirit to reveal stuff he wants us to confess.
c) People invited to come to the front and write with a red non-permanent pen on the OHP a word which represented something they wanted to confess before God and the group e.g. "jealousy", "anger", "lack of trust" etc.
d) When people have finished coming forward, leader prays a spontaneous prayer of confession on behalf of the group and then wipes off the red pen so that the OHP is clean. Again a spontaneous prayer of forgiveness is prayed over the group.
e) Next the leader invites the Holy Spirit to come and for members to bring a song/tongue/prophecy/word of scripture as the Spirit leads. A cluster member who plays bongos is designated to be ready to support a spontaneous song. Let the worship begin!

4. MYSTERY PRAYER STATION! Member of cluster has been asked to prepare a prayer station. She does it on God's promises for us. Having explained what God has been teaching her and why she has chosen this subject, she has handwritten all the verses she can find about God's promises and lays them out around the room on big sheets of paper. We have ten minutes to walk around the room reading the verses and receiving from God with worship music on in the background. Some people pray for each other.

5. BREAK Tea/Coffee cake.

6. NOTICES about whole church events and cluster events/news. One of the notices is that two members have been called to minister in the area next to our focus, so we all gather round to pray and prophecy for them and send them out!

7. TALK Theme: Despite horrendous difficulties Job continued in his walk with God – he didn't quit.

8. GROUP DISCUSSION in groups of three or four share "How are you walking with God? What does your walk look like at the moment?". Encourage groups to pray for each other about their struggles and hopes.

9. END Final prayer to tie up & general prayer offered from Cluster leaders.

Become

Mission Focus:	University Students
Venue:	Starbucks Cafe – given free with discount coffee!
	7.30-9.30pm, Thursday nights in term time.

Chill & Mix:
(30-40 mins)

Opening 30-40 minutes with a live activity background – quality music – secular DJ – cool vibe – sweets/chocs on tables. Team welcome on door with Become T-Shirts and clear explanation that this is a Christian community with all very welcome. Team also explain... grab a coffee, grab a table, grab a chat... it's fun, vibrant. Games such as JENGA on tables. During this 40 mins of social stuff – team spot newcomers.

Front-led Intro:
(10 mins)

Leader(s) give formal welcome, again clear who/what we are. Update on ongoing "Soap Swap Challenge" – 1st week given bar of soap to swap for something more valuable... review who's got furthest so far... one has MP3 player, another a special T-Shirt.

Games Time:
(30 mins)

Last week this was led by the church children's team doing "Velcro Man" and eating doughnuts on a string. This week it's... Teams of four; each given a celebrity/historic character and dress-up clothes. A team member to dress up and go out onto the street and get passers by to guess who they are! Prize for the winning team.

Talk Time:	A leader gives five minutes on a fairly
(20 mins)	challenging life-related "God-thing." Followed by invite to chat this theme on tables for five minutes (with get out... don't have to). For the next five minutes the speaker applies the theme and then explanation that as Christians we build community by praying for one another (again get-out clause)... so pray round tables if want to for a final five minutes.
Chat to close:	Chat and Out
(10 mins)	

This has been going just five weeks and has grown from 45 to 75. Several not-yet-Christians are so enthusiastic that they are inviting other not-yet-Christians along. They have a residential weekend away next week to build community (50 came).

Generator Cluster A

(All age cluster meeting, 13 June 2004)

Venue: An average-sized house!

Theme: **What's in a name?**

Vision: Generator is a cluster whose vision is to build families into extended family involving all ages. They aim to enable and facilitate all aspects of Christian life to be shared in the family producing a follow-on from the cluster to members homes. Singles and couples without children are linked to families as adoptive aunts & uncles.

Advanced preparation

Find Scriptures about us being precious and special to God

Choose song on CD and put lyrics up on flipchart paper on wall

Prepare and photocopy name sheets

Get sticky labels and pens

Heat up barbecue!

Leaders

This session was led by a couple but it could easily have been led by just one person.

10:45 People arrive, bringing contributions of food and drink for the barbecue

11:00 Adults and children gather together in the lounge, sitting on chairs and cushions and the floor. Leader asks what we've got to give thanks for – adults and children contribute, and we sing them to fit "Thank you Lord for this fine day."

Session is entitled "What's in a name?" and is about the good and bad names we are called, and how they can affect us.

Everyone gets into small groups, either family groups or with people we know well. Some groups may use the garden to give more space. Every adult and child is given a piece of paper headed "What's in a name?" Underneath "My name is ...." there are two columns, headed "Good names" and Bad names".

All write down names we have been called, both good and bad. Add names we call ourselves (these usually seem to be bad!)

Gather everyone together in lounge again.
Leader asks what we do with precious things (care for them, look after them etc). Shares some Scriptures about how precious we are to God.
Play a CD (song called "Son you are my treasure") and let people read the lyrics .

In groups again write down in the good names column, the names that God calls us.

Give each person a sticky label and get them to write on it the name they would like God to call them (eg Precious, Special, Pearl, Heir etc) and encourage them to wear it for the rest of the day.

Tear off the list of bad names, pray against the power of those names, and claim the names that God calls us. Then crumple the paper up and burn them outside on the barbecue.

11:45 Finish with a barbecue lunch together

Generator Cluster B

Venue: Average-sized House

Theme: **Share and feed**

Advanced preparation
Simple talk on testimony (in future weeks, not as much introduction was needed)
Someone planned the simple worship session
Everyone brought food/drink to share

Outline of Session

10:30 Welcome & refreshments
Explained the concept of share and feed (Share our testimonies of what God is doing in our lives, share by praying for one another, and share food together. Fed by each others' testimonies and by food).

10:45 Worship (Prayer and songs to CD)

10:55 Word (short, child friendly talk about the importance of testimony. Looked at how central to the New Testament is the testimony of ordinary people who's witnessed Jesus at first hand or who had heard about him – especially in Acts/ Got people to brainstorm the effects of testimony – encourages, builds faith, expectancy, etc)

11:10 Sharing of testimony and prayer – got people into small groups of about 6 adults/children. Encouraged them to share what God had been doing in their lives. Adults were asked to engage the children in an age-appropriate way. Then the group prayed for one another.

11:45 Sharing of food – everyone brought a contribution of food and drink.

(This format was very simple but very powerful. We started to have share and feed weeks every four/five weeks, so people knew what to expect and came prepared to share.)

Generator Cluster C

(All age cluster meeting, 21 September 2003)

Venue: Education Room, Kelham Island Industrial Museum
Theme: **Jesus is the way, the truth and the life**

Advanced preparation

Draw maze on flipchart; prepare talk about maze; print mazes
off internet
Wrap parcel with scripture cards
Write & print instructions for each prayer station
Make up children's worksheets
Pack up pens, crayons, paper, Bibles, concordances,
Communion items, etc
Worship leader to prepare worship and get OHPs of song lyrics

10:30   Arrive and put out activities on tables; leaders to pray for
session (3 leaders – one doing talk and memory verse
game, one doing Communion, one leading worship)

10:45   Call to worship (introductory song) + Welcome/notices

10:55   Encourage children to front for talk
(Simple talk about life being full of choices – which way to go? Give
examples suitable for all ages. Use a maze to illustrate and get child to find
the way through. Make point that just as there's only one way through the
maze, so there's only one right way to live and that's to follow Jesus. He's
the way, the truth and the life. If you're faced with a difficult choice, think
WHAT WOULD JESUS DO?)

11:05   Memory verse game – John 14:6 - (younger children to
pass the parcel to music; unwrap words of memory verse
and pass to older children who have to work out what
the memory verse is - stand up with it in order at end -
read it together)

11:15   Three prayer stations (Way, Truth & Life)
Introduce them – a mixture of activities to help us focus
on Jesus being the way, the truth and the life. Older
children can decide for themselves what's appropriate.

316

Adults – help younger ones to engage in what we're doing.

The Way
- Easily understandable version of Luke 4:14-21 such as 21st Century Children's Bible. Ask people to write on a card something they feel challenged to do in response to this passage. Make two copies – one to keep and one for accountability within the Cluster.
- Selection of mazes of varying degrees of difficulty

The Truth
- Pieces of flipchart paper on table, along with pens, Bibles and concordances. Ask people to write down truths and scriptures about Jesus. Teach others, including older children, to use concordances. (Use this as basis for worship in future Cluster meeting.)
- Worksheets about Jesus – e.g. colouring by number to reveal scriptures, codes to crack, quizzes, etc.

The Life
Table with Baptist style Communion administered by Cluster Leader, who is available to pray for people. Go to this station as individuals or as families.

11:45 Guitar playing draws people into worship (shakers and percussion instruments available for children)
12:00 Blessing (followed by lunch in nearby pub, where we meet non-Church family members)

A to B Cluster

Vision:

Working with addicts and homeless to create a community of restoration through Jesus.

Venue:

A rented clubroom that is bare boards and shabby walls but with a kitchen and servary hatch onto the room. The building is run down but opposite the city centre 24 hour pharmacy.

Beginning Section:

For the first half hour folk drift in, welcome one another, sit at simple metal frame tables and serve and receive tea, coffee, sandwiches and buns. Conversation ebbs and flows, rises and falls. Team members circulate and draw in folk to serve. Some team members are prayed with before they go out to invite in folk from the streets and doorways.

Middle Section:

A couple of songs are sung to a single acoustic guitar. Singing is approximately to tune and volume variable. A member of the team shares a simple down-to-earth personal experience, which leads to two or three calling out experience from the tables.

Then one of the leaders with long hair and tattoos gives a very short talk with the arresting theme, "What Jesus wants us to hate." He then lists some of the destructive things in our lives and how with the help of Jesus, we can move into freedom.

End Section:

Discussion of the theme is encouraged on the tables as more drinks and food are shared. Prayer is suggested on the tables or folk can ask for prayer... as needs of the coming week are shared and practical responses planned. A prayer read together ends the meeting and folk drift off over the next half hour, some team already going to address practical needs.

Divine Cluster - Harvest

Introduction and Welcome

UP

- Read Psalm 100 together
- Sing a song, simply led.

  We are trying to use simple, accessible ways of worship that will be easy for people to engage with and meet God through.

- Give opportunity for testimonies and thanksgivings from members of the cluster – things you want to give thanks for from the past week or so. End time by thanking God all together out loud.

  Sharing our stories from the week is a great way to catch up and lead us into worship together.

- Meditation based on collected items to illustrate harvest theme.

  We want to use our imaginations and thoughts to encounter God.

IN

- Someone brings a short word from Luke 10, sharing a few thoughts and leading into discussion in groups (incl. talking about identifying people of peace, and thinking of things the cluster can do as a group to reach out to those in the neighbourhood). Feedback of discussion.

  We want to let the bible be part of our community we allow it to challenge and inspire us.

  At times it is more appropriate for cluster leaders to share, and sometimes other people will bring a word.

  At most clusters discussion and application, as a group, are key features of the evening.

OUT

- In same groups identify one or two people of peace. Pray for them together and for each other.

    We want to share our struggles and victories.
    We are going into our mission fields as team.

- Commission – Light a candle to represent your place in the community Ask Jesus Spirit to fill you as you go.

- Take an apple to eat and then plant the seeds to represent thankfulness for the fruit of the past year and preparing for the new season ahead.

    Through simple acts we allow God to prepare us to go out
    into his worldand commit our journey to him.

Home Cluster

Vision:	**Young adults in the creative arts**
UP:	Experiment with worship and spirituality
IN:	Experience god and community in creative ways (focus of this meeting)
OUT:	Engage in mission within the post-modern world

<u>Hands – Equipment List</u>

<u>General Equipment</u>

The list is not long or complex – each of the stations can be done with different sized groups and in different sized rooms, although it is preferable if there is plenty of clear floor space. If you want to add to the atmosphere, you can dim the lights, use drapes and candles, play a CD of suitable background music and play a PowerPoint of lots of images of hands on loop through a laptop and projector.

<u>Preparation of Stations</u>

All stations can be set up so that there are a number of chairs and floor cushions around each one to allow time for reflection. Each one has quantities/sizes to suit a group of about 30, but you can scale these up or down according to the size of your group. Each station has some directional text along with a biblical passage for participants to read. There are also physical activities which need to be set up prior to the meeting. These are detailed below:

1. Doubts – Photocopy a left hand and a right hand. Reproduce 2 copies of each hand scaled up to A3 or A2 size and stick the sheets onto card. Buy 4 red ink pads (approx. 1in.x1in.).

Cut out a circular hole (approx. 2cm diameter) in the centre of each hand so that the ink pads can be taped onto the back of the card with the red showing in the centre of each hand. Place these two pairs of hands besides the instructions for the station. (Instruction card speaks of the cross of Christ and invites the placing of a fringer into the centre of each hand image)

2. Grace and Peace – Make a white linen cross (approx. 2m wide by 3-4m long). Place it on the floor with newspaper/plastic sheeting beneath to soak up any excess paint. Use white tape to make the word GRACE across the cross and the word PEACE down the centre so that they intersect at the letter A. Place plates of poster paint around the outside of the cross on newspaper. (The instruction at this station invites dipping hand in coloured paints and making a hand print somewhere on the linen. At the end peel off the invisible tape!)

3. Purity and Beauty – Arrange large bowls of water and towels together surrounded by cushions or comfy chairs. (Instruction card invites to wash one another's hands and gives suggestions for active reflection)

4. Justice – Arrange blank sheets of A4 and coloured pens on the floor. Alternatively, you can write off to Christian Aid and ask them to send you a free activity pack which will include names and addresses as well as pre-prepared post-cards to send to influential world leaders pleading with them to bring an end to injustice on current issues. (Instructions suggest either illustrating injustice or writing something practical, such as a card to world leaders)

5. Communion (optional) – Set up communion on a central

table for people to return to at the end of the stations. This can be served in whatever way people feel comfortable.

Floor Plan

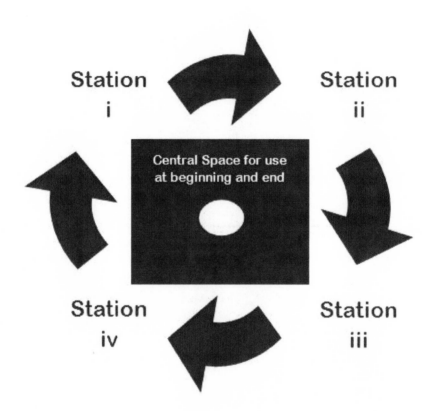

Leading the Session

1. Invite people to gather in the middle.
2. Take them through a meditation about Hands to focus on God and off ourselves and recent events.
3. Encourage them to make their own way round the stations i-iv (approx. 10 mins. per station).
4. Ask them to gather back into the middle for communion (optional).
5. Finish with a "Clenched Fist" action prayer involving clenching fists and opening hands, and leading through to invoking blessing.

Walkabout Cluster

Vision: To build community around shared social concerns

Values: To try not to do "church" but seek the Kingdom. Experimentation with gatherings that are socially and activity focused.

Gatherings: The cluster gathers and is split down into smaller groups to do different activities in the community. These groups then gather back to share a meal. We find that this completes the experience, gives people the opportunity to talk about what they have done, reflect, pray and give thanks. Splitting into smaller groups also gives people from different cells in the cluster the chance to work together in an activity based setting, which builds relationships between the cells. Working together (OUT) builds community (IN) and increases dependence and thanksgiving to God (UP).

Activities: Some of the following have been done using sub-groups to do different activities on the same day or evening gathering. On other occasions all the sub-groups were doing the same thing.

Recycling collection: Knowing that we have a poor recycling service from the local council we produced some flyers that we distributed around some streets in the local area. They notified people as to who we were and that we wanted to encourage better recycling from the council. We gave each household a plastic bag and asked them to fill it with waste plastic cartons / packaging etc and to complete a petition asking the council to increase their recycling collections. A week later we collected both the plastic and the petition sheets, took the plastic to a recycling centre and collated the petition responses and sent them to the council.

Old people's home: We've built an ongoing relationship with a local old people's home where we do a regular event for the residents. We combine a couple of World War Two songs with a game (bingo or picture bingo) with some old hymns and a parable or other short reading. We repeat the event in the two day rooms of the home and have been getting to know both the residents and the staff so that we're now known as 'the choir' by some. We'll also be going back there to carol sing around the home in early December and give the residents a Christmas card and a small gift. We've found that we can repeat pretty much the same format and that the use of old time songs allows the residents the best opportunity to join in and get involved rather than simply being spectators.

African Vocational Training Centre: As a cluster we've got a link to a Salvation Army carpentry training centre in Kampala, Uganda. It trains orphans with skills to enable them to earn a living for the rest of their families. We've had an African evening, quiz nights, promise auctions, and developed our own Good Gifts cards to raise money for the centre. This means that some Cluster evenings we have a pile of fun but also look to achieve some good from the time together. So far we've raised half the money to initially build the centre and then also contributed towards it's ongoing running and development.

Litter collections: We've gone to local parks and playgrounds to collect litter and clear them up - as with the old people's home this has often been a sub-group of the Cluster and is something that we've been able to involve the kids in.

Go-global Cluster

Mission Focus: Internationals

Core Value: Finding a place of belonging acceptance, and supporting each other through cultural adjustments.

General Pattern of Week Night Gathering:
Arriving at 7:15pm people share informally. Each member brings a food dish to contribute to the sit down meal. After thanks each explains the food they have prepared. There are 8-10 nationalities. Japanese, New Zealanders, Philippinos, Koreans, Chinese, Malaysian, English, Germans, Italians.

At approx 8:30pm after tea and coffee, the group of 20 people divide into 2-3 groups. Usually the established Christians share in one group and the younger not yet Christians are helped in their discovery in another group. They meet in separate rooms in the home, and use a member's house across the road if necessary. Leadership in the groups is shared around. Musical worship is seldom part of the group. Individual life situations are shared, and discussion is encouraged in the groups, with things explained carefully because of language and cultural differences. The meeting finishes approx 10pm.

Example of theme development:
It is advent so each weekly meeting after the meal themes of Hope, Peace, Joy and Love were developed to introduce and explain Christmas traditions to those from non Christian cultures. The week on love was divided into three stations for three groups to move around. At one they made chocolate in a heart shaped mould. At the second they were helped to make a small gift box in red paper (symbolic of love and happiness in

China) At the third there were artistic scrap books illustrating Christmas decorations, floats, displays, stable and crib. As each group shared each practical activity they explained questions of... how do I express love to my family, then to my friends, then to God. Lastly what makes me feel loved? The chocolate hearts in the gift boxes were taken away to give to someone to whom they wanted to express love.

All week relationships:
Some members meet during the week and share hospitality or do other activities together. Teaching others how to make and cook their national dish. Going for walks or visiting famous sites and buildings.

Appendix 4

Comparing and Contrasting to Other Smaller Expressions of Church

These particularly expand Chapters 4 and 7

1. Cell Church
2. Base ecclesial community (BEC)
3. Household and Simple Church

Comparisons to Other Small Faith Community Models

So what is the difference between cluster based church and cells, base communities, household church, etc? At the beginning of chapter four, I recognised that all were radical departures in how we are church or how we do church. A brief comparison with each should be helpful here.

Cell Church: The main difference is that cell church tends to minimise the importance of the mid-sized group or congregation. Cell emphasises cell and celebration and in its purest form, dispenses with congregation altogether[1]. This may be appropriate in cultures and continents where Christendom has never existed and where extended family is still the strong foundation in society. As we have argued here, it's precisely because western Christendom has distorted biblical congregation over the centuries and then invested so much in the resulting non-missional structure, that we need the liberation of its recovery.

Furthermore, it may be significant that the largest Anglican cell church worldwide – The Church of Our Saviour in Singapore – had in 2001 begun to introduce clusters. They explained to us that this was to gain more mission muscle and evangelistic effectiveness as cells together engaged in impacting their neighbourhoods. This being precisely one of the advantages that we have observed of clusters at St Thomas' and other UK cluster churches...

---

[1] Ralph Neighbour, Where Do We Go From Here, Touch, 1991

We have also already identified the difference in terms of leadership development. Cell leaders when growing to the next level of leadership become cell supervisors and cease to lead faith communities. They merely support and encourage cell leaders and then the next level is zone pastors who oversee the supervisors of cell leaders. In the cluster model, this pattern of support is similar, but the crucial difference is that it is combined with growing to lead the next size of missional community.

At the cell level things need be very little different. Healthy missional clusters are often made up of healthy missional cells. All the principles of cell life and multiplication fit perfectly with clusters. In fact St Thomas' small groups are based on similar values and some adopt a recommend modification of the four W's pattern for meetings (Welcome, Worship, Word, Witness and Wonders). However, with the focus on clusters, the type and model of small group can be more varied and less prescriptive than the cell system.

Base Ecclesial Communities[2] (B.E.C.'s): Here again there are differences and similarities. The BEC's, like cells, see themselves as fully church as do clusters. But again the BEC movement tends to develop this one model of church in the small, whereas the constituent small groups that make up clusters can vary widely. In some ways, Base Communities are more like clusters than small groups. They may be typically larger than cells and like clusters their defining identity is mission which is seen much more widely than just personal evangelism. Also, clusters share with the Base Community

---

[2] Jeanne Hinton, Walking in the Same Direction - New ways of Being Church, WCC, 1995 and Ian Freestone, A New Way of Being Church, Sold Out Publications, 1995

Movement a much less programmatic approach than cell church. This should not be surprising as the Latin American BEC's were one source of inspiration for Mike Breen for his journey of developing clusters through pastoral bases at Brixton. A significant difference is that BEC's reject any directive or hierarchical leadership, emphasising collaborative, shared leadership in everything and at all times. Another big difference with BEC's, which largely come from the Roman Catholic tradition, is that they are added to a completely unchanged priest-led parish congregation in inherited mode.

Household and Simple Church: This movement of house churches[3] has much in common with BEC's and clusters. The extended family size and dynamic is again a guiding principle. House or household churches see sharing food as a central focus of gathering, as do many of our clusters. House churches and simple church are strongly missional communities and share the lightweight, low maintenance value of clusters. Also the role of the apostolic and prophetic ministries in holding together a movement of household churches has parallels with a mission movement of clusters.

When clusters are planted separate from an existing church, or when clusters are only loosely linked to one another or to an inherited mode church, then they can be seen as a close relation of household church. When developed in this way, clusters would tend to be slightly larger than house church but exhibiting very similar dynamics. However, when clusters are developed in the networked church fashion exemplified by St Thomas', Sheffield, then there the similarities end.

Most household churches have little or no larger celebration

---

[3] Wolfgang Simson, Houses that change the world, Authentic, 1999 and Robert & Felicity Dale, Simply Church, Karis Publishing Ltd, 2002

level. Furthermore, they would see central resourcing and a huddle structure as institutionalisation and there is a much looser associational connection to one another – not a networked church. There's a very flat structure and each house church has high autonomy and that's the prime place of shared leadership. In this they have more in common with BEC's.

Appendix 5

An Illustrative Cluster Leader's "Job Spec"

1. Not a starting requirement
2. More a journey
3. Growth in character and skill

Goals for Cluster Leaders

Much of the following to be done through delegation/ involvement and community building.

- ☐ To know God, to hear from God and to listen for his guidance
- ☐ To be the ears and legs of God's Word to his people
- ☐ To develop vision for the cluster, see it owned, put into action and kept alive
- ☐ To provide empowered and empowering leadership through serving the community
- ☐ To gather people together and to build teams
- ☐ To take responsibility for the cluster and to pray for it
- ☐ To be accountable to church leaders and to be teachable
- ☐ To maintain the respect of the cluster
- ☐ To know ones limits and be able to say "No"
- ☐ To facilitate, support and care for the small group leaders
- ☐ To identify and apprentice future leaders
- ☐ To ensure quality engagement with God's Word
- ☐ To ensure the cluster pursues each phase of UP-IN-OUT
- ☐ To take the lead, especially in organising 'outs'
- ☐ To reveal God and by electing Grace, be a blessing to others, especially the lost
- ☐ To ensure organised management of the cluster
- ☐ To grow the cluster and appropriately prepare it for multiplication
- ☐ To discern where the whole group is at, including individuals on the fringe
- ☐ To offer an extended family welcome and to create and build 'community'

- [ ] To lead by example. To model the lifestyle and instruct where necessary
- [ ] To encourage the use of gifts, knowing that you as a leader do not have to have them ALL
- [ ] To make time to see people on a one-to-one basis
- [ ] Manage pastoral issues by dispersed care and reference to church leaders/specialists

Appendix 6

The 3 Phases of St Thomas' – Sheffield

Paul Maconochie's Summary of the Changes

This particularly expands on Chapter 14

1. Phase One – Mega church:
1994-2002
2. Phase Two – Scattered church:
2002-2003
3. Phase Three – Networked church:
2004 to present

The 3 Phases of St Thomas' – Sheffield
Paul Maconochie's Summary of the Changes

Phase One – Mega Church
Crookes, Ponds Forge, and The Roxy

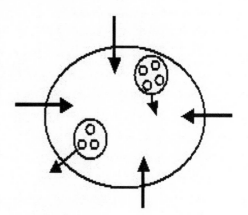

- Systematic, skilled teaching
- High quality music in worship
- High level programmatic resources
- High profile
- Relies on 'in-drag'
- Pilot clusters formed from small groups
- Most meet monthly, mid-week
- 1 or 2 clusters start to rotate in and out of Sunday services
- The first 'natural' clusters appear

Phase Two – Scattered Church
FEB 2002 – 2003

- Basic resources
- Main units of the church = missional communities across the city
- Strain on resource – based ministries
  Focus on 'un-churched'
- Clusters main expression of Sunday 'church'
- Huddles developed to support cluster leaders
- Lack of central resources leads to some separation between clusters
- Cluster leaders forced to embrace 'low maintenance' leadership

staff, basic resources

Phase Three – Networked Church

- Great resources and programmes
- Expressed through clusters across the city
- Seasons of 'gather' and 'spread'
- Reaching different kinds of people
- Clusters operate as 'extended families'
- Clusters can be 'Sunday church' or mid-week
- Every leader in huddle
- Central resources available

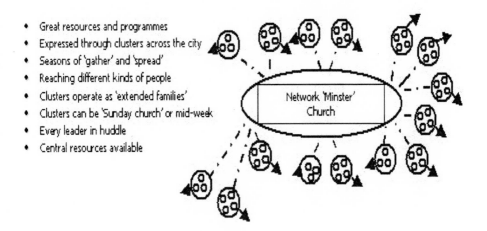

Network 'Minster' Church

Author Contact Information

Bob Hopkins
ACPI Office
Philadelphia Campus
6 Gilpin Street
Sheffield
S6 3BL
admin@acpi.org.uk
www.acpi.org.uk

Mike Breen
mike@3dministries.com
www.3dministries.com

Lightning Source UK Ltd.
Milton Keynes UK
03 June 2010
155035UK00002B/18/P